SEAFOOD LOVER'S
PACIFIC NORTHWEST

Restaurants, Markets,
Recipes & Traditions

FIRST EDITION

Karen Gaudette Brewer

GLOBE PEQUOT
Guilford, Connecticut
Helena, Montana
An imprint of Rowman & Littlefield

For Mom, who steered me toward writing,
and Dad, who instilled a reverence
for the outdoors.

•••———— •♦♦♦ ————•••

Globe Pequot is an imprint of Rowman & Littlefield

Distributed by NATIONAL BOOK NETWORK

Copyright © 2014 by Rowman & Littlefield

All photos by author unless otherwise noted.

Permissions managed by Kale Kim.

Maps: Alena Joy Pearce © Rowman & Littlefield

British Library Cataloguing-in-Publication Information available

Library of Congress Cataloging-in-Publication Data available

ISBN 978-0-7627-8114-0

∞™ The paper used in this publication meets the minimum requirements of American National Standard for Information Sciences—Permanence of Paper for Printed Library Materials, ANSI/NISO Z39.48-1992.

All the information in this guidebook is subject to change. We recommend that you call ahead to obtain current information before traveling.

Contents

About the Author

Karen Gaudette Brewer is an award-winning food, culture, and lifestyles writer based in the Pacific Northwest. Her first food memory is the sound of her mother shake-shake-shaking hot homemade doughnuts in a brown paper bag of sugar. Her second is sharing piping hot *taiyaki* in Japan with her aunties. She's an avid cook and feels incomplete when she goes more than a week without a meal of wild Alaskan salmon or halibut.

VALENTINA VITOLS

She began her professional writing career as a journalist with the Associated Press in San Francisco, where she covered energy and transportation and slowly got to know the wonders of the Bay Area food scene. Later, at the *Seattle Times*, she chronicled the people, restaurants, and ingredients behind a region on the rise as a culinary powerhouse. She continued sharing the stories of Northwest farmers, purveyors, and artisans as food writer and editor at PCC Natural Markets, the nation's largest consumer-owned natural foods cooperative. Most recently, she joined the editorial team at allrecipes.com, the world's largest digital food brand, where she helps millions of home cooks answer that all-important question: What's for dinner?

Born and raised among the moody and majestic forests of Washington State, she makes her home in Seattle with her husband, sportswriter and broadcaster Jerry Brewer, and their son, Miles. This is her first book.

●•◦•———— ◦●◆◦ ————•◦●

Acknowledgments

It's cliché for a reason: It takes a small army to make a book happen, to bring a region's stories to light. I am fortunate to be surrounded by such a battalion of know-how and talent. Thank you to my editor, Tracee Williams, and her team at Globe Pequot Press, for your faith in my writing, your flexibility, and your passion for the subject. Thank you to the multitude of chefs, home cooks, restaurateurs, fishmongers, shellfish growers, historians, regional specialists, ecology groups, tribes, fellow seafood fans, and others who made time in your busy lives to contribute to this project. I am honored to share your stories and our Northwest traditions far beyond our shores.

The author's elementary school playshed, already instilling a reverence for salmon.

Thank you to Jen and Kerry at The Business of Books in Seattle for preparing me for this adventure. To Holly Wyrwich, proofreader extraordinaire, and Kale Kim, who makes rights management look easy. Many thanks to the Seattle food and writing communities, whose warmth, knowledge, and humor is unmatched in the nation, of this I am sure (special thanks to Chris Nishiwaki for the oysters and pearls of wisdom). To Nancy Leson, whose deft skill at storytelling was an inspiration during my days as a cub food reporter at the *Seattle Times*, and Tan Vinh, who makes outdoor culinary adventures seem fun and accessible to anyone. To Tara Austen Weaver and Julie Christine Johnson, whose unflagging enthusiasm for the craft of storytelling has helped so many fellow writers push forward. To the Hi-Life in Ballard and Chinook's at Fishermen's Terminal, who always welcomed me and my laptop for long writing breakfasts and dinners.

To the Three Ks: Who knew "leadership camp" at Leavenworth would be so fruitful for each of us? To TYB and Nicole, who make goals both big and small seem achievable. To Tiffany, my partner in crime, ambition, and style. To Flying J, my oldest friend, who always grounds me. To the amazing moms of my PEPS group: May we continue to dream, for ourselves and for our little ones. To the Coniglios, who helped keep my family fed and positive as day-to-day life morphed into a circus act to make this project happen. To my Portland cousin, John Gaudette, for sharing his knowledge of all things Oregonian. To my nephew Aaron, whose passion for music renews my passion for words. To Kim and Kurt, for their ceaseless encouragement. To my husband, Jerry, my north star. Thank you for always making space for my dreams. And to Miles, my little cookie. May we have many, many more trips to the beach.

●•• ———————— •♦♦• ———————— •••

Introduction: Your Turn to Explore

You may have come to love the Pacific Northwest while gazing upon it from the air, plunging through the cloud bank toward Seattle, Vancouver, or Portland to soar above a landscape awash in waterways of every shape and size, fringed by sleeping volcanoes and jagged young mountain ranges, the evergreens a serrated edge along the horizon.

We're an unsolved mystery, a region so removed from the Old World that we were among the very last to be mapped and "discovered." We're the faraway corner of the lower 48 and the Canadian province farthest west, the uncharted territory, the paradise yet unfound. We're the coastal Pacific Northwest: misty, woodsy, elusive. Except when the sun comes out, and the whole region feels compelled to call in sick and spend the day outdoors, because, hey, it's probably going to rain tomorrow.

We're remote and yet strangely familiar: You know us from somewhere. Beyond software and jet planes, running shoes and video games, farm goods and timber, we produce flavors with a distinct sense of here. So prized are our oysters, they lure pilgrims from as far as Thailand, Malaysia, and the United Arab Emirates, eager to taste Pacifics, Kumamotos, and Olympias near the tideflats where they grow best. Sea salt gathered from what's been called the best-tasting bay along the Oregon coast captures the imagination of chefs and home cooks alike. Many of us notice the subtle flavor differences between the different

PHOTO COURTESY OF IRON SPRINGS RESORT

salmon species, between salmon caught in rivers rather than in the ocean, and between spring Chinook from the Columbia and Copper River kings from Alaska. (Note: Both are delicious.) We strap GoPro cameras to our crab pots and have made thousands of YouTube videos of our fishing, foraging, and seafood dining adventures—we just can't help ourselves.

The next time you pass a map or find yourself near a laptop, check us out. So cherished is Oregon's coastline, the state has protected the entire 363 miles of dramatic headlands and smooth sands for public use. Now shift your gaze to Washington and British Columbia. Squint a bit. When you ignore our borders, the Puget Sound, Strait of Juan de Fuca, and Strait of Georgia meld into the majestic, shore-tickling, island-filled waterway called the Salish Sea.

Our coast and waterways have played host to a multitude of fur barons, logger barons, oyster barons, tourism barons, and global explorers over the years, their names mingling on the map with native words in a cacophony of triumph and tragedy. Now it's a new age. Restore and protect are the words of the day as we struggle and strive to preserve our edible treasures for the generations to come. Add one more word: celebrate. Once you realize how lucky we are to live amid this bounty, every meal seems like a special occasion.

Our Edible Treasures

When it comes to seafood traditions, our region has legion. The East Coast has clambakes and blue crab feeds. The South has crawfish boils, the Midwest, fish fries. We head for the coast in droves to brave sideways rain and bone-chilling, damp cold for the simple pleasure of plucking buckets of fresh, sweet razor clams from the sands beneath the retreating tide, already imagining how creamy they'll taste breaded and fried.

We make space on our grills for glistening slabs of salmon and plump, briny oysters; catch, cook, and crack sweet Dungeness crab on beaches within view of nearby islands; burn our tongues as we slurp clam chowder while in line for the ferry; and wine and dine loved ones over fragrant bowls of Penn Cove mussels, crusty bread at hand to sop up the glorious broth. We recalculate the grocery budget (or, butter up a fishing friend) to afford each fresh catch as it comes available through the year: delicate petrale sole, succulent black cod, fat spring Chinook, sweet spot prawns, vibrant sockeye.

Our summers are magnificent but short. Our rainy season sometimes seems eternal. Seafood keeps our insides connected to the outside, keeps us feeling just a little bit less tamed.

Meet some of our favorites, listed here by their degree of quirkiness and cultural importance to the region. You'll be glad you did.

Geoduck (say gooey-duck)

Coastal British Columbia and Washington's "king clam" has many claims to fame. It's the world's largest burrowing clam species, with a shell up to 8 inches and a siphon of up to 3 feet—so large it cannot fit inside its

shell like other clams. This makes geoducks look exceptionally odd, with a strong resemblance to a certain part of the male anatomy that causes shoppers to sometimes blush when offered a closer look. It's also the tongue-in-cheek mascot of Washington's Evergreen State University (motto: "Let it all hang out.").

"Everybody looks at it, and they're kind of aghast when they see it. It's such a strange, phallic-looking beast," said Kevin Davis, chef-owner of Blueacre Seafood in Seattle. "Sautéed geoduck body is something most people will never have in their life, but you should seek it out. Most of the time it gets chopped up and cooked in soup or served in sashimi or sushi. It's rich and unctuous, not firm and chewy like you would think."

Locals have harvested wild geoducks for generations; its name is derived from a Native American word meaning "dig deep." True to its moniker, this deep digging can be comical: Upon spotting a potential geoduck in the sands below, a geoduck lover will suddenly dig as if possessed, then sprawl along tideflats, cheek jammed against the wet sand, and plunge an arm into the hole in hopes he'll catch this speedy bivalve before it buries itself even deeper. Commercial geoduck fishers bypass this whole messy process and dive to pluck them from the muddy seafloor.

Speaking of commercial fishing, geoducks rose to international prominence over the past few decades after years of obscurity, and in 2012 they were a $270 million industry. Geoduck meat is a prized delicacy in China at celebrations and banquets; demand has driven prices sky high (at times $100 or more for a single clam) and launched an entire farming industry. Chefs serve it raw and thinly sliced to show off its bright, briny flavor and slightly crunchy texture, or as an ingredient for Chinese hot pot, gently sautéed, or in soups and stews. Try Seattle Chef Ethan Stowell's recipe for Geoduck Crudo with Fennel and Radish ("In the Kitchen" chapter).

Wild Pacific Salmon

If you were dropped into the Northwest sans calendar or smartphone, you likely could guess the time of year by observing the five species of wild Pacific salmon, and the locals' reaction to them. Winter is when families pull out their best smoked salmon for bragging rights and to make gorgeous, cozy salmon chowder. March and April mean spring Chinook surging into rivers such as the Columbia, Fraser, and Rogue, fat and glistening; spring also is when native tribes hold ceremonies to celebrate the first salmon catch of the year. When you see chefs beeline to airports, it's May, when the first Copper River salmon arrives from Alaska. In summer, tenacious sockeye and coho cruise the fish ladder at Seattle's Ballard Locks as children on summer vacation shriek in delight, little hands and noses pressed up against the viewing glass in wonder. Fall is salmon festival time, as most species, after spending as many as 5 years away at sea to feed and mature, finally make their homecoming to the rivers and creeks where they were born to spawn and die, their bodies feeding the ecosystem, beginning the cycle anew.

Wild salmon is the quintessential Northwest dish, and for good reason: It's darn good eating, rich and satisfying to body and appetite. It's packed with heart-healthy fats that also help us think better. And, it's not just humans who enjoy and rely on salmon for sustenance. Bears, killer whales, bald eagles, and other treasured creatures rely upon a healthy salmon population for their survival. Unfortunately, a combination of overfishing, habitat damage, chemistry changes in the ocean, and previous misguided preservation efforts have resulted in dwindling runs along many of the hundreds of rivers and tributaries colonized by these fish. Salmon is an anadromous species, which means it spends part of its life in fresh water and part in the salty sea. Part of its allure is the clockwork regularity of its homecoming, but also, lately, the uncertainty of how many will make the trip (and how much fishing the powers that be will allow, in turn affecting the market price). In 2009, more than 680,000 coho salmon returned to

Oregon rivers, twice that of 2007; television reporters described certain creeks so choked with fish, it seemed possible to walk across their backs. Food banks were able to freeze more than 40 tons for future eating, according to a report in the *Wall Street Journal*. Why the dramatic fluctuation? Lower temperatures in 2008 North Pacific waters lured plumper plankton just as the salmon were gorging themselves to fatten up for the epic swim home. Billions of dollars of modifications to hydroelectric dams made them less lethal to fish. Lawsuits also forced the US Army Corps of Engineers to spill some water over the dams rather than run it all through turbines to produce electricity, a change that boosts survival rates for young fish. In 2013, coho numbers had fallen again, though fall Chinook on the Columbia River had its biggest run since the government began tracking the species at the Bonneville Lock and Dam in 1938.

We seem to celebrate salmon at every turn. Zoos and aquariums hang salmon-themed light displays at Christmas. Special programs in schools educate future generations about the life cycle of salmon and its role in tribal traditions. Northwest wineries create special vintages to raise money for river research. In Washington, the Salmon-Safe program rewards businesses that ease their environmental impacts to better accommodate salmon. Clean water advocates encourage locals to hit the car wash rather than scrub their cars in their driveways, to avoid sending soapy water, oil, and grease down storm drains and into salmon habitat. One popular car wash chain employs a pair of smiling salmon in its advertising; says one fish, "Thanks for the tasty stream!"

The storied fish sometimes receive more consideration than people, as when the occasional winter storm wreaks havoc in the normally mild climate. The "snowpocalypse" of 2008 paralyzed hilly Seattle in part due to reluctance to salt the roads for fear of harming Puget Sound and nearby streams, though it turned out that sanding the roads can also be harmful. The nation's largest dam removal project along the Elwha River on the Olympic Peninsula is another example of the region's growing devotion to salmon survival and recovery; when complete, the glacier-fed Elwha is expected to freely flow from the Olympic Mountains to the Strait of Juan de Fuca, giving access to more than 70 miles of spawning and rearing habitat, much of it within the pristine confines of Olympic National Park.

Due to commercial fishing restrictions in Washington and Oregon, most wild salmon you'll enjoy in restaurants and from fishmongers here actually hails from Alaskan waters, though salmon from the Columbia River, Neah Bay, Nootka Sound, and points south are available as well,

Salmon: Farmed or Wild?

How do you prefer your salmon? In the Northwest, it can be as polarizing a discussion as whether you support gun rights, pumping your own gas, or how the left lane should be used on the interstate. (*Note*: We infamously fail to use it as a passing lane.) Those who oppose farmed salmon point out that salmon pens kept in coastal waters can pollute the sea, that they attract devastating pests such as sea lice, that they eat unnatural diets, and that escapees weaken wild salmon populations by competing with them for food and transferring parasites and diseases. The contingent against eating wild salmon argues that we'll wipe out wild populations entirely if our appetite for wild fish continues to grow. Well-managed salmon farms with quality feed and pollution controls are the future, they say. Some restaurants agonize over which option to offer customers as wild salmon prices climb. For more on this topic, check out the Monterey Bay Aquarium Seafood Watch at montereybayaquarium.org/seafoodwatch.

often caught by tribal fishermen who are granted extensive fishing rights by treaty. Note that salmon not labeled "wild" on a menu or at a fish shop typically is farm-raised. Because of improved handling methods, salmon frozen fresh at sea is nearly indistinguishable from fresh. Another note: In the Northwest, most smoked salmon is hot-smoked per the tradition of local tribes—moist, flaky, fully cooked, and quite different from lox—though gravlax and lox are available.

King (Chinook, Tyee, Tule, Chin, Blackmouth)

Meriwether Lewis of the Lewis and Clark Expedition wrote that Chinook, when fresh, tasted better than any fish he had ever eaten. Rich, coral pink, and buttery, it's the largest of all Pacific salmon species. Typical length and weight is about 3 feet and 30 pounds, though the fish can grow longer than 4 feet and top 120 pounds. King salmon tolerates high cooking heat the best of all salmon species and does well on a grill, or seared in a pan and finished in the oven. Leftovers make for an incredible breakfast hash. Try the rare ivory or white king salmon when you spot it on a menu or

in a smokehouse—a delicacy. Also not to be missed is king salmon from the Copper and Yukon Rivers in Alaska, especially rich in oil and flavor because of the extraordinarily lengthy journeys these particular fish make to reach home (the longer the migration, the more fat a fish accumulates to make the trip, the higher the oil content, and the richer the flavor).

Find kings fresh summer through early fall, with spring Chinook available late winter through spring. "If you're here the first weeks of spring, and can get spring Chinook from the Columbia, it's as good as you're ever gonna eat in your life," says Kevin Davis of Blueacre Seafood in Seattle. Winter feeder kings are salmon in another life-cycle stage you might encounter on a restaurant menu, and they are particularly delicious. "You'll talk to people who fish, or have eaten a lot of salmon, and they don't even eat the fish that goes back to the river," Davis says. "Once they're there, they're spawning. They use all their energy to create reproductive organs when they enter the freshwater system, (so) they stop eating and go downhill. People who fish want the ones that are out in the ocean, the feeder kings, the ones eating and getting fat."

Try Chef Tom Douglas' recipe for Washington Chardonnay–Steamed King Salmon ("In the Kitchen" chapter).

Waterways: How We Live

City Fisherman Coco Hoke

Step into Coco Hoke's backyard in Seattle's woodsy Magnolia neighborhood and you'll often smell the pleasant aroma of his smokers transforming his most recent catch (salmon, lingcod, mahimahi) into a tender, almost candy-like treat.

He built his first smoker from plywood lined with metal and developed and refined his brine and methods over the years as most home smokers do: through trial and error. Now he smokes so much fish that he vacuum-packs his extras and shares with family, friends, and neighbors. His son-in-law recently gifted him a state-of-the-art smoker, earning a big grin.

One of the perks of living in Seattle is its easy access to the water: He's out fishing and crabbing with friends daily through the seasons, a happy ritual. Over the years, he's noticed there aren't as many fish as there used to be 20 years ago. You really have to know where to look now, he says.

Like all fishermen, he has favorite catches, including this gorgeous Chinook.

"I fought him for 40 minutes," Hoke says. "Then I had people over and we barbecued and ate him."

PHOTOS COURTESY OF RICHARD HOKE

Sockeye (Red)

Some diners prefer the intensity of sockeye: Its deep, vibrant red color, its richly textured, firmer flesh, its glistening roe (eggs), and its intense salmon flavor. They turn gloriously red when spawning, making them a favorite at fish

ladder viewing windows at locks and dams. They're also one of the smaller Pacific salmon species, with typical length of 1½ to 2½ feet and weight from 4 to 15 pounds. Kokanee—sockeye that don't migrate to the ocean—rarely exceed 1 foot in length. Most Copper River salmon on the market is sockeye, because of its abundance. Find sockeye fresh summer through early fall.

Coho (Silver, White)

Lean and delicate, Coho's orange-red flesh is moderately fatty and flakes well. It is a good species to try for those who are new to the distinct flavor of salmon. Typical adults weigh 8 to 12 pounds and swim past in a flash of silvery chrome topped with black spots, hence the name; the skin of mature adults takes

on a reddish glow. Find it fresh June through September, and enjoy it at its best grilled, broiled, or baked. Try Ivar's Mukilteo Landing Grilled Coho Salmon with Fennel Leek Jam, Candied Beets & Red Chard ("In the Kitchen" chapter).

Pink (Humpy)

Small (typically 2 to 4 pounds) and abundant, it's the species most likely to be found canned because of its size. Its nickname is from the distinctive hump this species develops along its back when it spawns.

Chum (Dog Salmon, Calico, Keta)

This plentiful species has a meaty, firm texture and mild flavor due to a lower oil content, the result of spawning near river mouths and not needing to migrate as far upstream. It has long been overshadowed by its counterparts, though an effort is under way to boost its allure (hey, it worked for geoducks!). When spawning, males have pronounced, canine-like fangs and their scales take on a striking reddish calico pattern. Adults typically weigh 8 to 15 pounds. It's available fresh late summer through spring and is highly prized as a traditional source of dried winter food. Chum roe, known as *ikura*, has bright red-orange beads about the size of peas; each provides an intense burst of salmon flavor. These salmon eggs are prized as a flavor enhancer and garnish for deviled eggs, sushi, and seafood dishes.

Steelhead

Beautiful steelhead are Washington's state fish, fast and sleek migratory rainbow trout that, like salmon and sturgeon, spend part of their lives out at sea before returning to their natal streams to reproduce. They generally are blue-green or yellow-green with a pink streak along their sides, a white underbelly, and small black spots on their fins and back. Steelhead acquire even more silvery markings and cover thousands of miles over the course of their lives. They garner great respect from local anglers for the fight they put up when lured. Loss of habitat has placed several steelhead runs under the protection of the federal Endangered Species Act. As with king salmon, conservation groups and efforts abound. Many anglers are vocal about the desire to preserve this fish for future generations, flocking to message boards and Twitter to complain when restaurants and fish markets offer their beloved steelhead.

Pacific Halibut

Sweet, flaky, and moist, halibut is among the most popular fish in this region. It's also one of the best-managed populations, thanks to the International Pacific Halibut Commission, the oldest such body in the world. The commission was formed at the behest of fishermen concerned about overfishing . . . way back in 1914. Halibut is also the prized catch of the nation's longest continuously operating fishing fleet: wooden halibut schooners that have journeyed from the Seattle neighborhood of Ballard to Alaskan waters and back each year since 1913. Pacific halibut is the largest of the flatfish and can grow to 500 pounds and 8 feet in length. Delicate baked halibut cheeks are a special treat. Find it fresh from early spring to late fall. Try Ivar's recipe for Dungeness Crab–Crusted Halibut with Tomato Shallot Fondue ("In the Kitchen" chapter). At home, I like to brush a fillet with olive oil, add salt and pepper, then wrap it in foil with cherry tomatoes and pop it atop the grill. By the time the fish is mostly opaque and flaky, the tomatoes will have burst from the heat, making for a juicy summertime meal.

The Olympia Oyster

These wee, easy-to-slurp oysters are the only ones native to the West Coast, and they flourish along Washington's Willapa Bay. The treasure-seeking 49ers from the Bay Area slurped so many during the 1840s Gold Rush, they spawned an oyster boom to go along with the timber boom fueled by construction in San Francisco. The West Coast's appetite for oysters nearly wiped out the Olympia, prompting the cultivation of the nonnative Pacific oyster. Now Olympias are being cultivated in the south Puget Sound and celebrated on menus around the region. These darlings, no bigger than a 50-cent piece, are sweet yet metallic, "like sucking on a copper penny," says Executive Chef Robert Spaulding of Elliott's Oyster House in Seattle.

Spot Prawns (Spot Shrimp, Spotties)

Despite their heft, these prawns, the largest on the West Coast, actually are shrimp, with glowy, pale orange shells and snow-white flesh as firm and sweet as lobster. Local forager and author Langdon Cook likes to eat them with a knife and fork after a very quick sauté in butter. Find them fresh between April and October, or catch your own with shrimp pots or traps in May in Puget Sound or along the Strait of Georgia in British Columbia. Vancouver's Granville Island celebrates them each May at the BC Spot Prawn Festival.

PHOTO COURTESY OF ALDERBROOK RESORT

White Sturgeon

White sturgeon are an ancient fish that spend their lives wandering the bottom of waterways throughout the Northwest, feasting on shrimp, smelt, and clams. Like salmon, they return to their home rivers to spawn (most famously, along the Columbia that divides Washington and Oregon, and the Fraser in British Columbia). Unlike salmon, they can live 100 years and longer, and, as the largest freshwater fish in North America, can eventually grow as long as a kayak and weigh half a ton. They can take up to 25 years to reach maturity—one reason overfishing in the late 1800s took such a dramatic toll on the population. Fans describe white sturgeon meat as a cross between halibut and chicken, boneless and tender. White sturgeon are available fresh year-round.

PHOTO LICENSED BY SHUTTERSTOCK.COM

Pacific Razor Clams

Light, sweet, and wonderfully meaty, razor clams are a delight panfried, deep-fried, or in pastas, soups, and stews. Unlike antisocial geoducks, these clams reside fairly close to the surface of surf-pounded, sandy beaches. That lures hordes of razor fans to race to the beaches during extreme low tides from late fall to late spring when state officials open the beaches to clamming. In the dead of winter, the crowds are small but determined, bundled up against the rain and wind, wearing gloves to rake, dig, or wield plastic tubes known as clam guns. (Watch your fingertips: The name *razor* stems from their brittle shells, which are razor sharp when broken.) In warmer weather, it can feel like a festival: Clam diggers seem to walk on water along the shimmering tideflats, then become silhouettes against the pinks, oranges, and purples of the lingering twilight. (I bet some of you already can picture the Instagram you'll create on your smartphone.) Local legend has it that razor clams were unusually reclusive in May 1980. Guess they also knew what scientists suspected: Neighboring volcano Mount St. Helens was about to erupt.

Like so many other local treasures, razor clams nearly succumbed to our voracious appetite for seafood. By the mid-1940s, Washington State's director of fisheries warned the coastal populations could not withstand the current level of harvest. Beachgoers can take 15 clams per person these days, and none can be tossed aside; back then, it was 36. Many diggers ditched the smaller clams they harvested, reducing the number available to mature for future harvests. By the mid-1960s, even the resort and business owners joined in the call for better razor clam management, afraid of the loss of an important tourist attraction dating back to the 1800s. The state restricted most commercial razor clamming and further limited when and where recreational clam diggers could forage and how many clams they could keep; the population has gradually stabilized. This is why most restaurants sell razor clams from Alaska. Oregon and Washington each have only one beach open to commercial harvest. British Columbia has more, but all three fisheries sell most of their razor clams as tempting bait for Dungeness crabs.

You know what this means: Time to buy a clam gun! And, to try The Depot's recipe for Pacific Fried Razor Clams ("In the Kitchen" chapter).

Dungeness Crab

Dainty and sweet, Dungeness crab is among the most versatile and universally enjoyed ingredients in Northwest cuisine. Unlike the East Coast's ubiquitous blue crabs cooked in Old Bay seasoning, Dungeness is at its best kept simple: boiled or steamed and enjoyed neat, like a tumbler of quality bourbon. During its peak in winter, the rich meat of a Dungeness barely needs melted butter or other adornment, and lends decadence to omelets, Benedicts, bisques, sandwiches, pasta, Asian noodle dishes such as yakisoba, stir-fries, and salads.

The crabs been harvested commercially along the Pacific coast since the 1880s (Oregon even named them the state crustacean in 2009 following a campaign by schoolchildren). On average, 25 percent of a Dungeness is meat, making it among the meatiest crabs available. While most Dungy fans dive straight in for the meat, others adore the green goo (crab brains) atop a bowl of sushi rice hot from the rice cooker. To revel in all things Dungeness, head to the Olympic Peninsula and the rain shadow (read: sunnier than usual) town of Sequim, Washington. Enjoy fresh crab for lunch, then hoist your backpack to stroll the Dungeness Spit. At 5½ miles, it's the nation's longest natural sand spit. Marvel at the Strait of Juan de Fuca as its waters tumble past. Find a nice driftwood log and savor a truly Northwest day. And when you get home, try Chef Tom Douglas' recipe for a decadent Dungeness Crab BLT ("In the Kitchen" chapter).

Black Cod, or Sablefish

If you've managed to live this long without tasting black cod, you're in for a treat. Velvet-smooth and buttery, black cod have a rich oil content that translates to exceptional flavor and melt-in-your-mouth, flaky meat (and plenty of those heart-healthy omega-3 fatty acids for which wild salmon also are legendary). Robert Spaulding at Elliott's Oyster House in Seattle dubs it "the bacon of the sea." You'll find it on many restaurant menus marinated in *sake kasu* or miso paste, then broiled (look for recipes from Ray's Boathouse and Uwajimaya in "In the Kitchen" chapter). Black cod resemble cod but are members of the *Anoplopomatidae* family, a group of fishes found only in the North Pacific Ocean. It's another species that dwindled in the 1970s because of overfishing, then recovered with stricter management of fishing rights. Find it fresh year-round, but chefs say it's at its best in winter.

Lingcod

Here's another local favorite with a perplexing name: lingcod is neither ling nor cod. It's speculated that early settlers misnamed this member of the Pacific greenling family because of its resemblance to European ling and its white, flaky, cod-like flesh. Whatever you like to call it, this versatile fish cooks up snowy white and mildly sweet, and can be enjoyed as you would halibut and other tender white fish. Try it in Mo's recipe for Fish Tacos ("In the Kitchen" chapter). Lingcod is native to the rocky shores of the Pacific coast and, like many other groundfish, was declared overfished in the late 1990s. Careful management of catch size has helped the lingcod population rebound during this decade. Try Olympia Seafood Company's recipe for Parmesan-Crusted Lingcod ("In the Kitchen" chapter).

The Pacific Oyster

While not native to the Northwest, the small and sweet Pacific oyster nonetheless has become its calling card—a totem species, if you will. Oyster farmers have widely cultivated the species in the Northwest since the early 1900s, when it first arrived from Japan. These days they do so using a variety of growing methods in the scores of coves, inlets, and bays tucked along the region's coastline, peninsulas, and islands. (Popular names you'll see on many a menu include Willapa Bay, Totten Inlet, Fanny Bay, Henderson Inlet, and Pickering Passage.) As fascination with oysters and regional flavor grows, each waterway is developing its own following. Local seafood consultant, branding maven, and former commercial fisherman Jon Rowley calls the local flavor imbued within each oyster its *merroir*, akin to *terroir*, which is the way the local terrain and climate flavor wine grapes. Shuck and slurp them raw, or try the baked oyster recipes from The Oyster Bar on Chuckanut Drive and OleBob's Seafood Market on the Long Beach Peninsula ("In the Kitchen" chapter).

Oregon Albacore

If you imagine the canned tuna fish of your childhood when you read the word "albacore," stop right now. This mild, firm-when-cooked tuna is on a whole other level, meaty and rich, utterly satisfying. It's why Bowpicker of Astoria, Oregon, uses albacore for its famous beer-battered fish and chips, to great effect. The Oregon albacore fleet catches each fish one at a time for higher quality tuna and less accidental bycatch of dolphins and other sea creatures, a high standard that has earned Oregon albacore a "Best Choice" rating from Monterey Bay Aquarium's Seafood Watch. During the season, typically late summer through early fall, you can buy fresh albacore directly from fishermen on the dock. Find high-quality local canned albacore at fish markets and farmers' markets.

PHOTO LICENSED BY SHUTTERSTOCK.COM

Penn Cove Mussels

The plankton-rich waters of Penn Cove, off Coupeville on Whidbey Island, host the nation's largest mussel farm, Penn Cove Shellfish, started in the 1970s by the Jefferds family. Not many people ate mussels in the Northwest before then, said Harry Yoshimura of Mutual Fish in Seattle. "They weren't real common here like they were in Europe."

These days, Penn Cove Shellfish grows and harvests about 2 million pounds of mussels per year from Penn Cove and from a second farm in Quilcene Bay, along Washington's upper Hood Canal. They've earned acclaim at international taste tests for their sweet flavor and tender texture. You'll find delightful *moules frites* at restaurants throughout the region, including Portland's Little Bird, Restaurant Marché on Bainbridge Island (a short ferry ride from Seattle), and up and down Whidbey Island.

Smoked Seafood

What do the Hawaiian husband of my hula dance instructor and the patriarch of my Norwegian neighbors have in common? Both smoke their own fish and brag about the results. It's a point of pride here in Seattle, along with foraging your own wild mushrooms, knowing the best place to catch a sunset (my vote is Golden Gardens Park), and finding the fastest shortcut to avoid I-5 traffic.

While smoked salmon is the standard, you'll also see smoked oysters, trout, prawns, sturgeon, halibut, black cod, and albacore. Some of the best smoked seafood is available from the stands at bigger farmers' markets, such as Wilson Fish of Olympia. In the Northwest, most smoked salmon is hot-smoked per the tradition of local tribes: moist, flaky, fully cooked, and quite different from lox.

Oregon Pink Shrimp

These wee, sweet shrimp are sustainably harvested along the Oregon Coast and are one of the few shrimp to earn a green "Best Choice" rating from the Monterey Bay Aquarium Seafood Watch program. It's also a top commercial catch in Oregon, second only to mighty Dungeness crab in value. You'll find pink shrimp frozen in many markets and fresh along the coast, and it's served in shrimp cocktail, dressed up as Shrimp Louie, and sprinkled atop salads throughout the Northwest.

Petrale Sole

In yet another case of mistaken identity, this favorite West Coast fish actually is a member of the flounder family, and has been fished off the coast of Oregon since the late 1800s. Its delicate white meat is at its best when lightly floured with herbs and panfried, or rolled with fresh herbs and baked. Petrale sole was declared overfished in 2009, but the population is slowly recovering thanks to more careful harvesting of it and other groundfish to reduce bycatch. Enjoy it at its best in winter, paired with lemon, leeks, and other congenial flavors. Try it coated in crumbs and panfried crispy, or the Petrale Sole with Tomato Concassé recipe shared by The Depot on Washington's Long Beach Peninsula ("In the Kitchen" chapter).

Pacific Lamprey

It's not an eel, or a snake, but an ancient, parasitic fish with a round, blood-sucking mouth that leeches off large fish and sea mammals to survive. Like the ponderous sturgeon that lurk in the Columbia, lamprey have not changed much through the centuries, and are the oldest fish alive, with a fossil record as far back as 500 million years. Lamprey, like salmon, are an anadromous species

that spend most of their lives in saltwater but return to their home rivers to spawn. Hydroelectric dams made it more challenging for many generations to return home; this, combined with overfishing, made their numbers dwindle. Why does such an ugly fish matter? It turns out lamprey are vital to the life cycle and survival of young, vulnerable salmon because they are tastier to predators. When the lamprey are missing from rivers and streams, more young salmon get snatched up by passing birds and other predators.

Lamprey also happen to be an important ceremonial food for tribes in the Columbia River basin, with an annual harvest along the slippery rocks of Willamette Falls on Oregon's Willamette River, followed by a festive lamprey roast (one NPR reporter described its flavor as a cross between a pork chop and mackerel).

Sea Urchin

Sea urchin's coral, or roe, or butter, is creamy and tastes intensely of the sea, with a rich flavor that lingers on the palate. Taste it stirred into Italian pasta dishes at restaurants such as Seattle's Anchovies & Olives; in a savory panna cotta at Roe in Portland; and atop rice and other seafood at sushi bars.

How to Use This Book

This is not an exhaustive list of every seafood eatery, fish market, or oyster slurping opportunity in the Pacific Northwest. Nor is it meant to be. It's a combination of the quintessential and the unique, a strong kickstart to your own explorations of this evergreen, misty corner of the country. Use it to get your feet wet, to help build your own bucket list of seasonal gustatory adventures.

Each regional section includes restaurants and eateries at every price range, plus recipes, activities, and how-to guides from some of our most talented and innovative chefs, fishmongers, and foragers. You'll meet fellow seafood fans who take their enjoyment of our local treasures to a whole new level, including a fifth-generation oysterwoman; a couple who throw a crab feed and an island campout for 50 guests each summer; and a man who turned an interest in sea salt into his livelihood—and, in the process, learned to identify subtle differences in flavor between each major salt waterway in the Northwest.

More about them later. For now, it's my hope that you discover something new or new-to-you to make your next meal, and many more after that, remarkable. If you're a fellow shutterbug, share photos and notes of your discoveries with the rest of us on Twitter, Facebook, or Instagram: #PNWSeafood.

WASHINGTON

To know Washington is to know water, boats, and bridges. The state Department of Ecology counts more than 28,000 miles of shoreline along places like Hood Canal, Puget Sound, Grays Harbor, Willapa Bay, Skagit Bay, Samish Bay, and the other lakes, rivers, salty sloughs, archipelagos, peninsulas, and countless inlets and coves that make our silhouette especially tricky to sketch. That's longer than the distance around the earth.

All that disconnected land is why car ferries remain a mainstay of getting around, despite the roughly 7,000 bridges that span these waterways, ravines, valleys, and other legacies of the glaciers that shoved their way through thousands of year earlier.

Traversing Seattle alone is nearly impossible without crossing a bridge, many of them historic drawbridges that open to let tall research vessels and pleasure boats pass through Montlake Cut to and from Puget Sound. The Tacoma Narrows Bridge, famous for collapsing in a 1940 windstorm, connects Tacoma to Gig Harbor and the Kitsap Peninsula, the roiling Narrows below home to giant Pacific octopus. The Hood Canal Bridge, famous for sinking in a 1979 windstorm (yes, there's a pattern), connects the Kitsap and Olympic Peninsulas over the lengthy, skinny fjord that's home to shellfish, crabs, and spot shrimp. The soaring Astoria-Megler Bridge, which connects the Oregon Coast to the Long Beach Peninsula across the mighty Columbia River, is doing just fine, thanks. All three bridges replaced long-standing steamboat and ferry routes and made it considerably speedier for motorists to reach Hood Canal, Port Angeles, and the coast.

They may slow us down. But such an abundance of inland waterways is part of what makes our seafood selection so desirable. Lynne Vea, a Seattle chef, cooking instructor, and television personality says, "We have fabulous ocean coast accessibility, but the protection that Vancouver Island and the Olympic Peninsula offer to such vast bodies of water as the Puget Sound, Hood Canal, the Strait of Juan de Fuca, and countless other waterways are, in my opinion, what makes this region so very desirable and offers a home to such a wide range of seafood."

Water. Boats. Bridges. Whew! When you're really in a hurry to see it all, especially on a short visit, consider going by seaplane. The perspective (and extra time) you'll gain from soaring above all this beauty is well worth it. (Note: US/Canada border crossings, by car, boat, plane, or train, require a valid passport.)

SEATTLE & ENVIRONS

N
W — E
S

WEST POINT LIGHTHOUSE

BALLARD
MAGNOLIA
FREMONT
INTERBAY
WALLINGFORD
Green Lake
EASTLAKE
SOUTH LAKE UNION
Lake Union
WATERFRONT
DOWNTOWN
CAPITOL HILL
CENTRAL DISTRICT
CHINATOWN-INTERNATIONAL DISTRICT
WEST SEATTLE
RAINIER VALLEY

Union Bay

Lake Washington

Puget Sound

Seattle–Bainbridge Island Ferry
Seattle–Bremerton Ferry

Duwamish Waterway

KENMORE
WOODINVILLE
ST. EDWARD STATE PARK
KIRKLAND
REDMOND
BELLEVUE
Lake Sammamish
Phantom Lake
Mercer Island
Pine Lake
SOARING EAGLE REGIONAL PARK
Beaver Lake
ISSAQUAH
COUGAR MOUNTAIN REGIONAL WILDLAND PARK
SQUAK MOUNTAIN STATE PARK NATURE AREA
TIGER MOUNTAIN STATE FOREST
Lake Alice
Lake Kathleen

To Tacoma (See Inset)

5
99
523
522
513
520
405
202
522
90
900
5
509
18

0   2   4 miles

INSET

Pacific
Puyallup
161
167
18
161
167
99
5
161
509
512
7
203
18
90
16
Gig Harbor
Tacoma
5
5
Puget Sound

0   5   10 miles

Seattle, Tacoma & the Eastside

Seattle is a city of neighborhoods, and for the most part it eschews giant restaurants in favor of intimate, casual spaces. Surrounded by water, filled with fishermen, it has ready access to such top-quality seafood that many higher-end restaurants print their menus and update specials daily, sometimes throughout the day. Football stadiums, ballparks, malls, even the airport boast seafood spots so locals can get their fix.

Thus you can choose to dine at a comfortable seafood chain (Anthony's, Ivar's, Duke's), at a small and fresh neighborhood seafood spot (Rock-Creek, Seattle Fish Company, Jack's Fish Spot), at an iconic seafood house (Ray's Boathouse, Palisade, Elliott's Oyster House), or at a plucky oyster bar (The Walrus and the Carpenter, Taylor Shellfish Queen Anne, Emmett Watson's). Don't miss the list of unexpected seafood finds for inspiration at restaurants where shellfish and salmon aren't the primary focus.

As prices continue to climb for iconic wild salmon and halibut, menus at every price range are featuring less-celebrated delights, from petrale sole and black cod to shellfish from seemingly every cove, inlet, and bay tucked along the region's waterways.

Speaking of shellfish, Seattle is in the midst of its raw seafood renaissance. Many eateries and even supermarkets have added raw bars that feature ceviche, Hawaiian-style poke, and crudo. Oyster bars are popping up like fall mushrooms and many higher-end restaurants are offering at least a few options on the half shell at dinner. It's very possible to thoroughly tour the Salish Sea without leaving your seat at the (oyster) bar.

As Frank Bruni wrote in the *New York Times*, "To eat in an around Seattle, which I did recently and recommend heartily, isn't merely to eat well. It is to experience something that even many larger, more gastronomically celebrated cities and regions can't offer, not to this degree: a profound and exhilarating sense of place."

Anchovies & Olives, 1550 Fifteenth Ave., Seattle, WA 98122; (206) 838-8080; ethanstowellrestaurants.com. Ethan Stowell grew up in a sleepier Seattle in the years before Microsoft, Costco, and Amazon were household names, and as a young boy wandered the shores of Lake Union catching crayfish with bacon on the end of a string. He hooked salmon from the pier in nearby Edmonds and heaved crab pots off the dock in the town of Langley on Whidbey Island.

What wows him the most of the local seafood array is our shellfish. "Some of the stuff we do here is some of the best in the world," he said, naming geoduck, mussels, clams, and spot prawns as prime examples (see his recipe for Geoduck Crudo with Fennel & Radish in the "In the Kitchen" chapter, along with the recipe for Grilled Washington Sardines with Wild Watercress Salad, Anchovies & Olives). His team highlights many of them on the menu at Anchovies & Olives, his Italian-inspired seafood and pasta eatery on restaurant-rich Capitol Hill (A&O is among the many restaurants in Stowell's ever-growing culinary empire). He delights in introducing diners to seafood dishes they may have overlooked, such as geoduck crudo, whole fish, and grilled sardines. His team offers a daily array of raw shellfish and finfish, a surprise for many unaccustomed to raw seafood outside of sushi bars and ceviche at the occasional Mexican restaurant.

The decor is understated and sleek, which places full focus on the food, including toothsome pastas extruded by Lagana Foods, in which Stowell also has a hand. Fans rave about the big flavors of bigoli with anchovies, chile, and mint; bucatini with Manila clams, *guanciale*, and spicy *pomodoro*; spaghetti with creamy *uni* (sea urchin) butter; and linguini with Dungeness crab, lemon, black pepper, and tarragon. Oyster lovers should mark their calendars for Oyster Power Hour, A&O's Sunday through Thursday happy hour, which includes four types of oysters on the half shell from Penn Cove, Hama Hama, and other small farms, all for a pittance.

AQUA by El Gaucho, 2801 Alaskan Way, Pier 70, Seattle, WA 98121; (206) 956-9171; elgaucho.com. Mention El Gaucho in Seattle or Portland, and thoughts immediately turn to top-quality steak in a swank, supper club atmosphere. But this waterfront special occasion restaurant, hidden at the end of Pier 70 near the Olympic Sculpture Park, offers El Gaucho's trademark elegance with seafood as the star. At least, when you're not gobsmacked by the panoramic view of Elliott Bay, Magnolia Bluff, and the Space Needle.

The extravagant menu is not Northwest-centric, but AQUA does serve a selection of beautifully shucked Taylor Shellfish Farms oysters, available by the half dozen, and a variety of dishes that feature Dungeness crab, including its delectable crab macaroni and cheese with black truffle and Parmigiano Reggiano. King salmon and halibut make appearances during their fresh seasons.

Ballard Annex Oyster House, 5410 Ballard Ave. NW, Seattle, WA 98107; (206) 783-5410; ballardannex.com. Ballard Annex is famous for its daily happy hour, when hordes of younger diners slurp oysters for $1.50 a pearl. Later, you'll find them huddled over Staub enameled cast-iron kettles of mussels, lounging in fragrant broth. Geoduck chowder, lobster rolls, clam linguini, and halibut fish-and-chips round out the standards on the menu, and you can enjoy your shellfish baked, steamed, or raw.

The ropes, nooks, and tiles of the natty, nautical design is enhanced by an oyster bar: three steam kettles at the ready to pop open clams and mussels; tanks of whole Dungeness crab and Maine lobster; and daily specials that include a hearty bouillabaisse on Sunday.

The Annex has dual citizenship; its menu offers standards from the East Coast and West. For homesick East Coasters, it serves Maryland blue crab cake and Old Bay french fries. Tired of debating whether blue or Dungeness crabs are best? Order the East vs. West crab cake showdown and settle it. Then sit back and ponder which concoction you'll order from the bar (a round of Scurvy, perhaps?) to wash it down.

Blueacre Seafood, 1700 Seventh Ave., Seattle, WA 98101; (206) 659-0737; blueacreseafood.com. This spacious and urbane fish house imparts a feeling of being inside a glossy blue aquarium. And when the menu arrives—updated twice daily with the latest arrivals from area waters—you'll see you're in excellent company.

Depending on the season, you can splurge on dishes such as wild Alaska feeder king salmon, succulent *kasu*-marinated Neah Bay black cod, gorgeous seared Hawaiian tuna, or a tray of gleaming local oysters on the half shell. Or you can cozy up to a bowl of razor clam chowder, nibble on

PHOTOS COURTESY OF BLUEACRE SEAFOOD

Dungeness crab and bay shrimp tater tots, or hit the bar at happy hour for Dungeness crab poppers, smoked seafood dip, and smoked salmon potato skins. Find their Totten Inlet Mediterranean Mussels Steamed in Sherry with Garlic & Smoked Paprika in the "In the Kitchen" chapter.

Chef Kevin Davis's Louisiana roots are apparent throughout the menu, as well as flavors and influences from cuisines around the globe. His skill with seafood is legendary; fellow chefs throughout the city (and plenty of diners) are quick to praise his ability to coax full flavor from fish. Davis credits his catch. He prides himself on knowing the optimal time to serve each type of fish throughout the year, from whom to buy it, and the best ways to prepare it. He once foraged for geoduck with Anthony Bourdain, celebrity chef and potty-mouthed hero of the Travel Channel's *No Reservations* and *CNN's Parts Unknown*, then served him sashimi and panfried geoduck right on the beach. Bourdain's proclamation: "This is (bleeping) amazing!"

Blueacre is the second Seattle restaurant for Davis and his wife, Terresa, who also own the popular Steelhead Diner at Pike Place Market, and who met and fell in love working together in the restaurant industry. They derived its name from blackacre, the generic legal term for property. Blueacre is a nod to Terresa's legal background, and to the couple's vision of a sustainable future in which fish are managed responsibly and our oceans and waters are safe from harm. To wit, they carry only seafood from US waters that's been responsibly caught or sustainably raised.

Chandler's Crabhouse, 901 Fairview Ave. N., Seattle, WA 98109; (206) 223-2722; schwartzbros.com/chandlers-crabhouse. Come here on a Tuesday in summer, and you'll see Lake Union come alive with sailboats competing in the friendly racing rivalry known as Duck Dodge. That is, if you can tear your eyes away from the feast in front of you: rich Dungeness crab, just plucked from the giant live tank at the entrance; beautifully arrayed house-smoked mussels, scallops, and clams; and fresh, seasonal ceviche.

Chandler's Crabhouse, like fellow fancy longtime waterfront seafood spots Palisade and Ponti Seafood Grill, doesn't get much press because its menu lacks edginess and it's been around forever (in this case, since 1988, when its clientele likely channeled *Miami Vice* for fashion inspiration). But when treated to warm service, high-quality seafood, and a lovely view, it's easy to see why crowds keep coming back.

Chinook's at Salmon Bay, 1900 W. Nickerson St., Seattle, WA 98119; (206) 283-4665; anthonys.com. When you tire of watching ferries skim along the Seattle waterfront, head north to Fishermen's Terminal, grab a booth inside bright, airy, and cheerful Chinook's, and take in a knockout view of the North Pacific Fishing Fleet through the wall of windows with a side of straightforward comfort classics.

The seafood at this casual, family-friendly spot is local and fresh, and the salmon is wild. You can try it baked, broiled, in salmon cakes, or panfried. Halibut, sturgeon, lingcod, and Dungeness crab: The gang's all here. The menu ranges from creamy, saucy pasta dishes with shellfish, to fried oysters and razor clams, to oysters on the half shell, plus a variety of seafood salads, soups, stews, and chowders. But where Chinook's really shines is breakfast. Try the salmon cakes and eggs, salmon hash, trout and eggs, or a luscious seafood scramble. Make sure to order the hot, fresh scones with marmalade.

If fish-and-chips are more your speed, head next door to Little Chinook's and enjoy a basket outside in the plaza, which overlooks the terminal that 700 commercial fishing vessels call home (Note: Young kids adore checking out the boats and seabirds). Chinook's also offers guest moorage. Boaters, contact the Fishermen's Terminal office at (206) 787-3395 for details.

Anthony's Homeport

If you're near Puget Sound or a major river in Washington or
Oregon, chances are high you're near an Anthony's restaurant.
Founder Budd Gould opened his first seafood restaurant in
1969 in what was then the sleepy Seattle suburb of Bellevue,
Washington. Through the decades, the company built or
acquired additional restaurants, fish bars, and casual eateries
along a bucket list of scenic Washington waterfront locales,
including along the Columbia River; perched above Tacoma's
Commencement Bay; overlooking the marina and Jetty Island
in Everett; facing Mount Rainier on picturesque Gig Harbor;
admiring the Olympic Mountains on Seattle's Shilshole and
Elliott Bays; and on Sinclair Inlet in Bremerton. They're a
favorite haunt of multigenerational groups, with something
on the menu for everyone and reliable preparations of all
the Northwest classics: salmon, halibut, lingcod, albacore.
Chinook's, an Anthony's restaurant at Seattle's Fishermen's
Terminal, offers a literal window onto the North Pacific Fishing

Fleet, a stunning backdrop while you polish off your salmon cakes, fish-and-chips, or seafood pasta.

In 1984 Anthony's opened its own wholesale seafood company to ensure the freshness of its seafood supply and serves only wild fish from responsibly managed populations. It remains privately held by the Gould family and members of Anthony's senior management team, and prides itself on creating a positive work environment. Anthony's counts more than 200 employees who have remained with the company 10 years or longer.

For more than 20 restaurants throughout the Northwest, visit anthonys.com. For their Anthony's Barbecued Oysters with Citrus Garlic Chive Butter, see the "In the Kitchen" chapter.

PHOTOS COURTESY OF ANTHONY'S RESTAURANT

Coastal Kitchen, 429 Fifteenth Ave. E., Seattle, WA 98112; (206) 322-1145; coastalkitchenseattle.com. Despite its fish focus, Coastal Kitchen is a neighborhood eatery most famous for its breakfasts, which typically require an hour-long wait on weekends. A recent renovation added an oyster bar, with bivalves from both coasts every day at breakfast, lunch, dinner, and happy hour.

Coastal Kitchen is committed to serving only sustainably raised and wild-caught fish, and features a seasonally changing menu that rotates through the cooking styles of seafood-centric spots around the globe, from Italy's Amalfi Coast to Veracruz, Mexico. Each meal of the day offers highlights from that season's chosen cuisine, along with standards such as fried oyster po' boys, Manhattan fish chowder, steamed clams, petrale sole, and cod-and-chips.

Duke's Chowder House, Three Seattle locations (Alki, Green Lake, Lake Union), plus Kent, Tacoma, and Tukwila; dukeschowder house.com. Casually cool, Duke's restaurants emphasize beachy fun with upscale pub food served amid a wealth of historic photos, nautical decor, and often, a killer sunset. Duke's prides itself on the traceability of its seafood: Each fish has a source code so chefs know where it's from, where it was processed, and often the boat that caught it. Owner Duke Moscrip, a former Bothell, Washington, high school basketball star, stockbroker, and among the original owners of Ray's Boathouse in Seattle, travels to Alaska and the Washington coast to meet with suppliers and ensure the quality of his seafood, whether it's a future decadent Dungeness-stuffed halibut fillet or meaty Alaskan weathervane scallops due to become a pleasing ravioli. The main chowder is his grandfather's recipe, rich with bacon and fresh herbs; Duke's also offers several other warming options, including Dungeness crab and Jack Daniel's whiskey chowder and lobster Pernod chowder.

The upstairs deck of Duke's on Alki Beach in West Seattle is among the best places to linger on a balmy summer's night. Watch twilight descend as the sun finally slips behind the Olympics around 9 p.m. Watch ferries slip past as the stars come out. Watch the parade of preening teenagers, lovestruck couples, ice cream–eating families, and the occasional wedding party posing on the beach. Then order another round and watch some more.

Unexpected Seafood Finds

With fresh seafood so abundant in the Northwest, nearly every Seattle-area restaurant has at least one offering on the menu, especially when favorites (Copper River salmon, halibut, spot prawns, razor clams) are in season. Here are some heavenly bites.

Crab Beignets, Loulay Kitchen & Bar (Downtown Seattle; thechefinthehat.com/loulay): What could possibly make beignets or Dungeness crab more special? Their marriage. These fritters served with harissa aioli manage to be puffy and light yet rich with sweet crabmeat at Chef Thierry Rautureau's newest restaurant in the Sheraton Hotel. Loulay also wins raves for its flaky, perfectly done wild salmon.

Crab Bisque, Nordstrom Grill (Downtown Seattle): On a cold, gray day (of which Seattle has legion), this creamy, nuanced soup, rich and sweet with Dungeness crab and a hint of spice, truly hits the spot. Nordstrom Grill is tucked discreetly behind the menswear in the basement level of its namesake department store. Its fresh seafood specials are reliably good—as are the cocktails.

Dungeness Crab Melt, Cafe Nola (Winslow, Bainbridge Island; cafenola.com): This charming bistro famous for its french toast also serves up a satisfying Dungeness crab melt, "all crab, no filler" as one friend praised, served with Roma tomato and cheddar atop grilled focaccia. Also tasty: the smoked salmon omelet with goat cheese, cherry tomatoes, and spinach.

Freshly-Shucked Oysters, Sound Seafood at Safeco Field (SoDo, Seattle; seattle.mariners.mlb.com/sea/ballpark/): Slurp fresh, local oysters grown by Taylor Shellfish Farms as you take in a Mariners game. Also on the menu: crab rolls, salmon sandwiches, smoked salmon chowder, oyster po' boys, and Pacific cod dredged in batter made with local Manny's Pale Ale.

Grilled Octopus, Cafe Juanita (Kirkland; cafejuanita.com):
Some diners plan return visits to James Beard Award–winning chef Holly Smith's intimate restaurant, which celebrates the cuisine of northern Italy, specifically for this appetizer that cradles tender grilled octopus with fennel, smoked bone marrow, and green sauce atop chickpea puree.

Havana Seared Scallops, Paseo (Fremont and Ballard, Seattle; paseoseattle.com): Yes, everyone goes for the sandwiches, thick with grilled pork, roasted pork, or grilled chicken, the juices dripping down to your elbow with each bite. But the seafood is worth standing in line for, too. Sea scallops are seared in garlic tapenade to your level of spiciness, and topped with fresh sprigs of cilantro. Cash only. Plan on a long wait.

Mussels and Squid with Ham Hock and Braised Beans, Miller's Guild (Downtown Seattle; millersguild.com): This new restaurant from James Beard Award winner Jason Wilson (Crush) prides itself on transparency; even its online menu lists the source of nearly all meat and fish, much of which is butchered or filleted right in the kitchen and prepared in the 9-foot-long custom-made wood-fired grill. In this dish, Penn Cove mussels and Monterey Bay squid cozy up with two comfort food classics. Also try the grilled wild Alaska peel-and-eat coon-striped prawns.

Oyster Sliders, Jolly Roger Taproom (Ballard, Seattle; maritimebrewery.com): Come for the beer, stay for the sliders. This taproom for local brewery Maritime Pacific Brewing Co. welcomes everyone from partygoers to families and serves tasty sliders hand made from locally grown oysters, fresh mahimahi, or fresh ground chuck, served with your choice of house-made sauces. The killer happy hour includes buffalo clam strips and the taproom's signature clams and mussels.

Penn Cove Mussels and Frites four ways, Le Zinc (Capitol Hill, Seattle; le-zn.com): How do you like your *moules*? Choose from *moules au Roquefort* (mussels steamed with sweet onions, white wine, cream, and Roquefort Papillon); Provençal (dry vermouth, roasted garlic, tomatoes, and maitake mushrooms; *marinière* (shallot, garlic, white wine, and house-made butter); or *moules au fenouil* (fennel, pork belly, Pernod, sweet onions, and tomato). Then move on to the absinthe fountain at this French gastropub, developed by the folks behind Pike Place Market favorite Maximilien.

Peter Canlis Prawns, Canlis (Queen Anne, Seattle; canlis .com): Named for the venerable restaurant's founder, these plump tiger prawns are sautéed in dry vermouth, garlic, and lime, and have been pleasing well-heeled crowds at Canlis for decades. You also can count on expert preparation of any seasonal fish featured on the menu.

Petrale Sole with Sauteed Leeks, Altura (Capitol Hill, Seattle; altura restaurant.com): This decadent dish celebrates all the delicious hallmarks of a Northwest winter: Tender petrale sole is served perched atop sauteed leeks and alongside microgreens, Dungeness crab, and tender, succulent mussels. So good, you may skip the dessert course altogether.

Pizza with Clams, Bar del Corso and Serious Pie (Beacon Hill and Downtown/South Lake Union, Seattle; bardelcorso.com and tomdouglas.com/seriouspie): Clams on pizza? Don't knock it till you try it. At Bar del Corso, wee clams in their shells perch atop pizza alongside cherry tomatoes, molten from their time in the eatery's wood-fired oven. At Serious Pie, Penn Cove clams join *pancetta tesa* and lemon thyme.

Seafood and Green Onion Pancake, Korean Tofu House (University District, Seattle): This popular hole-in-the-wall seems constantly packed with hungry University of Washington students huddled over steaming bowls of fragrant, spicy, sinus-clearing soup, served with an array of *banchan*, or side dishes. The seafood pancake is thin, crispy, and not too greasy, packed with shrimp and green onions. For more information, call (206) 632-3119.

The Seafood Special, Blind Pig Bistro (Eastlake, Seattle; blindpigbistro.com): Blind Pig has a deft hand with seafood, particularly in the raw. Longtime *Seattle Times* food writer and KPLU-FM radio commentator Nancy Leson raves about their scallop ceviche with avocado and lime ice. While the exact same dish may not be available or in season, chances are darn high you'll love whatever else is.

Smoked Oyster Pancake, Revel (Fremont, Seattle; revel seattle.com): Revel made its mark serving refined Asian street eats mixed with whimsical comfort food favorites (think plump, meaty dumplings; rice bowls brimming with tender short ribs, pickled vegetables, and greens; a dessert of ice cream sandwiches crafted with slabs of pound cake). The smoked oyster pancake is a filling, savory delight, seasoned with Old Bay. Also much loved: the albacore rice bowl with fennel kimchee.

Smoked Salmon Deviled Eggs, RN74 (Downtown Seattle; michaelmina.net/restaurants/locations/rnwa.php): Crowned

with crispy shallots and gleaming *ikura* (salmon roe), each bite is a symphony of creamy, salty, and sweet. Another great dish at this modern French bistro from celebrity restaurateur Michael Mina: bay scallops atop a trio of winter squash (kabocha, spaghetti, and delicata), served alongside dainty, wild Northwest mushrooms.

Stir-Fried Clams with Basil, Facing East Taiwanese Restaurant (Bellevue; facingeastrestaurant.com): These fragrant, tender clams hit the spot after a long wait for a table at this perennially packed Eastside eatery. Another seafood hit on the menu: savory seafood sweet potato–flour pancakes featuring yearling oysters, shrimp, or both.

Sushi, Sashimi, and Bento Boxes, Maruta Shoten (Georgetown, Seattle; marutashoten.com): Widely considered some of the best supermarket sushi around, the bento boxes at this mid-size Japanese market are packed with fresh, high-quality fish; rice; pickles; potato salad; and vegetables (and psst . . . what's left is half-price after 5 p.m.). The grocery half of the market offers popular Asian recipe ingredients, rice crackers, and candy.

Whole Crab Curry, Little Uncle (Capitol Hill and Pioneer Square, Seattle; littleuncleseattle.com): Local food blogger Jen Chiu (*Roll with Jen*) advises that if you ever see the whole-crab curry special on the menu, order it immediately. In lieu of this treasure, the Dungeness crab fried rice and mini curried rockfish fritters should set your soul at ease.

Elliott's Oyster House, 1201 Alaskan Way, Pier 56, Seattle, WA 98101; (206) 623-4340; elliottsoysterhouse.com.
When the shy Seattle sun comes out to play, it's hard not to want to linger on the deck or near a window at Elliott's, to watch green-and-white ferries lumber past on sparkling Elliott Bay, take in a hauntingly beautiful sunset behind the rugged Olympic Mountains, and slurp just one more oyster.

Oysters on the half shell arrive on a footed platter nestled in fresh ice, gleaming like jewels with Champagne mignonette glistening in a small cup in the center. Each week, Elliott's shucks about 7,000 oysters behind its 150-foot oyster bar and offers more than three dozen options at a time. Its menu reads like a Northwest geography lesson: Barron Point, Peale Passage, Totten Inlet, Mystery Bay, Sun Hollow. Each is listed with its growing method (beach, suspended bag, rack and bag, tumble bag, long line).

"The oyster is one of the totems of Northwest seafood," says Executive Chef Robert Spaulding, who has served oyster lovers from as far as the

United Arab Emirates, Malaysia, and Thailand traveling to Seattle just to taste the locally grown Pacifics. "When we talk to people around the world about what kind of seafood comes from the Northwest, they're going to mention salmon and crab. But increasingly, they'll mention oysters."

This waterfront seafood house also offers a full range of aquatic treasures: steamed, chilled, or marinated Dungeness crab; gorgeous king crab

Oyster New Year & the Puget Sound Restoration Fund

This perennially sold-out November bash is widely considered the biggest oyster party on the West Coast and features more

than 30 varieties of fresh local oysters, an expansive seafood buffet, live music, dozens of local wines and microbrews—even an oyster luge for the iciest of slurping. It's a chance to knock back oysters with the men and women who grow them and to celebrate oysters in all their briny goodness.

Proceeds support the Puget Sound Restoration Fund, a nonprofit founded in 1997 dedicated to restoring marine habitat, water legs complete with a special post-crab hand-cleaning ritual; and a full spectrum of salmon, lingcod, and other fish. See the "In the Kitchen" chapter for Elliot's Grilled Copper River King Salmon recipe.

Oyster aficionados should definitely pay a visit for its weekday Progressive Oyster Happy Hour (Mon through Fri, 3 to 6 p.m.) in the Elliott's lounge, starting at only a dollar apiece at 3 p.m.

PHOTOS COURTESY OF ELLIOT'S OYSTER HOUSE

quality, and native species in Puget Sound. PSRF collaborates with industry, tribes, government agencies, private landowners, and community groups toward the vision of a clean and healthy Sound that is productive, full of life, and capable of sustaining the region.

PHOTOS COURTESY OF ELLIOT'S OYSTER HOUSE

So far, PSRF has restored hundreds of acres of shellfish and salmon habitat to health; planted 10 million native oysterseed at 70 sites with the help of more than 100 partners; launched three community shellfish farms to improve water quality and restore habitat; and began monitoring the potential impacts of ocean acidification on shellfish communities. Teams from Elliott's volunteer to seed, tend, and harvest the oyster beds on the Henderson Inlet Community Shellfish Farm.

Flying Fish, 300 Westlake Ave. N., Seattle, WA 98109; (206) 728-8595; flyingfishrestaurant.com. This venerable Seattle fish house was in the midst of transition during the writing of this book. Longtime owner, chef, and 1999 James Beard Award winner Christine Keff had sold it to Xiao Ming Liu, chairman of Fortune Garden Group, which owns 15 high-end restaurants in China. In an unusual partnership, Liu kept Keff onboard to help his Chinese chefs translate their flavors and dishes to the Northwest palate.

Keff opened Flying Fish in 1995 after admiring the seafood grills along beaches in Thailand where that day's catch was prepared to order. That Asian influence pervaded many of her trademark dishes, from salt and pepper Dungeness crab served with sesame noodles, to seared ahi tuna in a soy ginger reduction, to spicy red curry coconut mussels. The menu consistently features about a dozen fish in various preparations, such as grilled sturgeon and Neah Bay king salmon, as well as Northwest oysters sourced from small family farms.

In 2010, she presciently moved Flying Fish from then-trendy Belltown to quiet South Lake Union just before Amazon.com and other businesses added office towers and flooded the neighborhood with thousands of workers. She is lauded by fellow chefs for her pioneering work with seafood sustainability. Keff worked with fishermen and distributors who harvested their catch with the least disruption to oceans and life cycles. Her Hawaiian tuna supplier tagged the fish so it could be followed all the way to market—one of the only ways to combat seafood fraud.

The Grill at Seattle Fish Company, 4435 California Ave. SW, Seattle, WA 98116; (206) 939-7576; seattlefishcompany.com. After years of selling fresh seafood, crab cakes, and other staples to its community, this popular fish market has expanded its casual eat-in options for lunch and dinner to include grilled prawn skewers, grilled salmon, pan-seared scallops, fish tacos, fresh steamed crab, and po' boy sandwiches with fried oysters or shrimp. And several varieties of fish-and-chips. And chowders and soups.

The late Dave Harris, founder of The Other Coast Cafe in Ballard, developed the grill's menu. As one local put it, it's the perfect spot to enjoy high-quality, well-prepared seafood and not have to change out of your jeans. Not that that stops most Seattleites, but still.

Seattle's Oyster Bars & Oyster Hot Spots

Have your heart set on a certain variety? Call ahead to check availability, or plan your visit for late fall, winter, and early spring, when most varieties finish spawning and grow plump and flavorful. For the budget-minded, be sure to check each bar's website for happy hour specials, when the luscious bivalves often drop to $1.50 apiece or less.

Ballard Annex Oyster House (Ballard; ballardannex.com): Home to the a pair of legendary early and late-night happy hours, this natty, nautical-themed outpost along bustling Ballard Avenue gets packed with fans of raw and cooked bivalves.

Blueacre Seafood (Downtown; blueacreseafood.com): Belly up to the curved stainless-steel-topped bar crowned with glittering ice and choose from a dozen varieties sourced from waters throughout the Northwest, just right with a fabulous cocktail.

The Brooklyn Seafood, Steak & Oyster House (Downtown; thebrooklyn.com): The shuckers behind the copper-topped, circular bar pry open half a dozen to a dozen local varieties daily. They're the perfect eats before a show at Benaroya Hall or a lecture at the Central Library.

Elliott's Oyster House (Seattle Waterfront; elliottsoysterhouse .com): A classy, oyster-centric dining experience on the Seattle waterfront with a 21-foot oyster bar, more than two dozen options, and views of Elliott Bay and passing ferries. Oysters get the star treatment, served atop altars of ice that place them eye level when set on your table. Admire, then indulge.

Emmett Watson's Oyster Bar (Pike Place Market; 206-448-7721): If you're sleuth enough to find this tiny dive, tucked into an obscure corner of Pike Place Market, squeeze into a booth and pick out your oysters and beer from the paper bag menu. Relax. Feel smug that you found this laid-back treasure. Repeat.

Frank's Oyster House & Champagne Parlor (Ravenna; franks oysterhouse.com): Oysters arrive displayed on long trays of ice. Wash them down with a Champagne cocktail. Frank's is good to visit with landlubbers as well; the menu includes *poutine*, fried chicken, deviled eggs, and rich desserts.

F.X. McRory's Steak, Chop & Oyster House (Pioneer Square; fxmcrorys.com): Muscle your way through rowdy crowds after a Seahawks game, Sounders match, or Mariners homestand for peel-and-eat prawns, Dungeness crab cocktail, and oysters on the half shell at this venerable steak house and watering hole.

Little Gull Grocery (Northlake/Wallingford; westwardseattle .com): This 22-seat oyster bar and grocery offers a refuge to duck in and savor your favorite local oysters after a jaunt along the nearby Burke-Gilman Trail or post-kayak on Lake Union.

Shuckers (Downtown; fairmont.com/seattle/dining/shuckers): This oyster lair inside Seattle's grand Fairmont Olympic Hotel offers carved oak paneling, a tin ceiling, and oysters prepared nine ways, including Rockefeller, casino-style, house-smoked, panfried, and Provençal.

Taylor Shellfish Melrose Market (Capitol Hill; taylorshellfish farms.com): Tucked into Melrose Market, a collection of fine food purveyors, Taylor offers an array of live shellfish from its farms along Hood Canal and Samish Bay, as well as live Dungeness crab. Slurp and crack, or take classes to learn tips from the pros. Taylor opened two new oyster-centric joints in 2014 in Seattle's Queen Anne and Pioneer Square neighborhoods.

The Walrus & the Carpenter (Ballard; thewalrusbar.com): Bright, white, and beachy-chic, this temple of local seafood delights keeps the shucker and his cascades of ice front and center with a bar that wraps around. Savor oysters from Hama Hama Oyster Company on Hood Canal and a variety of other Northwest locales.

Whole Foods Market Westlake (South Lake Union; whole foodsmarket.com/stores/westlake): An oyster bar in a super-market? It a match made in heaven at this high-energy Whole Foods that anchors one of Seattle's fastest growing neighbor-hoods, packed with youthful tech and life-sciences workers. Watch the calendar for the 69-cent oyster happy hour at the in-store bar, featuring plump oysters on the half shell with a dozen wines, hard ciders, and craft beers on tap to enjoy alongside.

Harbor Lights, 2761 N. Ruston Way, Tacoma, WA 98402; (253) 752-8600; anthonys.com. This landmark seafood house tucked along scenic Ruston Way has had a front-row seat as Tacoma morphed from city of lumber mills and shipyards in 1959 to butt of jokes in the 1980s for its sulphurous "aroma," to its current era: home to a branch of the University of Washington, a renowned glass museum, a second Tacoma Narrows Bridge, and host of the US Open golf championship in 2015 at nearby Chambers Bay.

Over the decades, Harbor Lights largely has stayed true to its roots and menu, serving home-style seafood dishes, often in colossal portions, with consistently stiff drinks. The waitstaff is warm and knows the many regulars by name. You can't beat the view: Commencement Bay sparkles from every angle on a sunny day and pulses with angst in stormy weather.

Ivar's, Three waterfront restaurants and 24 fish bars throughout Washington, including SeaTac Airport, Safeco Field, CenturyLink Stadium, and Husky Stadium; ivars.com.
It's hard to imagine Seattle without Ivar's and its iconic namesake, the late Ivar Haglund. The local folk singer, entrepreneur, prankster, and marketing mastermind opened a small aquarium on the Seattle waterfront in 1938, then founded Ivar's soon after to sell his now-famous clam chowder and fish-and-chips to the aquarium's droves of visitors. If Ivar's stacked the cups of clam chowder it sold in 2012, it would be the equivalent of 3,199

PHOTO COURTESY OF IVAR'S RESTAURANTS

Space Needles high (the height of about 134 Mount Rainiers). Each year, Ivar's now sells almost 2 million orders of cod-and-chips.

Over the years Ivar added waterfront restaurants and fish bars throughout the region and managed to keep the public's attention via now legendary stunts and capers. He hosted international clam eating contests; rolled a baby seal in a baby buggy through downtown Seattle to visit Santa

Claus; and issued his own clam stamp in 1960 (promptly revoked by the US Postal Service). For decades, he also sponsored an Independence Day fireworks display over Elliott Bay. Despite its founder's goofiness, Ivar's full-service restaurants are renowned for pleasant customer service.

Ivar's Salmon House on north Lake Union is built to resemble the ceremonial longhouses of Northwest coastal tribes and is packed with historic photos and tribal art. It also offers a view of downtown Seattle, accented in winter by Seattle's beloved Christmas ships, and by a flotilla of kayaks and rowing shells come summer. Long a brunch favorite with University of Washington sports fans, it offers sailgating parties for those who want to brunch and then cruise to nearby Husky Stadium via the Montlake Cut.

Seafood Lover's Pacific Northwest

Ivar's Mukilteo Landing, 710 Front St., Mukilteo, WA 98275; (425) 742-6180; ivars.com. Being stuck in line for the ferry from the waterfront town of Mukilteo to Coupeville on Whidbey Island is a pleasant experience due in no small part to this waterfront eatery, just 30 minutes north of Seattle. Watch the ferries come and go from the scenic dining room or outside deck. Chef Anderson shares two of his best sellers in the "In the Kitchen" chapter.

Lark, 926 Twelfth Ave., Seattle, WA 98122; (206) 323-5275; lark seattle.com. Like several Seattle seafood hotspots, warm and rustic Lark is not strictly a seafood restaurant. Yet Chef Johnathan Sundstrom has become known for his expert preparations and devotes a whole page of his small-plate, shareable dinner menu to seafood choices.

His signature seafood dish indisputably is his roasted eel with the ancient, syrupy condiment saba, an ideal blend of sweet and savory, perched precisely atop a rich mound of aioli potato salad. As for the local catch, his halibut preparations are swoon-worthy: Neah Bay or Alaskan halibut lounging in porcini broth, sitting pretty with spiced cashews in curry sauce with hearts of palm, buddying up to baby leeks. Fans rave about king salmon so fresh you can taste the sea. Penn Cove mussels are steamed with bacon, apple, and shallots. Geoduck ceviche is perky with chile, mint, and cherry tomatoes. And of course, local oysters on the half shell. Sundstrom hails from a long line of now-prominent Seattle chefs who worked with Tom Douglas earlier in their careers. Sundstrom was chef de cuisine at Dahlia Lounge, working closely with Douglas to develop the restaurant into one of national prominence. He steeped himself in the study of heirloom foods and the latest cooking methods, and he built relationships with farmers and foragers. Within six months of taking the helm at Seattle's Earth & Ocean, *Food & Wine* magazine named Sundstrom one of its Best New Chefs for 2001. In 2007 he was named Best Chef Northwest by the James Beard Foundation.

Mashiko, 4725 California Ave. SW; Seattle, WA 98116; (206) 935-4339; sushiwhore.com. Casual, fun, and breezy, like so much in West Seattle, Mashiko was Seattle's first sushi bar to serve only sustainable seafood—what Chef Sato likes to call guilt-free sushi—back in 2009. That means no hamachi (yellowtail), farm-raised salmon, *unagi* (freshwater eel), bluefin tuna. Basically, some of the most popular items at sushi bars.

The Future of Our Northwest Catch

The charming photos in black and white that cover the walls of many local fish-and-chip joints, ferry terminals, and seafood markets show wild salmon so big, they make modern minds speculate whether Photoshop was involved. Spring Chinook salmon, swimming home up the still-untamed, undammed Columbia River after gorging on smelt, krill, and herring in the Pacific, once regularly topped 80 pounds—heftier than most golden retrievers. Our forebears assumed this supply was permanent and were stunned to watch it dwindle.

These days, a plump but relatively paltry 30-pounder is revered, in part because we now recognize all the natural and man-made obstacles this delicious fish endured to join us for dinner. These days, increasingly careful management of who, how, and when commercial fishermen, tribal fishermen, and folks like your Uncle Sven can cast nets, drop crab pots, or come home with a bucket of clams—paired with conscientious chefs and greater consideration of how logging, development, and industrial pollution affect habitat—has helped to stabilize many local fish populations and even helped some, such as lingcod and white sturgeon, to come back from the brink.

Kevin Davis of Seattle's Blueacre Seafood shared a story about a light bulb moment. Earlier in his career, a young sous chef came up to him with a magazine article about overfishing. "This is what your generation left us to work with in the future," the young chef told him. Davis felt disrespected, and the jab stuck in his craw. Then, he realized the kid was right.

"It was my generation and the generations before me that were not paying attention. It wasn't part of our culture. I decided to make it part of my culture," Davis says.

While executive chef at the late Oceanaire Seafood Room (whose space Blueacre now fills), Davis began hosting events for the Marine Stewardship Council, got involved with the salmon preservation group Long Live the Kings, and became an ardent student of sustainability. He observed where fish came from, which populations were imperiled, and which means of harvest produced the best catch with the least harm. Today he, like Tom Douglas and many other Seattle restaurateurs, supports efforts to protect Alaska's Bristol Bay and its famously abundant wild salmon population from potential toxic runoff and pollution from Pebble Mine, a proposed mine that would be among the largest in the world. Sushi Chef Hajime Sato of West Seattle's Mashiko transformed his cozy bar into a sustainable sushi paradise.

"Some people tell me I'm destroying sushi culture by saying you shouldn't eat certain things," Sato told *Seattle Metropolitan* magazine in 2013. "I say, if there are no fish left, we'll have no sushi culture at all."

In 2004, PCC Natural Markets shifted its seafood department to carry only sustainable options; Whole Foods is making strides toward this goal as well. Ray's Boathouse, Seastar Raw Bar, and other big seafood destinations are taking another tack: Their leaders are exploring whether to include the latest farmed salmon from boutique operations on the menu as a way to preserve the wild salmon that's left for future generations and keep salmon affordable to customers.

Who's right? Only time will tell. What can you do as a diner or shopper to make a difference? Most experts suggest you choose smaller, faster-growing fish (sardines, mackerel, anchovies, shellfish) and/or choose fish from populations that are well-managed, such as Alaskan halibut (in the US, the Monterey Bay Aquarium Seafood Watch website and app are helpful resources; in Canada, consult Ocean Wise, a similar conservation program led by the Vancouver Aquarium). Will you be run out of the Northwest if you eat something marked red on the Seafood Watch list? No. But you might want to take a photo of it for your kids and grandkids.

At first, his customers were wary. But after a few months, they returned, and in 2014 Mashiko celebrated its 20th year of crafting high-quality sushi, sashimi, and *izakaya* dishes, including divine *gyoza*. (Sato hails from Utsunomiya, Japan, that nation's *gyoza* capital.)

Sato is philosophical about the transition to sustainable seafood. People don't expect to eat whale at a sushi bar, he points out, but one reason is that its hardships are all over the news, just as awareness of the overfishing of bluefin tuna is growing. You don't hear about the plight of eels as frequently. His goal is to raise awareness, do his part, and, in turn, to encourage better management of fisheries to ensure delicious variety in the sea for generations to come.

But back to the food. Dreamy oysters poached with sake and soy. Northwest albacore seared with garlic sauce. Seared black cod with *tarako* mayonnaise. Oregon Bay shrimp croquettes. And that's just the local stuff.

Sato can be endearingly bossy, as you might notice from his website. Ask him about his many hobbies and passions (tropical fish, racing his motorcycle, pet adoption). And make sure to use the bathroom, which features luxury Japanese toilets.

Ray's Boathouse, Cafe & Catering, 6049 Seaview Ave. NW, Seattle, WA 98107; (206) 789-3770; rays.com. When you're 40 and considered a classic, how do you stay relevant? In 2002, Ray's Boathouse won the James Beard America's Classics Award, which honors legendary family-owned restaurants across the country. It reflected the restaurant's evolution from dockside cafe known for home-cooked meals to full-fledged restaurant in 1973 to the Boathouse's enduring reputation as a special-occasion restaurant, its iconic red neon sign beckoning where Salmon Bay flows into Puget Sound.

A recent remodel of the Boathouse resulted in a long bar facing picture windows onto Shilshole Bay, a perfect place to perch with a plate of gently seared albacore and gaze upon the lingering sunset behind the rugged Olympic Mountains. But Ray's is about more than sunsets. Many local chefs credit former Ray's chef Wayne Ludvigsen (and, in turn, seafood marketing guru Jon Rowley) with changing how they think about seafood.

In the early 1980s, when the focus was squarely on exotic fish, Ray's shifted gears and focused entirely on high-quality Northwest fish and shellfish. It offered perfect seafood, simply prepared. It was among the first Seattle restaurants to serve Copper River salmon. It threw a party to celebrate the comeback of the Olympic oyster, the only oyster native to the West Coast. It helped form what is now considered Pacific Northwest cuisine: pure foods, fresh—even wild—ingredients, served with a sense of place. See the "In the Kitchen" chapter for Ray's Boathouse Black Cod in Sake Kasu recipe. At lunch, head on up to the Cafe for good eats and one of the best decks in the city.

RockCreek Seafood & Spirits, 4300 Fremont Ave. N., Seattle, WA 98103; (206) 557-7532; rockcreekseattle.com.
Eric Donnelly earned a following for his skills with seafood at Toulouse Petit, the party-rocking, New Orleans–style restaurant in lower Queen Anne with a seemingly endless menu at every meal. In 2013 he opened his own space that feels like dining in a stylish, modern fishing lodge and offers a near transcendent experience with seafood. This is among Seattle's very best.

While the restaurant sources its seafood globally from well-managed fisheries, the menu is awash in treasures from coastal waters, rivers, and inlets. Whole fried smelt from the Columbia River is creamy goodness, from head to tail. Ivory Neah Bay king salmon melts in the mouth, as does Neah Bay black cod Provençal with sherry, lime, caramelized shallots, and Provençal herbs. That particular preparation makes you wish you'd ordered more baguette (from the delightful Macrina Bakery) to sop up the heavenly sauce. Try Donnelly's Neah Bay Yelloweye Rockfish recipe found in the "In the Kitchen" chapter.

Each night more than two dozen seafood options await, many as small plates so that you can try a bite of this, a bite of that. Oysters on the half shell hail from several Washington locales; the bar offers oyster shooters and raw bar shots for those who prefer their shellfish with some adornment.

PHOTOS COURTESY OF ROCKCREEK SEAFOOD & SPIRITS

Pike Place Market

This jewel of downtown Seattle teems with all manner of food-stuffs, from gorgeous, juicy local strawberries to impossibly fresh peaches to phenomenal, freshly strained Greek yogurt to Italian delicacies. Here are its best bets for local seafood.

Emmett Watson's Oyster Bar (206-448-7721): Teeny, tiny, authentic. If you're sleuth enough to find this tiny dive, tucked into an obscure corner of the market (roughly beneath The Pink Door in Post Alley), squeeze into a booth (literally: four average adults are a tight fit), and pick out your oysters (raw or broiled). Then peruse the handwritten menu printed on brown paper bags and choose from spicy shrimp soup, clam chowder, fish-and-chips, steamed mussels or clams in garlic broth, or chilled gazpacho. Enjoy the people-watching: families, hipsters, old timers, tourists. Relax. Feel smug that you found this laid-back treasure. Repeat.

Il Bistro (ilbistro.net): First, you have to find Il Bistro (notice a trend?), hidden as it is down an unnoticed staircase near Pike Place Fish Market, past the yammering fishmongers who fling salmon through the air before an adoring crowd. Your reward is a cozy space with arched doorways, dim lighting, and a hearty seafood linguini made with fresh pasta, clams, mussels, calamari, white prawns, and salmon, all bathed in a white wine herb broth. This Italian spot, famous for its romantic ambience, late-night happy hour, and quality cocktails, has made its home in the market for more than 30 years. Be sure to perch a spell at the marble-topped bar, tended by top-shelf Seattle barmen.

Jack's Fish Spot (jacksfishspot.com): Enjoy a cup of steamy hot cioppino or piping hot fish-and-chips perched at their postage stamp of a counter in the Sanitary Market side of Pike Place. Watch the daily chaos of the market ebb and flow around you, then take home some fresh seafood for dinner.

Lowell's Restaurant & Bar (eatatlowells.com): Yes, it's the place from *Sleepless in Seattle*. Yes, it has a lovely water view. Yes, it has one of the best slogans ever: "Almost classy since 1957." It's also a breakfast hotspot in the market and opens at 7 a.m. with plenty of seafood options. Try the house-cured lox, made from fresh wild king with a dill brine. The salmon is wrapped and weighted for a week, then sliced thin and served with a toasted bagel, house-pickled red onions, and cream cheese and capers on the side. Lowell's serves omelets stuffed with Dungeness crab (celebrity chef and local boy Mario Batali's favorite breakfast, as told to *GQ*) or smoked salmon, and Benedicts crafted from either. Can't decide? Choose the San Juan Benedict, which gives you one of each. If you really want to go for broke, order the Hangtown fry, flush with plump local oysters, bacon, scallions, eggs, and Parmesan. Dang.

Marché Bistro & Wine Bar (marcheseattle.com): This lovely French bistro is the spot to feel fancy: Enjoy oysters on the half shell, wine glass at your side, or savor dry-roasted mussels with preserved lemon, bacon, confit garlic, and shallots.

Matt's in the Market (mattsinthemarket.com): If there's local seafood in season, it'll be on the specials sheet for dinner. Matt's serves pure, delicious preparations paired with excellent service and a picture-perfect view of the Pike Place Market rooftops, Puget Sound, and lumbering ferries, plus a lingering Northwest sunset, if you're lucky. There's a feeling of accomplishment when you first find Matt's, tucked atop a stairwell in a prime perch above the action at bustling Pike Place Market. It's like joining a secret club. Dining at Matt's is your chance to see the multitude of mesmerizing, fresh, and local ingredients you passed downstairs in the market stalls mingle in blessed harmony on your plate.

Pike Place Chowder (pikeplacechowder.com): This spot offers a full array of seafood chowders, including chowders and bisques crafted from clams, seared scallops, Dungeness crab, and smoked salmon. Come prepared to wait in line (read: don't show up if you're already starving), as this tiny shop often is mobbed during the lunch rush. Makes sense, as it's won the national Great Chowder Cook-off enough times to garner a berth in its hall of fame.

Seatown Seabar & Rotisserie (tomdouglas.com): The Dungeness crab BLT is legendary. Seatown also is a good spot to enjoy local oysters on the half shell and watch happy visitors pose for photos outside. For non-seafood lovers in your group, the chicken pot pie is divine. Be sure to stop by the nearby Rub with Love Shack for Chef Tom Douglas's seafood rub.

Steelhead Diner (steelheaddiner .com): This bustling, contemporary diner perched along one of the market's steep hills offers sweet views of Elliott Bay and combines comfort classics (mac and cheese, red beans and rice) with fresh, seasonal options that change daily. Seafood standouts include crowd-pleasing Dungeness crab and bay shrimp–stuffed tater tots; substantial Alaskan razor clam chowder with apple-smoked bacon and a truffle oil drizzle; caviar pie; Angry Georgia Bank sea scallops, spicy with Spanish chorizo, serrano peppers, cracked basil and toasted garlic; and troll-caught grilled Alaskan king salmon with port-soaked local Chukar cherries and a smoky almond and rosemary brown butter sauce. Save room for dessert and the standout chocolate pecan pie with bourbon chantilly cream, baked with locally crafted fair trade Theo Chocolate.

Salty's Waterfront Seafood Grills, Three Northwest locations; saltys.com. It's impossible to have a conversation that involves the phrase "epic brunch" without also uttering "Salty's." Along with omelet stations, a chocolate fountain, a Make Your Own Mary Bloody Mary bar, and the usual brunch fare, Salty's offers a bounty of fresh seafood: crab legs, oysters on the half shell, chilled peel-and-eat prawns, Dungeness crab, freshly shucked oysters, blackened salmon, and seafood paella.

The first Salty's opened in Portland, Oregon, along the Columbia River in 1978, then expanded on the Puget Sound in Des Moines, Washington, in 1981. The flagship restaurant on West Seattle's Alki Beach, added in 1985, offers a jaw-dropping view of downtown Seattle. The chain remains family-owned by Gerry and Kathy Kingen.

Sea Garden Seafood Restaurant, 509 Seventh Ave. S., Seattle, WA 98104; (206) 623-2100; seagardenseattle.com. This much-loved Cantonese-style seafood house, reopened in 2014 after fire damage. It wins raves for its consistently good food, attributable to its burbling tanks of Pacific Northwest crab, prawns, geoduck, and fish, and the kitchen's deft skill at seasoning dishes just so since 1981. Favorite dishes include the spicy salt-and-pepper prawns and squid; fresh crab dressed in black bean sauce or ginger and green onion; honey walnut prawns; and Chinese greens and panfried geoduck. Be forewarned: They'll bring the live crab right to your table before cooking to make sure it passes your muster. Sea Garden also excels at Peking duck, wonton soup, salt-and-pepper pork chops, and noodle dishes. It's a fun place to gather with a big group late at night, before or after karaoke at nearby Bush Garden or a Mariners baseball game.

Seastar Restaurant & Raw Bar, 205 108th Ave. NE, Bellevue, WA 98004; (425) 456-0010; 2121 Terry Ave. #108, Seattle, WA 98121; (206) 462-4364; seastarrestaurant.com. John Howie opened his first Seastar in Bellevue in 2002, fresh from running the show at Palisade, the Magnolia waterfront special-occasion restaurant. This was back when the concept of raw seafood still seemed largely limited to sashimi at sushi bars. Now, some higher-end supermarkets sell poke, shellfish crudo appears on menus throughout town, and ceviche seems as normal as a shrimp cocktail. While he was not alone in pushing the raw front, the size and scale of his restaurants made an impact.

Bellevue's Seastar trends more toward business diners; Seattle's, at the base of the Pan Pacific Hotel in South Lake Union, seats more tourists, though each also is peppered with locals. The raw bar at both offers a range of delicacies, from sashimi favorites scallop, salmon, and ahi; to shrimp poke with red chiles, sesame, and soy; to scallop ceviche with a touch of habañero. It changes daily based on availability; be sure to call ahead if you have a favorite in mind.

For those who prefer their seafood warm, the menu is awash in flavor, with steamed local clams with herbs, pine nuts, butter, and white wine; the showstopping Seastar Iced Shellstock Bowl featuring Dungeness crab legs, fresh shucked oysters, scallop ceviche, grilled and chilled large black tiger shrimp, and Alaska king crab; and the ever-popular sesame-peppercorn-crusted ahi in a ginger-soy reduction.

Seastar offers its Northwest king salmon applewood grilled or roasted atop a cedar plank to great effect, and could wind up being a trendsetter yet again. After years of hearing they should shun farm-raised salmon, Seastar hopes its customers will change their minds after sampling the salmon it sells from SweetSpring near Olympia, an eco-farming operation that is careful enough with its elimination of contaminants and disease to earn a vaunted Monterey Bay Aquarium Seafood Watch green seal of approval.

Seatown Seabar & Rotisserie, 2010 Western Ave., Seattle, WA 98121; (206) 436-0390; tomdouglas.com. If you've lived in the Seattle area for at least a year, chances are high you've swooned over a perfect burger and coconut cream pie at the cacophonous and merry Palace

Kitchen, savored a dinner date at the warm and plush Dahlia Lounge, shared a potato pizza at Serious Pie, held a working lunch over Indian-style crepes at student union–like Assembly Hall, ravaged the eggs Benedict at urbane Lola, or raised a pint at rowdy Brave Horse Tavern. Or maybe all of them. And that's not even the entire collection of ever-popular, Tom Douglas–helmed establishments.

What began with the Dahlia Lounge and a coveted James Beard Award for Best Chef Northwest in 1994 has become an empire, recognized in 2012 with a second Beard Award for Best Restaurateur.

But assortment of restaurants and awards and cookbooks aside, Douglas has a passion for sustainable seafood, taking care to serve species from healthy populations and habitats.

"We'd like to be able to buy some of it again in 5 years because we didn't eat too much of it," he said.

He's just as fervent about quality ingredients. During his career in Seattle he's watched the focus of seafood dining shift from fancy preparations to the quality of the fish itself. In the '70s and '80s "it was more about the flash than about the seafood on their plate," he says. Then overfishing hit the news, and diners and chefs alike grew more conscious about what was being served. New methods of handling the catch at sea resulted in superb fish that could shine even on its own, such as in his recipe for Washington Chardonnay–Steamed Salmon, one of his favorite meals to cook at home (see the "In the Kitchen" chapter).

PHOTO COURTESY OF TOM DOUGLAS RESTAURANTS; PHOTO BY EVA MRAK-BLUMBERG

Shiro's Sushi, 2401 Second Ave., Seattle, WA 98121; (206) 443-9844; shiros.com. Sushi chef Shiro Kashiba has the respect of every chef in town who handles fish or dreams of handling fish as well as he. There's his legendary pickiness, honed decades ago during an apprenticeship in Tokyo that called for shopping the famed Tsukiji fish market. Slowly but surely, he helped raise the bar on seafood quality throughout the region. There's his exquisite mastery of sushi and sashimi, pleasing local palates since 1970, when he helmed Seattle's first full-service sushi bar. "I think he's the best chef in Seattle," says chef and restaurateur Ethan Stowell.

These days, Kashiba's behind the bar only a few days each week, but his trademark smile, impeccable *omakase* (chef's choice) plates, and beloved dishes such as rich and buttery broiled miso black cod keep patrons loyal. His connection to Jiro Ono of the documentary *Jiro Dreams of Sushi* has sparked renewed interest in Kashiba's craft, as has the success in New York of fellow Ono apprentice (and onetime Shiro's employee) Daisuke Nakazawa.

Puget Sound's Best Fish & Chips

Who in the Puget Sound region makes the very best? Well, it comes down to a host of factors. Breaded or battered? With rice flour, cornmeal, crushed crackers, or panko? True cod, lingcod, halibut, albacore, or salmon? And are those chips hand-cut or from a freezer bag? You'll have to try them all and see. Lucky you!

Airport Diner (Bremerton; bremertonairportdiner.com): Pilots land at this airport just to enjoy the halibut fish-and-chips, served in a dining room where model airplanes dangle from the ceiling and the active runway is within view. Located en route to Hood Canal and a good stop when headed home from camping or when visiting Bremerton's blackberry festival.

Anthony's HomePort Shilshole Bay (Ballard, Seattle; anthonys .com): Snag these panko-breaded beauties in the bar, served with perfectly crunchy coleslaw, bright with ginger. Watch stand-up paddleboard yoga lessons float past, along with fishing schooners and the occasional cruise ship.

Bait Shop (Capitol Hill, Seattle; baitshopseattle.com): Seattle retro bar maven Linda Derschang tackles seafood, designing a fun and relaxed fish-and-chips joint that feels like the inside of an old boat (in a good way). Beer-battered Pacific cod, hand-cut fries, and a frozen cocktail machine. Boom.

Emerald City Fish & Chips (Rainier Valley, Seattle; emerald cityfishandchips.com): Fried fish with Southern flair and a touch of spice, for eat-in or takeout. The fish-and-chip options include Alaskan cod, catfish, halibut, salmon, oysters, prawns, clam strips, and crab puppies (hush puppies filled with crab) and come with coleslaw. Grab a shrimp, catfish, or oyster po' boy sandwich, or nosh on shrimp cocktail.

Ivar's Seafood Bars (multiple locations, including most major sports stadiums; ivars.com): Locals swear by these simple and solid fish-and-chips, always made from wild Alaskan true cod, salmon, or halibut.

Little Chinook's at Salmon Bay (Interbay, Seattle; anthonys .com): Piping hot, crisp, and succulent true cod, served within steps of the North Pacific Fishing Fleet at Fisherman's

Terminal. Enjoy in booths at this casual counter eatery, or take your fish-and-chips to go and soak in the sun and salty breezes. A great spot for kids, who'll thrill over the bobbing boats and waterfowl.

Marination Ma Kai (West Seattle; marinationmobile.com/ ma-kai): Beer-battered cod or rockfish with a panko crust comes with miso or kimchee tartar sauce. Hand-cut fries are twice fried and served with house-made ponzu vinegar. Plus, there's Hawaiian-style shave ice!

Nisqually Bar & Grill (Olympia; 360-491-6123): Biker bar on the outside, wonderful fried goodness inside. Hand-battered fresh true cod fillets, coleslaw, and fries. Visit on all-you-can-eat Fridays.

Northern Fish/Fish Tales Bistro (Tacoma; northernfish.com): Battered cod, served with fries still in their jackets. Enjoy them on the lovely dock outside, then take home fresh fish for dinner.

Pacific Inn Pub (Wallingford, Seattle): This unpretentious local spot offers hand-dipped, light and crispy breaded cod piled atop a mountain of piping hot fries. The cut of the fish is what makes it especially good, its fans say.

Pike Street Fish Fry (Capitol Hill, Seattle; 206-329-7453): Local cod, oysters, smelt, salmon, halibut, catfish . . . this tiny joint where night owls refuel after catching a show at Neumos has it all.

Spud (Seattle and the Eastside; spudfishandchips.com): Some customers boast they've been regulars at these iconic (and independently owned) fish stands at Jaunita Green Lake and Alki Beach for 50 years.

The Three Lions Pub (Redmond; thethreelionspub.com): British expats longing for the thick chips of home say this place fits the bill, with breading on the fish that stands up to a sprinkling of malt vinegar (and football on the telly to boot).

Tides Tavern (Gig Harbor; tidestavern.com): The wild-caught halibut-and-chips tastes even better by the windows or out on the deck, where you can while away hours watching the boats sail by and daydream about living in a house overlooking this whole tranquil scene.

Sushi Kappo Tamura, 2968 Eastlake Ave. E., Seattle, WA 98102; (206) 547-0937; sushikappotamura.com. This sleek sushi bar in the shadow of the Ship Canal Bridge and a short jaunt from the University of Washington is included on best-of lists both local and national for its attention to detail, plush sashimi, and sensational desserts. Its cooked seafood wins raves, too, as do local treasures such as Shigoku oysters on the half shell served with *momiji ponzu*.

Chef Taichi Kitamura hails from Kyoto, Japan, and learned from local sushi legend Shiro Kashiba. Sushi Kappo Tamura is his latest venture after Chiso and Chiso Kappo in Fremont. The chef's selection served at his 10-seat sushi bar is well worth the splurge.

Tanglewood Supreme, 3216 W. Wheeler St., Seattle, WA 98199; (360) 708-6235; tanglewoodsupreme.com. It takes a bit to track down Tanglewood Supreme, tucked along an alley amid sleepy Magnolia Village. Like its surroundings, this seafood bistro is a relaxed, mellow place, where the pristine seafood does most of the talking.

Here, local oysters on the half shell arrive with green apple-shallot mignonette, lemon, and chervil. A pretzel-roll sandwich is replete filled with house-cured "salmon pastrami." Alaskan albacore loin comes dressed with pea vines and a medley of lentils in chanterelle broth with grain mustard. *Seattle Times* restaurant critic Providence Cicero named the curry-sauced Alaskan weathervane scallops paired with small green eggplants and puffs of naan one of her best bites of 2013.

Taylor Shellfish Melrose Market, 1521 Melrose Ave., Seattle, WA 98101; (206) 501-4321; taylormelrose.com. You could call this place a fish market, but it's more of a gathering place. Tucked into trendy Melrose Market, a collection of fine food purveyors, Taylor offers a sleek buffet of stainless steel tanks teeming with fresh, live shellfish (farmed geoduck, Mediterranean mussels, and Manila clams) from its farms along Hood Canal and Samish Bay, as well as tanks of live Dungeness crab and a chowder bar.

Oysters include Kumamotos, coppery Olympias, meaty Pacific oysters, hard-to-find Shigokus, and local favorite Totten Island Virginicas, an East Coast oyster perfected in West Coast waters. Choose your favorites and enjoy them right there on the spot at the 30 in-house seats (if there's room), or take home your bounty armed with cooking and serving tips from the pros behind the counter.

A Very Ballard Day

One splendid way to while away a summery day is to wander the northwest Seattle neighborhood of Ballard. Beyond the quirky shops, trendy restaurants, and one of the region's top farmers' markets on Sunday, Ballard also is home to the North Pacific Fishing Fleet and the Ballard Locks, with its famous fish ladder and lovely gardens.

Fishermen's Terminal, below the Ballard Bridge on Salmon Bay, is home to hundreds of active fishing vessels that ply Alaskan waters and the Bering Sea for halibut, wild salmon, king crab, black cod, and more. Among this fleet is a small flotilla of 100-year-old halibut schooners that represent the oldest continuously operating fishing fleet in the nation. You also might spy weathered crabbing vessels from the Discovery Channel show *Deadliest Catch*. Pay your respects at the fishermen's memorial to those who have perished at sea, grab some fish-and-chips from Little Chinook's, and inhale the salty breeze. Pick up fresh seafood and cooking tips at Wild Salmon Seafood Market for dinner later, or, along the terminal's west wall, where fishermen and women sell directly from their boats.

Head to the west end of Salmon Bay and you'll encounter the Hiram M. Chittenden (Ballard) Locks (nws.usace.army .mil/Missions/CivilWorks/LocksandDams/ChittendenLocks .aspx), which lift and lower boats of all sizes to connect salty Puget Sound with Seattle's freshwater lakes. Watch the locks in action—always fascinating, and sometimes amusing when drunk boat passengers interact with the crowd on shore—then visit the fish ladder, where Chinook, coho, and sockeye salmon zoom past the viewing glass in flashes of silver, green, and red. Catch sight of Chinook July through November, with best viewing the last two weeks of August; sockeye is plentiful June through October, with best viewing in July; and coho can be seen August through November, with best viewing the last two weeks of September. Steelhead fans can catch a glimpse November through May, with best viewing the last two weeks of February and March.

Surrounded by gardens and lawns, the locks also serve as a strolling and picnicking haven for locals, who turn out in droves for free summer concerts. Within walking distance is the Lockspot Cafe, a grizzled, 90-plus-year-old institution with an old-school bar and a walk-up

fried fish window. Head to Shilshole Bay for dinner at Ray's or Anthony's (local seafood and a killer sunset), or visit bustling Ballard Avenue for an array of local oysters at The Walrus and the Carpenter or Ballard Annex. Ballard Brothers on 15th Avenue NW offers wild seafood salads and more, fast-food style. And remember that each July, downtown Ballard fills with the aroma of salmon sizzling over an alder fire for Ballard SeafoodFest, which celebrated 40 years in 2013.

In a nod to its wired, smartphone-carrying clientele, Taylor offers online ordering with in-store pickup. For the huge percentage of apartment- and condo-dwellers on Capitol Hill, the shop also offers private parties, so you and your friends can crack, shuck, and slurp to your heart's content with no muss or fuss at home. The venerable shellfish farmers opened a new shellfish bar in Seattle's Queen Anne neighborhood and will open an oyster bar in Pioneer Square, both in 2014.

These in-city "shellfish delis" are Taylor's latest efforts to connect with a younger crowd of shellfish lovers. Taylor also buses oyster lovers out of Seattle to its Totten Inlet oyster beds in distant Shelton, Washington, on select winter nights with extreme low tides for its popular Walrus & Carpenter Picnics (see details in the "To the South" chapter), which also serve as fund-raisers for the Puget Sound Restoration Fund. There, guests wander the mudflats by the light of lanterns and the moon, and shuck and slurp 'til they can shuck and slurp no more. And now you know why Seattleites own so much fleece and like to dress in layers.

The Walrus & the Carpenter, Barnacle and Narwhal Oyster Truck, 4743 Ballard Ave. NW, Seattle, WA 98107; (206) 395-9227; thewalrusbar.com; thebarnaclebar.com; narwhaloystertruck.com. Bright, white, and beachy-chic, this temple of local seafood delights places the shucker and his cascades of ice front and center, with a marble-topped bar that wraps around the action. And it's a good thing there's so much eye candy; with no reservations taken, you'll likely wait a good bit, especially after adoring reviews from the *New York Times*, local bloggers, Yelpers, Urbanspooners, TripAdvisors, the *Seattle Times*, and seemingly everyone else who has ever stepped foot in this tiny dining room.

O, oysters! This wee space somehow manages to produce 6 to 12 oyster varieties each night, from coppery Olympias that hail from Shoal Bay, to Penn Cove Select from Whidbey Island, to Treasure Cove from Case Inlet. Should you arrive with an oyster avoider, the menu offers other local delights, such as grilled sardines, satisfying with walnut, parsley, and shallot, and smoked trout with lentils, walnut, onion, and crème fraîche. Pickled herring arrives with green olive tapenade and bread crumbs. There are also amazing cheese and decadent desserts. It's a small, well-edited menu that somehow delivers on every type of craving. And, in the new Northwest tradition, Chef Renee Erickson graciously lists her purveyors on her website, from farmers and shellfish growers to ranchers and beekeepers. To balance out all those oysters, consider the steak tartare, perfectly seasoned and topped with egg yolk.

Barnacle may be an overflow location for the lines at Walrus, but this intimate bar has its own game going on, with a copper counter that stretches the length of the room, stunning Moroccan tile work, well-crafted cocktails, and a divine array of savory enticements: canned, pickled, smoked, and cured seafood plates, house-made charcuterie, hand-sliced serrano ham, and fresh seasonal vegetable dishes. Don't miss the octopus terrine, which *Seattle Metropolitan* magazine declared one of its best bites of 2013.

As if these two seafood havens were not enough, Erickson also has the **Narwhal Oyster Truck.** This beautifully renovated 1960 Divco dairy truck plies Seattleites with easy-to-eat ocean delights such as fried Hama Hama oysters battered with cornmeal, flour, and cayenne pepper; toasted rye with smoked herring butter and pickled shallots; and her famous smoked trout salad. Look for the Narwhal Oyster Truck at the Queen Anne Farmers' Market, at Hilliard's Beer in Ballard, and perhaps serving fresh oysters and Champagne at your stylish Seattle friend's wedding.

Westward, 2501 N. Northlake Way, Seattle, WA 98103; (206) 552-8215; westwardseattle.com. It's easy to miss Westward, so distracting is the view of the downtown Seattle skyline as you cruise along the north shore of Lake Union. Then you spot its flickering fire pit. Then, you find yourself bundled up in a wool blanket on an Adirondack chair around said fire, cocktail in hand, plate of oysters alongside, pink sunset gleaming on the sides of the skyscrapers across the lake. You may never leave.

Chef Zoi Antonitsas strikes a balance between Northwest and Mediterranean flavors and makes great use of her wood-burning oven to coax smoky loveliness from many dishes, including her warming Moroccan fish stew, rich with shellfish, cauliflower, potatoes, bread, and cod, and intense with curry-like Moroccan *ras el hanout.* Each seat in

PHOTOS COURTESY OF WESTWARD

the charming, retro-nautical space offers a view of lake and city (it's not just me who finds it fetching: Westward was a 2014 James Beard Award finalist for Outstanding Restaurant Design). If you're a lucky duck with a boat or know someone who has one, park at the dock for a quick meal or afternoon drink. Pop by Little Gull Grocery, the oyster shop inside, for treasures to take home and enjoy. Find Chef Antonitsas's recipe for Smoked Manila Clam Dip in the "In the Kitchen" chapter.

The Whale Wins, 3506 Stone Way N.; Seattle, WA 98103; (206) 632-9425; thewhalewins.com. This bright, chic space is an ideal antidote to Seattle's oft-gloomy weather, especially with the wood-burning oven at its heart that transforms meats and vegetables into swoon-worthy meals, many perfectly paired with pickles for ultimate umami.

Each menu features a selection of fish and shellfish plates as well, including divine sardines on toast with curried tomato; herring rillettes on toast with pickled shallot; roasted clams from Hama Hama on Hood Canal with dill, serrano ham, fennel, brown butter, and cream; and pan-roasted whole trout with lentils, piquillo peppers, olives, Meyer lemon, and cilantro vinaigrette.

Save room for dessert, which also hails from the oven, this time in the form of plump, pillowy brownies, moist and dense pound cake, and a variety of fruit desserts. It's yet another delightful space with good food from Seattle restaurant phenom Renee Erickson.

Wild Ginger, 1401 Third Ave., Seattle, WA 98101; (206) 623-4450; The Bravern, 11020 NE Sixth St., Bellevue, WA 98004; (425) 495-8889; wildginger.net. Like Lark, Wild Ginger is not strictly a seafood restaurant, but a pan-Asian restaurant that happens to work wonders with carefully sourced, fresh seafood. Tanks of live crab and lobster make that goal even easier.

Thai spicy clams feature fresh, local Manila clams in a spicy roasted chili paste with tomato, red pepper, palm sugar, and basil. Locally grown Mediterranean mussels come in two preparations: Cambodian, with turmeric, lime leaf, galangal, lemongrass, Thai chiles, and coconut milk; or Rayong, with spicy Thai coconut curry sauce, galangal, and pineapple. Otak Otak, a popular appetizer, features salmon in a red curry coconut sauce, wrapped in a banana leaf packet and steamed, then grilled. Yum.

Where to Buy in Seattle

Seattle is blessed with a multitude of high-quality fish markets, from those favored by chefs (Mutual Fish Company, Uwajimaya, Wong Tung Seafood) to many smaller operations tucked neatly into neighborhood side streets (Ballard's Fresh Fish Company, Seattle Fish Company in West Seattle, Mercer Island's Freshy's Seafood Market). Most offer bites to go, from hot cioppino to fish-and-chips to fish sandwiches.

Access to so much seafood also means most major supermarkets offer fresh fish and sometimes even live shellfish. Seattle Caviar Company in the Eastlake neighborhood offers sustainable roe options (including *ikura* and white sturgeon), with in-store tastings (and even carries gluten-free blini).

Here are some perennial favorites.

Gemini Fish Market, 1410B NW Gilman Blvd., Ste. B, Issaquah, WA 98027; (425) 961-0741; geminifish.com. This fun, friendly, family-owned fish market wins high marks from fans for its high-quality selection of Northwest favorites (spot prawns, Dungeness crab, Columbia River spring Chinook, a variety of bivalves) and specialties from around the globe, with a focus on seafood from sustainable stocks. Owners Kim and Jim Oswalt and Executive Chef Dave Gipson take pride in their signature recipes for crab cakes, salmon burgers, mustard dill halibut, and a variety of dips, spreads, rubs, sauces, and oven-ready recipes.

Jensen's Old-Fashioned Smokehouse

Mike Jensen's smokehouse resides near a bustling intersection crammed with ethnic markets, gas stations, an oil change center, and a Chinese restaurant that specializes in karaoke. But step inside his tidy shop and the cacophony dissipates—yes, just like smoke. The heady, sweet scent of smoked salmon envelops the senses until you can't stop pondering how best to enjoy his fish. In an omelet? Atop a steamy bowl of rice? Or perhaps stirred into a top-secret salmon chowder recipe?

Jensen grew up a ferry's ride across Puget Sound in Bremerton, watching his parents run their own retail smokehouse. Armed with a business degree with from the University of Washington, he decided to try his own hand at the craft. His became known as one of the premier smokehouses in Seattle, and he's still going strong more than 25 years later, supplying fish to local shops and many of the vendors at Pike Place Market.

Cutters handpick and fillet each fish, brine each batch, then slowly cook the salmon for up to 18 hours for rich, smoky flavor and color. Their ingredients are simple: salmon, water, sugar, salt, and natural alderwood smoke. Choose from their selection, or bring in your own catch for smoking.

10520 Greenwood Ave. N., Seattle, WA 98133; (206) 364-5569; jensenssmokehouse.com

Mutual Fish Company, 2335 Rainier Ave. S., Seattle, WA 98144; (206) 322-4368; mutualfish.com. The Mutual Fish Company is a retail and wholesale seafood market that's been owned and operated by three generations of the Yoshimura family since 1947 and has been a favorite of local restaurateurs and local home cooks for decades.

The small, bright shop in Seattle's congested Rainier Valley offers a wide variety of fresh, seasonal fish such as black cod, rockfish, albacore, and various species of salmon; tanks of live clams, mussels, and oysters from around the region; and a complete line of Asian groceries. Harry Yoshimura says Mutual has adjusted its offerings with the ever-changing demographics of the neighborhood and the changing tastes of its customers.

"Everything is becoming more Americanized," Yoshimura says. "Where in the old days, people used to eat a lot more fish heads and bones and a lot of the less expensive seafood, and now the trend is salmon and halibut, more filleted fish, and things that are a little bit easier to cook and don't smell up the house as much." Other changes over the years: Mutual now sells more fresh, raw oysters than shucked oysters in jars. And not many people ate mussels until Penn Cove Shellfish began growing them off Whidbey Island in the 1970s. "They weren't real common here like they were in Europe," he says.

With the way the world's changing, everyone's experiencing different types of seafood prepared in different ways. "You never saw ceviche in a restaurant before. You never saw Hawaii poke in a restaurant before, but now it's pretty much common," Yoshimura says. "You're seeing a change in cultures and everything, and various types of preparation from all over the world now."

Supermarket Seafood

Living so close to the water has its perks. Many major local markets offer a solid variety of salmon, halibut, cod, and sole, and most will cut it to order. Want to know your seafood is sustainable? Shop PCC Natural Markets. The local co-op was the first retailer to partner with the Monterey Bay Aquarium's Seafood Watch program to ensure all fin fish and shellfish offered in their stores are not harvested from dwindling stocks. Other local chain Metropolitan Market offers a poke bar (raw and cooked Hawaiian-style seafood salads) at its Magnolia location. West Seattle Thriftway is renowned for its fresh seafood and crab cakes.

Want live seafood? Hit the many Asian supermarkets in the region, including Asian Food Center (Bellevue), Uwajimaya (Seattle, Bellevue, and Renton), Lam's Seafood Market (Seattle), and 99 Ranch Market (Edmonds and Kent). Each boasts tanks of live seafood, and most will fry whole fish or steam whole crabs for you as a convenience.

Pike Place Market, Open daily year-round; pikeplacemarket.org. The nation's oldest continually operating farmers' market is famous for its fish-tossing fishmongers at Pike Place Fish Market, and it houses several other longtime fish and shellfish counters among its bustling arcades, including Pure Food Fish Market and City Fish. Don't miss the fresh cioppino at Jack's Fish Spot, run by a former commercial fisherman. Pike Place Market's seafood shops also are where many locals buy their smoked salmon to ship home to family and friends for the holidays.

Tacoma Boys/H&L Produce, 5602 6th Ave., Tacoma, WA 98406; (253) 756-0902; tacomaboys.com (with additional locations in Puyallup and Lakewood). The giant readerboard that faces Highway 16 boasts of juicy Cadillac peaches, freshly cut Christmas trees, and local asparagus, depending what time of year you're crossing the nearby Tacoma Narrows Bridge. But step into this grocery, a Tacoma landmark since 1985, papered with cheerful, hand-painted signs, and you'll find quality wild seafood, including bacon-wrapped scallops, stuffed tilapia, and wild salmon with cedar planks for grilling.

Tim's Seafood, 224 Parkplace Center, Kirkland, WA 98033; (425) 827-0195; timsseafood.com. Widely considered the best fishmonger on the Eastside, Tim's is known for the Hawaiian-style ahi poke and popular tropical fish including mahimahi and opah, as well as for meaty crab cakes, hot cioppino, dry-pack scallops, and top-quality ivory salmon.

University Seafood & Poultry, 1317 NE 47th St., Seattle, WA 98105; (206) 632-3900; universityseafoodandpoultry.com. Impossibly fresh fish, smoked salmon, wild game, and holiday meats keep loyalists coming back year after year to this U-District institution, marked by a neon fish sign. "It's not much to look at," all of them note. But when you finish grilling your salmon, pull your halibut from the oven, or prepare your smoked salmon appetizer, you'll be glad you stopped by.

Uwajimaya, Chinatown/International District, Bellevue, Renton; also in Beaverton, Oregon; uwajimaya.com. Uwajimaya has been selling a huge variety of fresh and live seafood, Asian groceries, and produce since 1928, growing a bit more each year. The flagship store has been an anchor in Seattle's Chinatown/International district for decades. Step inside and your eyes are drawn in a million directions, with aisles packed with snacks, noodles, rice, teas, fruits, vegetables, meats, and spices from Japan, Korea, China, Vietnam and elsewhere in Asia. But the seafood department is the tour de force, where tank after tank of live seafood bubbles and burbles. It's a virtual aquarium of crabs, clams, lobster, geoducks, spot prawns, oysters, snapper, mussels, and more. You'll also find sushi-grade seafood and ocean treats like creamy uni (sea urchin). See their recipe for Black Cod or Salmon Kasuzuke in the "In the Kitchen" chapter.

PHOTOS COURTESY OF UWAJIMAYA

Top Northwest Farmers' Markets for Seafood

The Northwest teems with bustling, high-quality farmers' markets that sell everything from foraged wild mushrooms and sea beans to local organic produce to milk from grass-fed cows. At the larger markets you'll often find fishmongers and smokers, too. Here are some best bets.

Portland, Oregon

Portland Farmers' Market at Portland State University, open Sat Mar–Dec; portlandfarmersmarket.org. This market features fresh seafood from Yakama Nation fisherman Simon Sampson and his fish business, **Columbia River Fish Company Treaty 1855**, which supplies fresh wild salmon to Portland-area restaurants and residents. You can also take home fresh Dungeness crab and clams from **Linda Brand Crab**; artisanal sea salt from **Jacobsen Salt Company** of Tillamook, Oregon; artisanal hot- and cold-smoked wild salmon from **The Smokery**; and clams, oysters, and wild troll-caught salmon, lingcod, and tuna from **Stonewall Banks Seafood** of Oak Grove, Oregon.

Upcoming: Plans are under way for a new daily, year-round, indoor-outdoor marketplace named for Oregon native and American cooking icon James Beard. The James Beard Public Market (jamesbeardpublicmarket.com) will be located at the west end of the Morrison Bridge in downtown Portland and will feature 50-plus permanent vendors, restaurants, a teaching kitchen, and an event space. Groundbreaking is planned for 2016.

Seattle

Ballard Farmers' Market, open Sun year-round; ballard farmersmarket.wordpress.com. Tucked between stalls selling fresh-baked pies, organic fruits and vegetables, locally foraged mushrooms, Jonboy caramels, and luscious Whidbey Island Ice Cream bars, look for **Wilson Fish** of Olympia, makers of smoked salmon some have called life-changing, plus flash-frozen wild albacore from **Fishing Vessel St. Jude**, and fresh salmon in season from the boats of **Loki Fish Co.** Fresh oysters? **Hama Hama Oyster Company** brings them from Lilliwaup on Hood Canal and **Taylor Shellfish Farms** from its tideflats around the state.

Vancouver, BC

Granville Island Public Market, open daily year-round; granvilleisland.com/public-market. This peninsula and shopping district is a hot spot for tourism and entertainment, not to mention wonderfully fresh fish. **Longliner Seafoods** carries wild fresh or smoked BC salmon and local halibut. It has its own smoked salmon pouches that require no refrigeration. **Lobsterman** has over 25,000 gallons of saltwater in tanks full of lobster, crab, clams, mussels, scallops, and oysters from the top fisheries in BC and beyond. **Finest at Sea** sells only wild products caught by its own fisherman through sustainable fishing practices.

Wild Salmon Seafood Market, 1900 W. Nickerson St. #105, Seattle, WA 98119; (206) 283-3366; wildsalmonseafood.com. Paula Cassidy's eyes sparkle when she talks seafood. It may be her livelihood as co-owner of this bustling seafood market at the heart of Seattle's Fishermen's Terminal, but it's her passion too. She and partner Jon Speltz were among the first in town in the early 1990s to stop selling farmed salmon. In the beginning, that meant selling wild salmon that was frozen at sea, then a new concept for most seafood shoppers.

"The first year was tough, then people caught on," Cassidy says. "We were here at Fishermen's Terminal, and we wanted to support the fishermen. We buy direct whenever possible."

Wild Salmon got its start as a cooperative for fishermen to sell their local catch. Now it's a full-service seafood market, packed with fresh fish, shellfish, smoked seafood, alder and cedar planks for baking and grilling, and a thriving shipping business, all within steps of the North Pacific Fishing Fleet.

Wong Tung Seafood, 210 12th Ave. S., Seattle, WA 98144; ngo -imagination.com/seafood. "Down-to-earth" is a common description for this seafood shop, and it is apt. It makes up for its lack of ambience with abundant live seafood and low prices. Pro tip: Be prepared to pay cash only. People rave about the fresh fish paste, a tough-to-find delicacy.

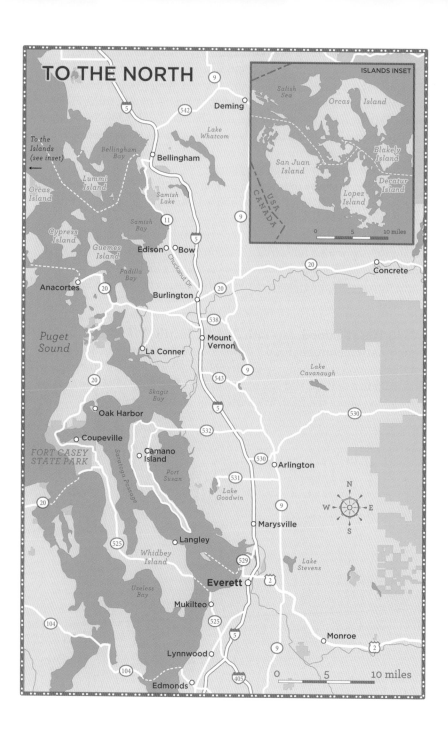

TO THE NORTH

ISLANDS INSET

Salish Sea

Orcas Island

San Juan Island

Blakely Island

Decatur Island

Lopez Island

USA
CANADA

0   5   10 miles

9

5

542

Deming

Lake Whatcom

Bellingham Bay

Bellingham

To the Islands (see inset) ←

Lummi Island

Orcas Island

Samish Lake

Cypress Island

11

Samish Bay

9

Guemes Island

Edison ○ ○ Bow

Chuckanut Dr.

Padilla Bay

Concrete ○

20

Anacortes ○

20

Burlington ○

20

538

Puget Sound

La Conner ○

Mount Vernon

543

9

Lake Cavanaugh

Skagit Bay

20

5

Oak Harbor ○

530

532

Coupeville ○

Saratoga Passage

FORT CASEY STATE PARK

Camano Island ○

530

20

Port Susan

531

Arlington ○

Lake Goodwin

9

N
W · E
S

525

Langley ○

Whidbey Island

529

Marysville ○

Lake Stevens

Useless Bay

Everett

2

Mukilteo ○

104

525

Monroe ○

5

2

Lynnwood ○

9

104

405

Edmonds ○

0   5   **10 miles**

To the North: Whidbey Island, Chuckanut Drive & the San Juan Islands

About an hour's drive north of Seattle, when you leave Interstate 5 and outlet malls in your rearview to head west, the landscape shifts. Glaciers crept through here eons before, leaving valleys, foothills, and sloughs in their wake. Farmland abounds: 100,000 acres in the Skagit Valley alone that dance with golden daffodils, a rainbow of tulips, and vibrant irises each spring. They produce the most flower bulbs of any county in the country. You'll see leafy green potato tops that hint at fingerlings below; acres of plump, juicy berries; apple orchards; and dairies that craft top-notch cheese, butter, and yogurt. Clouds of trumpeter swans and snow geese drift above the region's fields, forests, and rivers during each year's migrations.

The gradual return of the forest signals that you're closing in on Samish Bay, whose extensive tidelands, nutrient-rich currents from the nearby Georgia strait and clean water makes it a strong natural producer of shellfish. There's a diverse array of eateries at which to enjoy your loot. Crack open a beer at a picnic table, oysters warming atop a nearby grill, as you gaze at the San Juan Islands. Or enjoy that same view perched several hundred feet higher in an elegant cliff-top dining room, armed with an award-winning wine list to pair with your oysters. Or savor your oysters over a game of shuffleboard at a tavern a few miles down the road. So many oysters, no shortage of options.

Let's explore the roads from the shores of Samish Bay to the Salish Sea, where even the gas stations offer their own special clam chowder and smoked salmon.

Anacortes

This windswept town anchored on Fidalgo Island is your last stop before boarding ferries bound for the San Juan Islands and sits at the junction of the highway that cruises past Deception Pass and south along Whidbey Island. Vibrant berry stands line the main drag in summer, freshly picked from area fields. Most local markets offer fresh seafood, and you can buy

it right from the dock in the marina. Take heart that no matter where you dine, you're likely to have a decent meal due to the ubiquity of fresh fish. Some of the best seafood you'll enjoy may not necessarily be from a restaurant: Gas stations, grocery stores, and roadside stands all vie to sell fresh fish, smoked seafood, and clam chowder. If you're trying to piece the region's fractured topography together, the views from atop the forested hills of Washington Park on Fidalgo Island should solve the riddle.

Adrift, 510 Commercial Ave., Anacortes, WA 98221; (360) 588-0653; adriftrestaurant.com. Cozy and unpretentious, with warm, friendly service and a mix of booths, bar, and tables, Adrift is a favorite breakfast spot for the legions awaiting the ferry for the San Juans during the sunnier months and also popular with seafood fans for its fresh, local ingredients. Favorites include the decadent crab au gratin; light and crisp panfried Samish Bay oysters; and a refreshing ahi/toro poke salad. In late spring, do not miss their plump and sweet local spot prawn cocktail. Vegetarians and those who avoid gluten also will find options on the menu, and there are plenty of local brews on tap.

Black Rock Seafood, 8991 Stevenson Rd., Anacortes, WA 98221; (360) 293-2525. This locals spot cooks crab and shrimp on the premises in season, offers plenty of fresh seafood from nearby waters, and sells flavorful pickled herring. Call ahead before you visit if you have your heart set on a particular item, as they sell out quickly.

Puget Sound Prawns, B-dock in Cap Sante Boat Haven (off R Avenue) at the Port of Anacortes, 100 Commercial Ave., Anacortes, WA 98221; (360) 202-3024; pugetsoundprawns.com. Head to the docks on Friday and Saturday in season for live, local, wild shrimp, trap-caught by this cooperative of small-boat, family-crewed, local fishermen who have been fishing commercially most of their adult lives. Look for live wild coon-striped shrimp May through Sept, and live wild spot prawns late June through Aug.

SeaBear Store & Smokehouse, 605 30th St., Anacortes, WA 98221; (360) 230-1082; seabear.com. SeaBear is the life's work of Anacortes fisherman Tom Savidge and his wife, Marie. In 1957 they built a backyard smokehouse and began selling smoked wild salmon to local taverns. When customers asked that he preserve his salmon longer, Savidge developed a special pouch that preserves smoked salmon with no need for refrigeration. His innovation suddenly made it easy for tourists to take smoked salmon home or ship it to family and friends and vaulted SeaBear to national recognition. Now, SeaBear ships smoked salmon, lox, chowders, wild salmon burgers, bacon, chorizo, and other seafood to all 50 states. Its retail store offers these favorites, plus local artisan gifts, coffee, and Washington wines.

The Shrimp Shack, 6168 State Rte. 20, Anacortes, WA 98221; (360) 293-2531; shrimpshack.us. This big red-and-white shack alongside Highway 20 is a popular stop for many campers and daytrippers en route to Deception Pass State Park, despite some grumbling about portion sizes. Grab a seat at one of its picnic tables and hoist an oyster burger, shrimp burger, sockeye salmon burger, crab cake burger, elk burger, gator burger (you get the picture). They also offer more straightforward burgers and a kids' menu, along with deep-fried colossal prawns, clam strips, fish-and-chips, popcorn shrimp, and local Pacific oysters. Still hungry? They've got fresh seafood for you to take home, too, including local shrimp and crab in season.

Bow, Edison & Chuckanut Drive

These neighboring towns nestled in the northwest corner of Skagit Valley—the sweet spot between Samish Bay and civilization—often are mentioned in the same breath, typically by daytrippers up from Seattle or down from Bellingham to partake in the fabulous baked goods at Breadfarm and pie at the Edison Cafe; local cheese and butter from Golden Glen Creamery and Samish Bay Cheese; meals lovingly crafted from local produce and meats; and the luscious, strikingly fresh Samish Bay oysters served as shooters and fashioned into various fried concoctions. Park your car (or your bike) and wander a spell. The area's charm grows on you.

Blau Oyster Company, 11321 Blue Heron Rd., Bow, WA 98232; (360) 766-6171; blauoyster.com/story.htm. This family-run, straight-forward, working oyster farm traces its legacy back to 1935 and sits on Samish Island in Samish Bay at the bottom of a long, curvy road. Even mammoth tour buses from British Columbia brave this route after a trip to the Skagit Valley Tulip Festival because the oysters are good. When that happens, it sometimes takes eight shuckers shucking to keep up with demand.

Take home fresh oysters, clams, mussels, and crab. Got a hankering for panfried oysters? Head back into downtown Edison to the Edison Inn, which serves Blau's beauties.

The Edison Inn, 5829 Cains Ct., Edison, WA 98232; (360) 766-6266; theedisoninn.com. Test your shuffleboard skills to the beat of whatever song happens to be blaring as you tip back Northwest micro-brews and slurp oysters gathered just minutes from here by Blau Oyster Company on Samish Bay. The Edison is a laid-back, come-as-you-are, everybody's-welcome kind of spot, akin to hanging out in your cool uncle's basement lounge, complete with wood paneling, scores of framed old photos of the area, and solid bar food standards with cameo appearances from Skagit Valley produce, meats, cheese, and seafood.

It's been kicking since 1934, through two moves, Prohibition, and a series of owners. What has stayed the same is its easy access to fresh, creamy, dainty local oysters. On the menu: oyster shooters with house-made cocktail sauce or a splash of vodka; oyster cocktail; a hand-breaded grilled oyster scatter; and a hefty, panfried oyster burger. Urp.

Chuckanut Drive

There's a sense of wandering into a secret space as you approach Chuckanut Drive. The forest, largely absent through open valleys and sloughs, reappears as a canopy—a dramatic one come fall, when vivid foliage tumbles down amid the backdrop of stately evergreens. The winding road hugs sandstone cliffs; peek-a-boo views of Samish Bay, the San Juan Islands, the Olympic Peninsula, and Vancouver Island flicker past at regular intervals through the trees. Built for logging, this once was the only road from Burlington, 19 miles long, running past Larrabee State Park with its woodsy hikes and meadows and fat red and purple starfish, to Fairhaven, just outside Bellingham. It was paved in 1921 and gained notoriety as a liquor transport route during Prohibition (some of that era's "restaurants" have endured as actual eateries). Chuckanut became Washington's first scenic byway. In fair weather, cars and bikes share the road. On rainy days, you might be the lone soul puttering along, chancing upon a bald eagle or great blue heron, wondering how you got so lucky.

PHOTO COURTESY OF TAYLOR SHELLFISH; PHOTO BY KELLY CLINE

The Oyster Bar, 2578 Chuckanut Dr., Bow, WA 98232; (360) 766-6185; theoysterbar.net. Step inside the little hunting lodge-esque house perched on a cliff alongside twisty Chuckanut Drive and your breath will catch: A wall of windows looks onto Samish Bay, the San Juan Islands sparkling in the distance. In winter, a fireplace crackling along the wall bids you to linger; in summer, the sunset that sets the deck aglow in oranges, purples, and pinks. So linger you do, and settle in for a fantastic meal.

Here, the oysters come fried golden crispy with a Parmesan bread crumb crust; fresh on the half shell with iced grapefruit mignonette; or baked with spinach, tomatoes, bacon, dry sherry, and chives (recipe found in the "In the Kitchen" chapter). Much of the seafood on the menu hails from the Northwest, including Columbia River sturgeon, Dungeness crab, wild salmon, spot prawns, and Pacific halibut. In season, Taylor Shellfish Farms Manila clams are steamed with morels, leeks, and grape tomatoes in a roasted sweet corn and thyme broth. In warm weather, a chilled seafood salad is resplendent with Dungeness crab, prawns, avocado, papaya, and hard-boiled egg, dressed for the weather in serrano chile and peanut oil.

The restaurant got its start as a roadside oyster stand for Rockpoint Oyster Company in the 1920s, became a lunch counter due to its popularity, then shuttered during World War II when plant manager Zenzabaro Maekawa and his family were sent to a Japanese internment camp. Otis Amos bought the restaurant in 1946 and named it the Oyster Bar. Subsequent owners expanded the menu, renovated the restaurant, and added a wine cellar. Guy and Linda Colbert, the most recent owners, have run the Oyster Bar since 1987 to popular and critical acclaim. Like so many others in that time, they moved to the Northwest from Southern California in search of a healthier environment for their family. They never left. The folks at the Oyster Bar cure their own gravlax and obtain much of their produce during summer and fall from Morgan Farms just a mile south. They serve breads from The Bread Farm in Edison; berries from nearby Sakuma Farms; wild mushrooms, nettles, and huckleberries from local foragers; and oysters, clams and mussels from Taylor Shellfish, directly below the restaurant on Samish Bay. *Wine Spectator* has awarded its wine cellar its Best of Award of Excellence every year since 1990.

Parking can be tricky along this narrow stretch of road with limited official parking spaces. Leave yourself time to look for just the right spot.

Oyster Creek Inn, 2190 Chuckanut Dr., Bow, WA 98232; (360) 766-6179; oystercreekinn.com. If you can't bear to tear your eyes from the beauty of your surroundings, Oyster Creek Inn is ideal. Surrounded by windows, the intimate dining room offers views of ferns, waterfalls, moss-covered trees, and Oyster Creek below, where salmon come home to spawn each fall.

Each carefully crafted dish from Chef Thomas Palmer's kitchen also brings the outdoors in and celebrates the abundance of the Skagit Valley and Samish Bay, from a heavenly house-made Dungeness crab ravioli served with artisan house-made bread, to a warm seafood salad with butter lettuce, salmon, scallops, prawns, mussels, and clams, to a geoduck crudo. The oysters here also arrive on the half shell; baked as a gratinée with bacon, Parmesan, and spinach; and panfried, served atop fettuccine.

Oyster Creek Inn is situated near the historic bridge on a hairpin curve just past the entrance to Taylor Shellfish Farms. Like its neighbor, The Oyster Bar, it dates back to the mid-1920s, where it began as a small lunch and beer shack, then evolved over the decades to become its current enchanting incarnation.

Taylor Shellfish Samish Farm Store, 2182 Chuckanut Dr., Bow, WA 98232; (888) 766-6002; taylorsamish.com. First, you need to spot the driveway, easy to miss as distracted as you are by the scenery along Chuckanut Drive. Then, navigate the narrow drive down, down, down until you begin to wonder if you chose the right road after all. Then, you see it: Samish Bay sparkling before you, islands in the distance, and the small buildings and counter that serve as Taylor's Samish outpost.

This shellfish farming operation, headquartered on the Hood Canal, for generations has raised oysters, mussels, and clams in Samish Bay, where they still are sorted, washed, and bagged by hand. For visitors, this location is set up as part grocery, part picnic area. Step inside and select your favorite oysters from the bubbling tanks of Virginicas, Kumamotos, Olympias, and Pacifics, along with a bag of instant charcoal, lemons, cocktail sauce, or whatever else your heart may desire (even Goldfish crackers for the kids).

Settle next to one of the nearby kettle grills and picnic tables, set your oysters over the coals to warm, and savor the moment as you listen to the waves lap the shore, watch the seabirds carom past, and speculate just how long it would take to swim to the nearest island if you have one more beer. Note: The picnic area is on a first-come basis, and you'll want to bring picnic supplies and drinks. The farm store also carries wild salmon and halibut, pickled herring, Dungeness crab, geoduck, Mediterranean mussels, Manila clams, and smoked salmon and shellfish.

Waterways: How We Live

Shellfish at Sunset with Lynne Vea

Northwest summer sunsets seem endless. The sun's molten after-glow shimmers and fades into an inky violet twilight that lingers well past when the stars begin to flicker and glow. Seattle-area chef, television personality, and cooking instructor Lynne Vea and her husband, Brad, like to watch the spectacle next to a crackling campfire along the water, savoring the last few bites of the day's fresh catch.

Whenever they can get away, they boat with friends around the San Juans and Canadian islands in the Strait of Juan de Fuca, fishing, crabbing, and oystering. Vea's a fan of Westcott Bay Oysters on San Juan Island. "After we drop our crab pots (if the seasons coincide), we jet over to Westcott. Later, we slurp oysters while the crabs are boiling away."

At least once a year, they gather a gaggle of family and friends and meet at Taylor Shellfish on Chuckanut Drive for a sea-food feast.

"We buy a passel of whatever is in season, head up to Larabee State Park, and grill/steam it all up while watching the sun set over Chuckanut Bay," Vea says. "Inevitably, we will have

made several stops along the way through the Skagit [Valley] for supplies like cumin Gouda from Samish Bay Cheese and olive baguette from the Breadfarm in Edison."

Throw Your Own State Park Shellfish Cookout

Here's what Seattle-area chef and cooking instructor Lynne Vea totes along to make a quick and easy alfresco seafood cookout—whether she's found herself along the waters of Puget Sound or on the Pacific coast.

Must-Have Cooking Supplies:

Clams, mussels, oysters, scallops, spot prawns ... whatever is in season, in any combination. Plan between ¼ pound to ½ pound per person (three to six oysters per person, for example). Err on making extra: You can always use the leftovers for bisque or chowder.

A heavy-bottomed pot (that you don't mind getting smoky) with a tight-fitting lid

A big bowl for serving

Lots of paper towels

Slotted spoon

Charcoal and a charcoal chimney (with a lighter)

Newspaper

Butter

Local dry white wine

Fresh garlic

Lemons

Hot sauce

Local products like cheeses, sausages, fresh produce ... anything you can gather en route to your cooking destination

Great bread

Whether it be in a fire pit or a stand-up barbecue, start your coals in the charcoal chimney. While this preheats, beard the mussels and scrub any sand off the oysters. Cover the picnic table with newspaper.

When the coals are white, dump them in the pit or grill and immediately set the pot on top of the grate (or directly on the coals if it's a cold day) to begin preheating. Add the butter, wine, and garlic (the whole mixture should be about ½ to ¾ inch deep in your pot) and let it come to a boil. Drop in as much shellfish as you have on hand and put the lid on the pot. Let the pot come back to a full rolling boil and then cook for about 12 minutes, or until the clams and mussels and oysters are open and the shrimp are bright pink and opaque through. (Option: You may throw some oysters, curved side down, directly on the grate until they pop, if you like. Make sure you have tongs or a heatproof glove to retrieve them.) Throw any fresh produce you would like on the grill as well. Spoon the cooked seafood into the serving bowl and carefully pour the cooking juices over, leaving any silt or sand in the bottom of the pot. Serve with lemon wedges, hot sauce, all of your local treasures, and lots of bread for dipping!

Burlington

Like so many towns in the Northwest, Burlington started out as a logging camp. These days, it's a commercial hub at the junction of Interstate 5 and Highway 20, fringed by farmland and forests. Sakuma Brothers Farm just outside of town offers berry sundaes and other treats during harvest.

Skagit's Own Fish Market, 18042 State Rte. 20, Burlington, WA 98233; (360) 707-2722; skagitfish.com. This friendly, well-stocked, and beloved fish market just minutes from I-5 is a must-visit whenever you happen to be in the vicinity. Locals and tourists alike rave about its simple but memorable Dungeness crab sandwich; its fresh shrimp cocktail and local oyster shooters; its hefty halibut fish tacos and oyster burgers; and its array of pristine seafood from Northwest waters awaiting a hot date with your backyard grill, or with a campfire at nearby Deception Pass, or with your oven. The staff knows its stuff; many fish, have fished, or hail from fishing families.

Skagit's Own also is well stocked in provisions: hot sauces, local jams and syrups, local spice blends from Burrows Bay to season all that bounty, local canned tuna, spring roll wraps, local dairy products, and popular Asian sauces and marinades. Did we mention they also serve local Lopez Island Creamery ice cream by the scoop? Yes, they're going for sainthood.

Owners Tana Skaugrud and her husband, Eric, both hail from fishing families and began fishing off the Washington coast in 1998. A neighbor noticed crab pots in their yard and asked to buy some of their catch. The quality of their fish gained a reputation that blossomed into a successful farmers' market stand, and later, Skagit's Own.

Islands

Jewels, puzzle pieces, skipping stones: however you like to describe the scattering of curvy, woodsy islands throughout the southern Salish Sea, the San Juans and their neighbors are pure magic to visit. You reach them by ferry, seaplane, or personal boat, the scenery constantly changing as you cruise by or around one island after the next, each home to cabins, summer camps, hikes with breathtaking views from hilly peaks, and folks who appreciate being hard to reach. The islands also are home to a variety of shellfish growers, fishermen, and restaurants that transform their wares into fantastic meals best enjoyed as the sun sets behind the island next door.

Anderson's General Store, Guemes Island, 7885 Guemes Island Rd., Anacortes, WA 98221; (360) 293-4548; guemesislandstore .com. Just a 5-minute ferry ride from Anacortes, this little rural island with an independent streak is Dungeness crab central come summer, when crab fans flock to Guemes Island Resort to crab, clam, stargaze, and mellow out in hot tubs heated over wood fires.

Anderson's offers picnic supplies, s'mores fixings, eclectic gifts, and a small cafe that serves simple bistro fare with a Hawaiian influence. A wintertime menu featured ahi poke with soy ginger vinaigrette, Nisqually Farm oysters with lemon white truffle gremolata, coconut prawns with fennel kimchee, basil oil, and sweet chile coulis. If you're not staying on the island, Anderson's makes for a fun daytrip. Hop the ferry from Anacortes, grab some lunch, wander the beach, then head on back to the mainland.

Waterways: How We Live

Summertime Crab Feed with the Foushées

August is a beloved month in the Pacific Northwest, one of the few times of year along the waterfront and coast when it actually can feel hot. Locals bask in the sun, get out on the water as much as possible, and feast on local produce and seafood rolling into markets.

August is when Mikal and Charlie Foushée summon their families and their tight-knit group of friends from Seattle to Charlie's parents' place on Guemes Island, a quick ferry ride across the water from Anacortes. There, they pull up chairs to a series of long tables and celebrate summer with a giant alfresco feast of sweet, fresh Dungeness, elbows bumping as they reach for dishes of melted butter.

"A lot of family and friends come in from out of town. From Los Angeles, they come up and see the San Juans. It's so amazing," enthuses Mikal Foushée. "We put them on a boat, pull up some crabs, and have them clean and boil them. It's quite an experience for someone who's not from the Northwest."

Foushée grew up around Bainbridge Island, but still marvels at the beauty of this region's waterways. She and her dad would pop out on the water in a rowboat and go crabbing whenever the season was up, sharing the extra crabs with neighbors.

"Giving people crab is his favorite thing to do. It is a free gift from the sea that he can give everybody," she said.

Her husband, Charlie, and his sister, Marie, also grew up crabbing. A few years back, Charlie and Marie remarked how fun it would be to throw a big party on Guemes for friends and family. Now the annual gathering is 50 people strong. They crab on Friday and Saturday, play a beer-fueled kickball game, and cook the crab—around 40 last year—in a huge pot atop a gas camping stove, storing them in the fridge until dinnertime. Everyone pitches in with side dishes, a keg, rolls of paper towels.

Later that night, they camp on the waterfront lawn beneath the stars. They look forward to including everyone's children in the years to come.

"It's a fun experience, and we'll do it forever," Foushée vows.

Tips for Your Own Crab Feed

- Have a plan. Determine when you need to start crabbing to feed your crowd and how frequently you (and, hopefully, your team of helpers) need to check the crab pots, retrieve crabs, and cook them in advance of dinnertime. "That takes a fair amount of time and dedication to get 40 crabs," says Mikal Foushée.
- Ask friends to get crab licenses at their local sporting goods store so that you can capture enough Dungeness for the group. The 2013 daily per-person limit in Marine Area 7, home to Guemes Island, was five male crabs at least 6¼ inches wide between the points of their shells. Learn more at wdfw.wa.gov/fishing/.
- Delegate non-crab responsibilities. Who will bring the keg (or wine)? Who's in charge of breakfast and lunch the next day? Other important assignments: rolls of paper towels, garbage bags, fresh corn to boil or grill, salads, other side dishes.
- If a big crowd plans to camp on your lawn or beach, consider renting portable toilets.

Bay Cafe, Lopez Island, 9 Old Post Rd., Lopez Island, WA 98261; (360) 468-3700; bay-cafe.com. Lopez Island is rustic and lovely to start. This unassuming restaurant with terrific seafood, friendly ambience, and a mesmerizing water view from its sunset-facing dining room and sunny deck seals the deal. Fans make repeat visits while on vacation just to squeeze in as many meals as possible.

Dishes that earn top raves include clams and chorizo sausage with fennel, white wine, and tarragon; a tender sea scallop risotto with porcini mushrooms, leeks, and crème fraîche; expertly prepared halibut and salmon; and meaty Dungeness crab cakes. For non-seafood fans in your party, the Bay offers plenty of meaty options, including roast chicken, duck breast, pork tenderloin, and grilled rib eye or filet mignon.

Coho Restaurant, San Juan Island, 120 Nichols St., Friday Harbor, San Juan Island, WA 98250; (360) 378-6330; cohorestaurant .com. This cozy restaurant offers attentive service, an award-winning wine

See the San Juans by Sea

Elakah Expeditions (elakah.com): Excursions with this kayak tour operator range from daylong Lummi Island foraging trips, complete with sea-harvested meals prepared on the beach, to longer journeys through the San Juan Island archipelago. Trips from $65 per person.

San Juan Outfitters/Savor Seattle Tours (savorseattletours .com): This outfit offers a San Juan Islands gourmet kayak expedition, which they've dubbed a "pampered paddling" experience. Glide past resident orcas, remote islands, and other incredible scenery in your kayak, then enjoy entrees like grilled salmon with smoked sea salt and corn soup and grilled shrimp served with jalapeño corn bread when you arrive at a series of campsites, savoring the flavors as the sun sets.

Schooner Zodiac (schoonerzodiac.com): This tall ship offers various daylong and weekend sails throughout Puget Sound, some women-only. The PNW Seafood and Wine Excursion offers a cruise through the San Juans with stops at local wineries and an onboard winemakers' dinner featuring a special guest chef and vintners.

selection, an abundance of local ingredients, and a small but well-executed selection of regional seafood. Some highlights: a grilled octopus and shrimp pizza with roasted garlic, caramelized onion, and watercress; pan-seared lingcod bright with the flavors of coconut milk, lemongrass, and ginger; and expertly prepared salmon. There's also a three-course chef's tasting menu for those who don't mind dining early. Note: Make reservations, as this popular spot always draws a crowd.

Doe Bay Cafe, Orcas Island, 107 Doe Bay Rd., Olga, WA 98279; (360) 376-8059; doebay.com. Famous for its annual music festival, Doe Bay Resort and Retreat charms visitors with its reverence for nature, rustic accommodations and serene environs. Its waterfront cafe keeps up the charm offensive, serving organic produce from the resort's kitchen garden and the island's farms, orchards, and foragers, and seafood plucked from nearby waters. The flavors of each season meld into lovely seasonal dishes that rise far above expectations for an "end of the road" eatery far from the island's main village.

Doe Bay serves a Northwest take on Vietnamese pho soup with king oyster mushrooms, seasonal vegetables, baked tofu, and local spot prawns. A recent offering of local king salmon called for red onion port jam, dandelion

greens, salsify chèvre, quinoa cakes, and walnuts, served with garden-fresh microgreens. Effingham Inlet oysters come with a sorrel leek cream sauce. In warmer months be sure to call ahead to reserve space.

Friday Harbor Seafood, San Juan Island, Main Dock, Port of Friday Harbor, Friday Harbor, San Juan Island, WA 98250-9548; (360) 378-5779; interisland.net/fishcreek/. This floating market on the main dock in Friday Harbor offers tanks of live crab and shrimp and plenty of salmon, halibut, cod, red snapper, steamer clams, mussels, and oysters from throughout the Northwest, as well as smoked seafood and locally made cocktail and tartar sauces. Stop by and build a picnic lunch from smoked seafood, fresh oysters, shrimp cocktail, seafood chowder, and freshly steamed crab.

The Inn at Ship Bay, Orcas Island, 326 Olga Rd., Orcas Island, WA 98245; (877) 276-7296; innatshipbay.com. Dining here, in a historic 1869 farmhouse flanked by heirloom fruit trees, set on a bluff with unobstructed views of Ship Bay, is nothing short of magical. And seafood is featured prominently on the menu, with beautiful presentation. Seared black cod is accompanied by snap peas, tender fava beans, beets, and an addictive citrus-based sauce. Local spot prawns arrive with local spinach, and sparkle with the sweet zest of satsuma and pomegranate. Depending on the season, choose from troll-caught king salmon or wild halibut, each served with seasonal vegetables.

Jones Family Farms, Lopez Island, 1934 Mud Bay Rd., Lopez Island, WA 98261; (360) 468-0533; jffarms.com. Jones Family Farms is the secret ingredient in many fresh seafood dishes around the Northwest, its pristine Olympia oysters, mussels, littleneck clams, and locally sourced wild salmon and halibut taking a star turn on menus from Elliott's Oyster House, Little Uncle, Lark, and Barnacle Bar in Seattle, to San Juan Islands eateries such as Southend Restaurant, Doe Bay Cafe, and Coho Restaurant, to venerable Northwest destination restaurants such as The

Willows Inn and The Herbfarm. Chefs, including Robert Spaulding at Elliott's, offer high praise for the quality of their products, which are available at select local fish shops, grocers, and farmers' markets.

The Farm, which also raises top-quality pork and beef on woodsy and tranquil Lopez Island, got its start when Nick Jones got a free boat, leased a fishing permit from friends and tried his hand as a commercial fisherman. As his family grew, Jones and his wife, Sara, looked to the land and shore for their livelihood, developing a pasture-raised livestock operation and later adding their 5½ acre shellfish farm.

The Willows Inn, Lummi Island, 2579 West Shore Dr., Lummi Island, WA 98262; (360) 758-2620; willows-inn.com. Few Northwest places have managed to capture the imagination of urban dwellers so completely as The Willows Inn, with its tales of 20-something Chef Blaine Wetzel foraging the local woods for berries and mushrooms, moss, nettles, and fiddlehead ferns, peering into reef nets for the wild salmon he later will

Lummi Island

Is it or isn't it? While the US Geological Survey declares Lummi (and Guemes, for that matter) beyond the limits of the San Juan Islands archipelago, don't tell the island. Leaders bill it as the "most accessible" San Juan Island, tucked as it is within Rosario Strait, just a 6-minute cash-only ferry ride from the dock near Bellingham (co.whatcom.wa.us/publicworks/ferry/schedule.jsp).

Whatever its identity, this wooded, tranquil island is again on the map thanks to an increasingly famous restaurant called The Willows Inn. Its chef is the latest to discover what local tribes have recognized for generations—Lummi Island offers a bounty of riches on land and sea. It's also home to Lummi Island Wild, a salmon fishing cooperative that employs reefnets, a historic Pacific Northwest salmon fishing method practiced for centuries by local tribes using cedar canoes and cedar nets to catch wild sockeye and other species as they swim past on the high tide. The boats may be bigger and the nets made of nylon, but the harvest method remains true, resulting in high-quality, gently handled, sweet fish.

load into his smokehouse, and paddling a kayak at daybreak to harvest seaweed and sea lettuce. Any or all could be candidates for the day's meal.

Wetzel worked for 18 months in Copenhagen at Noma, named by many food critics as the best restaurant in the world. Now back at home in Washington, Wetzel has refined all he learned about locavorism in Denmark to suit the Northwest—and won critical acclaim from all corners in the process, including a declaration in 2011 from the *New York Times* that Willows Inn is "One of the 10 Restaurants (in the World) Worth a Plane Ride."

Seemingly every simple, well-presented, perfect dish on his menu incorporates wild edible plants, seafood that swims past the island caught by the inn's fishing boats, or ingredients from the inn's 7-acre farm that produces Wetzel's fruits, vegetables, eggs, and pork. A ranch within a mile raises Wetzel's lamb, beef, and duck. It's an entire ecosystem housed on and around one island, on display within one restaurant dining room in dishes both whimsical (a smoked oyster that arrives in a cedar box like a present, wisps of smoke curling up) and sublime (smoked salmon so intense and pure, past diners say they dream of it).

You'll need to factor in a long drive (about 2½ hours from Seattle) and an extremely short ferry ride near Bellingham to reach Lummi Island. Consider staying the night at the inn; you'll get first priority to reserve a table and can savor the 3-hour tasting menu without haste. The Beach Store Cafe on the waterfront serves full breakfast, lunch, and dinner if you make it a weekend (a very mellow, relaxing weekend). The Taproot Cafe, home to the inn's farm store, offers unique local products and food, plus a locally sourced menu, picnic-packing service, and a full bar.

Marysville

Marysville began as a trading post amid logging camps, the Tulalip reservation, and pioneer settlements, and in recent years has carried on that tradition, with the Tulalip tribe's resort and casino and outlet mall drawing crowds each weekend. Don't miss the strawberry festival the third week of each June, which started up in 1932.

Blackfish Wild Salmon Grill & Bar, Tulalip Resort Casino, 10200 Quil Ceda Blvd., Tulalip, WA 98270; (360) 716-1100; tulalipresort casino.com. Wild Northwest salmon is the star of the show at Blackfish, where it's smoked over alderwood coals with hand-carved ironwood sticks in the traditional tribal technique. This method creates fragrant, moist, flavorful fish and a sense of delight at experiencing salmon as many previous generations have enjoyed it. Yes, you're in a casino, but the restaurant's wood longhouse setting with its open fire pit, wood carvings, and large beams offers respite from the many diversions at this resort with its AAA Four Diamond hotel about 45 minutes north of Seattle.

The menu at Blackfish teems with coastal treasures, from wild steelhead and Alaskan halibut to local oysters shucked to order and a Pacific Northwest Bounty Bowl that features Dungeness and Alaskan king crab legs, prawns, mussels, clams, wild salmon, lobster saffron bisque, fingerling potatoes, and asparagus. Northwest wines and microbrews are abundant, and local ingredients are ubiquitous, including root vegetables, wild mushrooms, and berries. Don't miss the super clam fritter appetizer, made from a tribal elder's recipe.

Whidbey Island

You access this long, quirky, largely untamed island either by ferry from the city of Mukilteo to the south or via the breathtaking Deception Pass Bridge from the north: talk about upping the ante on scenery. As you explore the communities scattered throughout woods, amid valleys, and along waterways, you'll find uncommonly good mussels served everywhere from a dive bar in charming Coupeville to the multicourse delights at the Inn at Langley. Then, of course, there's the wildlife, the art, the military history and lighthouse at Fort Casey, the really amazing pie . . . better eat up, because you might be here awhile.

Fraser's Gourmet Hideaway, 1191 SE Dock St., Ste. 101, Oak Harbor, WA 98277; (360) 279-1231; frasersgh.com. This favorite date-night spot with its warm ambience, open kitchen, and water view boasts a wealth of enjoyable seafood dishes, from a tapas plate of bacon-wrapped dates, Manchego cheese, and smoked mussels; the spicy Singapore tiger prawns served with marinated glass noodles; Penn Cove mussels steamed in a fragrant curry cream broth; and several seafood entrees on the menu any given night, from a graceful poached sablefish to tender, seared sea scallops in sage and brown butter over pasta with spicy harissa oil.

Front Street Grill, 20 Front St. NW, Coupeville, WA 98239; (360) 682-2551; frontstreetgrillcoupeville.com. On a serene street in the historic Whidbey Island town of Coupeville sits the Front Street Grill, where broad windows and a stylish bistro atmosphere connect diners with the rippling waters below and the last flickers of sunset's glow. Enjoy mussels at Front Street with all manner of shellfish accoutrements, served any of 10 ways: romesco; pistou (with pistachio pesto); Rockefeller (with spinach, bacon, Pernod, and cream); the traditional white wine; Southwest (with diced tomatoes and peppers); coconut green curry; Mediterranean (with kalamata olives and fennel); San Daniele (with prosciutto, caramelized onions, and sage); Angry (with chorizo sausage, red wine, shallots, and chile oil); and in saffron cream. Whew. Five bucks adds linguine to any mussel dish.

The Inn at Langley, 400 First St., Langley, WA 98260; (360) 221-3033; innatlangley.com. Whidbey Island inherently is relaxing; its slower pace and easy access to nature encourage decompression. The 4-star Inn at Langley takes it to the next level, with rooms that overlook smooth-as-glass Saratoga Passage and the Cascades, plus a dining room adjacent to an herb garden that should get the centerfold of a gardening magazine, and a double-sided river rock fireplace.

In 2013, *Saveur* magazine named The Inn to its list of Notable Hotel Restaurants of the world; the previous year, Chef Matt Costello was a James Beard Award semifinalist for Best Chef in the Northwest. Multi-course dinners at the inn's restaurant, prepared with grace by Costello, offer the opportunity to sample and savor in one sitting the island's freshest seasonal produce, troll-caught wild salmon, Penn Cove mussels, meats, cheeses, locally foraged mushrooms, and more, paired with vintages from the inn's extensive wine collection.

Prima Bistro, 201½ First Street, Langley, WA 98260; (360) 221-4060; primabistro.com. Since 2006, this sunny, cozy bistro tucked above the Star Store has offered seasonal, French-inspired Northwest eats and a good selection of seafood small plates, including truffled wild prawns, house-smoked wild salmon, and local clams served with chorizo and semolina-crusted panfried Northwest oysters with truffle mayonnaise. Here, Penn Cove mussels are served either with white wine and shallots or white wine and curry; and the half dozen oysters on the half shell arrive with white wine mignonette. Prima offers vegetarian and kids' menus, a full cocktail bar, an extensive wine list, and a deck with a fantastic view over Saratoga passage on warmer days and nights.

Seabolt's Smokehouse, 31640 State Rte. 20, #3, Oak Harbor, WA 98277; (360) 675-6485; seabolts.com. Family-owned since 1978, Seabolt's offers smoked seafood galore, fresh fish (much of it caught by

Penn Cove Shellfish, Coupeville

Penn Cove Shellfish has farmed mussels in the famed nutrient-rich (and just plain pretty) mussel beds of Penn Cove since 1975, the oldest and largest mussel farm in America. The Jefferds family's mussels have earned acclaim at international taste test competitions for their sweet flavor and tender texture. What makes this little nook the most prolific mussel-growing area on the West Coast? The Jefferds family says the cove's shape enables it to absorb fresh mountain river waters and their minerals from the Cascade range to the east. The cove also sits in the rain shadow of the Olympic Mountains to the west, and all that sunshine helps plankton thrive. These days, Penn Cove Shellfish grows and harvests about 2 million pounds of mussels per year from Penn Cove and from a second farm in Quilcene Bay, along Washington's upper Hood Canal.

A serene street in the historic Whidbey Island town of Coupeville, facing Penn Cove, holds two fun, polar-opposite mussel experiences for the mussel maniac in your life: Front Street Grill and Toby's Tavern.

locals), and plenty of award-winning meals to enjoy in the smokehouse restaurant: hot clam chowder; beer-battered fish-and-chips; grilled wild fish sandwiches; Penn Cove mussels steamed with garlic, white wine, lemon, and butter; seafood gumbo and stew; halibut fish tacos; popcorn shrimp; seafood salads; and steamed or chilled fresh local Dungeness crab served with butter. Salmon fillets are cured to perfection then slowly smoked with alderwood in the traditional Northwest style.

Toby's Tavern, 8 Front St. NW, Coupeville, WA 98239; (360) 678-4222; tobysuds.com. Toby's Tavern lives up to its dive bar reputation in all the best ways: framed historic photos tacked to every wall, a hand-me-down back bar that's served patrons in venues all over the island, and fake parrots dangling from the ceiling, along with a five-man racing shell built by local legend George Pocock for the University of Washington back in the 1950s that's since been raced around the globe. It's a bar crammed with locals where the focus is very much on each other versus the (lack of) view. Enjoy Penn Cove mussels at Toby's drenched in wine and garlic out of a no-nonsense stainless steel bowl alongside a generous portion of crispy home-style garlic bread. Dump your discarded shells in another stainless bowl nearby and enjoy a glass of Toby's own microbrew, Toby's Red Parrot Ale.

How to Read a Tide Table

Isn't there an app for that? Well, sure. But it pays to understand the basics behind the ebb and flow of tides to maximize your enjoyment of the shoreline and know the best times to go clamming. There's nothing quite so alarming as hiking past seastacks for a better view of the sunset, only to realize the narrow strip of land you crossed to get there is rapidly disappearing into the thundering Pacific.

The basics: Tides are caused by the gravitational pull of the moon (and, to some extent, the sun). As the earth rotates on its axis, the moon's attraction causes the earth to bulge out in its direction and recede twice daily. Therefore, each day has two tides.

Each day on a tide table has four lines (or, a chart) to represent those tides. The smaller numbers are the low tides, the larger, high tides. The best tides for beach walking and clam digging are minus tides (when the measurement is below zero), and the best time to head out is an hour or so before the low point. On the other end of the scale are king tides—high tides that can cause coastal flooding.

Once you get the hang of it, be sure to check the tides for your anticipated location. Each point along a body of water can have slightly different tides because of differences in topography, and tides shift by 20–30 minutes each day. Find tide guides at sporting goods or boating stores, in mobile apps, or online at sites such as protides.com.

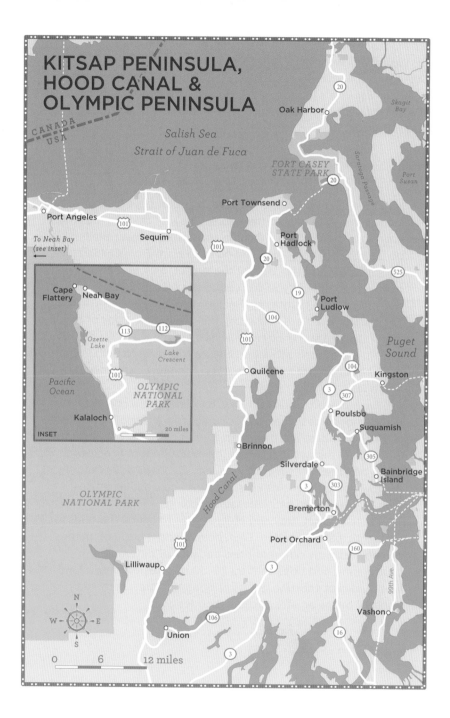

To the West: Kitsap Peninsula, Hood Canal & the Olympic Peninsula

The hardy people of this region of Washington built—and lost—many fortunes in timber, fishing, oystering, and other natural resource ventures over generations, including supplying lumber and oysters to fuel San Francisco's Gold Rush–era appetites for construction and consumption. While hiking, camping, fishing, and admiring the majestic scenery have long been big draws for tourists, many are making their way there to enjoy the restaurants, farms, creameries, and cideries along the Olympic Culinary Loop (olympicculinaryloop.com). This local agritourism effort celebrates the foods and recipes that hail from the region's many microclimates, its coastal proximity, and its Native American heritage: locally grown and foraged fruits, vegetables, herbs, and berries, locally hunted game, bountiful seafood, and handcrafted local wines. Note: This loop very handily dovetails with the Olympic Peninsula Waterfall Trail (olympic peninsulawaterfalltrail.com). Yes, you'll probably need every type of camera lens on this trip.

The Kitsap Peninsula might as well be an island, and sometimes it feels like one by how long it takes to join the "mainland." It's surrounded by water along its curvy shores, joined with the Olympic Peninsula by the Hood Canal Bridge and by a thin neck of land at its southern end at the aptly named Union. It's joined with Tacoma and Seattle by the Narrows Bridge, and ferries constantly lumber back and forth between Seattle and Bremerton and Edmonds and Kingston.

On a map, Hood Canal is a long, skinny fishhook, inlaid with bays, coves, and reaches, its narrow passages and muddy tideflats abundant with shellfish and fringed by evergreens. This 55-mile-long Puget Sound fjord ebbs and flows as much as 18 feet with the tides; mighty currents course through its veins. In stormy weather, the wind howls with fury; once, with enough intensity (120 mph gusts in 1979) to sink the floating bridge that connects the Olympic and Kitsap Peninsulas.

To the west, the Olympic Mountains loom, craggy and formidable. This remote corner of Washington remains largely untouched, undeveloped, even undiscovered. Sections of misty, mossy, wild Olympic National Park are celebrated by researchers for their lack of noise and velvety, star-bright skies; it is still possible to hike past waterfalls, along salmon streams, past pristine lakes, within temperate rain forests, through the foothills, and not see a soul.

These are places most easily traveled by boats and mountain goats; those of us in cars must go far afield, hug the curves of the fjords and foothills, which makes for a long, leisurely drive roadtrippers either adore or abhor. My advice: Focus on the journey as much as the destination. Shuck and slurp fresh oysters at the water's edge, the better to relish the cry of an osprey that pierces the heady stillness. Pull over and rent a kayak so you can paddle out and watch that osprey up close. Pull over later and wander a windswept, chilly beach to comb the sands for sand dollars, prized Japanese glass fishing floats, or the occasional message in a bottle. Pull over and explore.

Bainbridge Island

The charming town of Winslow with its cafes and shops is just a 30-minute ferry ride from downtown Seattle. If you take the car ferry (or bring your bike), trek to the Bloedel Reserve for lush, lovely gardens. The parks department offers a marvelous array of classes, including stargazing, shellfish gathering, and flyfishing.

Hitchcock, 133 Winslow Way E., Bainbridge Island, WA 98110; (206) 201-3789; hitchcockrestaurant.com. Just a ferry's ride away from Seattle sits charming Hitchcock, home to an applewood-fired oven, handmade pasta, a smoker, cozy booths, craft cocktails, antique banquettes, and memorable preparations of the fresh, local catch.

Depending on the season, the menu might reveal cold-smoked coho salmon from Neah Bay, bright with pickled scorzonera (a variety of the root vegetable salsify) and apple-horseradish foam; charred giant Pacific octopus, bathed in a cayenne pepper hot sauce and date-caper-parsley relish; or fresh albacore also plucked from Neah Bay, alongside delightful *pommes dauphine*, salsa verde, and rich duck egg aioli. Slurp oysters on the half shell from as close as Bainbridge Island's own Rockaway Beach, or from Willapa Bay or the Hood Canal.

Waterways: How We Live

Oysters in the yard with Andrew Welch

Andrew Welch makes the most of living on the water. Nearly every day of crabbing season, you'll find him and his young daughters, Hannah and Claire, heading out in their boat along Colvos Passage to pull up their crab pots. He fishes in front of his Gig Harbor home for salmon nearly every morning of the season. He even raises oysters from seed in bags on the beach.

It's a seafood lovers' fantasy, just a few steps outside his door.

"In the summertime, we'll go out and grab a dozen oysters when people come over," says Welch, who grows triploid, dainty Olympia oysters and creamy Kumamotos. "I've got about 500 this year. It's incredible."

Welch grew up crabbing each summer with his dad, who lived farther north along Agate Pass, which separates Bainbridge Island from the Kitsap Peninsula. Crabbing has become bonding time for him and his girls.

"They love them, and it's kind of cool when your 3-year-old can tell which ones are female and which ones are male, and which ones are keepers and which ones aren't," says Welch, who sells real estate with his wife, Allison.

Some of the dozens of Dungeness they pull up will get steamed for dinner. Some will become homemade crab cakes. Most will be shared with friends and neighbors, old and new. You can find the Welch Family Crab Cakes recipe in the "In the Kitchen" chapter.

He named his old boat *Hole in the Water*, after the boat of a favorite detective in the '80s TV drama *Simon and Simon*. His current boat lacks a name; the girls haven't decided yet, he says with a chuckle.

Restaurant Marché, 150 Madrone Lane N., Bainbridge Island, WA 98110; (206) 842-1633; restaurantmarchebainbridge.com. It's difficult to believe Restaurant Marché is Greg Atkinson's first restaurant. Atkinson is the legendary former chef at Seattle's venerable, nationally acclaimed, and beloved Canlis and is known for infusing its menu with seasonality and modernity in the mid-1990s. Atkinson is also author of *West Coast Cooking* and five other cookbooks that have helped define an entire cuisine. But perhaps he was biding his time for the perfect spot and the perfect moment. And he seems to have found it.

Tip Sheet: Gone Oystering

If you'd prefer to gather your own oysters, check with your favorite oyster farms for annual public harvest days or beach days. Or hit a beach open to public harvesting in your neck of the woods (Note: be sure to get a permit through your local government). Popular spots in Washington include Illahee State Park, Birch Bay State Park, Mystery Bay State Park, and Fay Bainbridge State Park.When this book went to press, Oregon did not allow public oyster harvest. In BC, check out recreational shellfish reserves on Baynes Sound, Nanoose Bay, and Kye Bay.

In Washington, the Bainbridge Island Metro Park & Recreation District (biparks.org.) offers regular shellfish foraging and cooking classes with author and forager Langdon Cook at waterfront locations around the state. The Puget Sound Restoration Fund (restorationfund.org/projects/csf/portmadison) also operates the Port Madison Community

Shellfish Farm on the Bloedel Reserve tidelands on Bainbridge Island and additional farms in Olympia and Blaine. An annual membership grants access to the bivalves in trade for volunteer hours to seed and harvest the oysters.

PHOTO COURTESY OF UWAJIMAYA

Floor-to-ceiling windows draw light into the comfortable, cozy space where he sends luscious king salmon through an applewood broiler. Plump local mussels are steamed in Pernod, served with heavy cream, a reduction with fresh fennel, and deep gold, twice-fried french fries hewn from Washington potatoes that manage to stay creamy in the middle. It's a small wonder they are considered by many local food writers to be among the region's best. The silky trout meunière is served in browned butter and plated atop potato gratin and sautéed greens. Definitely worth the ferry ride from Seattle.

Here's what to wear and bring:

- Rubber boots or shoes you don't care about: It's muddy and cold on the tideflats.
- A trash bag to line your car's trunk in case you haul home wet clothes.
- A lantern or flashlight, in case low tide falls after sunset or before sunrise
- Gloves.
- A bucket. Some recommend two: Sit on one and harvest/shuck with the other.
- Dress in layers so you can add or subtract warmth based on conditions. Pack a windbreaker, preferably waterproof (this is the Northwest, after all).
- An oyster knife/shucker (find them at hardware stores, kitchen shops, and many oyster farms).
- A cooler to haul home your loot
- Your favorite condiments (lemon, hot sauce, etc.). Some oyster farms offer special butters and cocktail sauce, but better safe than sorry if you prefer your oysters dressed rather than naked.

"When I go oyster picking, I bring a lemon, hot sauce, and a cold beer," said Langdon Cook. He also suggests you bring Tupperware to hold the oysters because most beaches require that you shuck them and leave the shells (future oysters will call them home).

Brinnon

Brinnon, halfway between picturesque Port Townsend and the Olympic Mountain hikers' paradise known as Staircase, is perhaps best known for its proximity to Dosewallips State Park. Its 5,400 feet of fresh and saltwater shoreline on either side of the Dosewallips River enable easy access to clams and oysters, plus a boat ramp so you can head out fishing or crabbing.

Since 1993, this north Hood Canal community has hosted the Hood Canal ShrimpFest each Memorial Day weekend, celebrating Hood Canal spot prawns and other local seafood with live music and family-friendly fun (facebook.com/BrinnonShrimpfest). As a bonus, tides typically are low enough during the festival for easy harvest of clams and oysters on nearby public beaches. Brinnon also is the setting for the murder mystery novel *Homicide on the Half Shell*. It's also home to the Halfway House restaurant and its stellar homemade pies.

Geoduck Tavern, 307103 US Hwy. 101, Brinnon, WA 98320; (360) 796-4430. The star attractions at this well-loved dive bar are its 1-pound Burger Dip (burger meets French dip sandwich) and its deck with views of Hood Canal and the antics of its wildlife: bald eagles, elk, kingfishers. Despite the name, there's no geoduck on the menu, though you'll find a grilled oyster sandwich, salmon burgers, clam chowder, and other coastal pub grub—plus, bar talk with local retired lumberjacks. Named one of the best bars in America (and a "rustic paradise") by *Esquire* magazine in 2011.

Cape Flattery & Neah Bay

The drive to wild and windswept Cape Flattery, the northwesternmost point of the lower 48 states, is a chance to count eagles and lift your spirits. Diane Schostak, a longtime Olympic Peninsula resident and executive director of the area's convention and visitors bureau, once counted 34. "You're driving with your chin on the dashboard, looking at the tops of trees," she said.

Hope your neck is flexible, because when you're finished gawking at eagles, you'll begin gawking at passing whales and at the dramatic rock formations in the sea from your vantage point atop 60-foot sheer cliffs. Neah Bay, the closest town to the cape, is on the Makah tribe's lands. Be

sure to stop by the museum at the Makah Cultural and Resource Center to admire Northwest tribal art and artifacts from tribal ancestors.

The Warm House Restaurant, 1471 Bay View Ave., Neah Bay, WA 98381; (360) 645-2077. This laid-back casual spot with views of the marina and outdoor dining in warm weather offers seafood caught by the tribe's fishing fleet in the nearby waters, a freshness you'll notice even in fried items like the lightly battered cod fish-and-chips with fresh french fries. Clam chowder is satisfying with fresh ingredients and fresh herbs, and the halibut burger is a treat.

Kalaloch

It's impossible not to want to stop and stare in this majestic spot on the southwest coast of the Olympic Peninsula where forest, river, and ocean converge. Nearby Ruby Beach offers coastal camping and hiking within

view of the Pacific and its lingering sunsets, as well as bird colonies and other wildlife frolicking within this wildlife refuge.

Creekside Restaurant, Inside Kalaloch Lodge, 157151 Hwy. 101, Kalaloch, WA 98331; (866) 662-9969; thekalalochlodge.com. When you're the only place to eat within miles, you don't have to knock yourself out to get diners. The same goes when you can offer an unparalleled view of the thundering Pacific. Yet the Creekside makes the effort, serving quality seafood dishes, locally grown organic produce, all-natural meats, and cozy, generous desserts. Seafood on the menu starts at breakfast, with smoked salmon hash and Dungeness crab Benedict. A juicy and slightly spicy salmon burger hits the spot for a post-hike lunch, and dinner offers different Northwest fish throughout the seasons. Request a table on the deck in good weather for a grand view of Kalaloch Creek where it mingles with the ocean. When the weather's lousy, get a window seat inside to enjoy the incoming storms with hot chocolate and a plate of warm cookies.

Lilliwaup

Hama Hama Oyster Company, 35846 N. US Hwy. 101, Lilliwaup, WA 98555; (888) 877-5844; hamahamaoysters.com. The folks at Hama Hama—the fifth generation of this oystering family and their farm, named for the local river—describe their business as an ecosystem, and it's easy to see why. They manage their Hood Canal tideflats and woodlands together, each landscape and its needs influencing the other.

Such thoughtful stewardship is a large reason they're still going strong since their founding in 1922, with their Blue Pool and other oysters appearing in fine restaurants and on kitchen tables throughout the region.

The little store on site is open every day of the year, save for Thanksgiving and Christmas. You can watch the oyster shucking in action and dip your fingertips in a touch tank filled with Puget Sound sea creatures to learn a bit about the local ecology.

In 2014, plans were under way to expand into a small restaurant to cook oysters and clams, with an outdoor eating area, all the better to savor the special compound butters that one friend remembered fondly an entire year after her visit to Hama Hama's annual oyster festival. Right now, visitors can only buy oysters and sit outside and shuck them.

Like Taylor Shellfish, its neighbor to the south, Hama Hama has grown in prominence by reaching out to new customers in places urban food lovers congregate: farmers' markets, cooking classes, chef dinners, oyster bars. Each spring comes time for Hama Hama Oyster Rama, an open farm day when visitors can come harvest their own oysters at low tide and barbecue them on shore, with live music, and tideflat tours with an ecologist. From time to time, they welcome a raucous party bus from Portland restaurant EaT Oysters, crammed with beer-fueled oyster fans who pile off and gorge themselves on freshly shucked bivalves.

For city dwellers who can't make the trek to Lilliwaup, Hama Hama ships shellfish (say that five times fast). Or, visit their booth at Seattle's Ballard or University District farmers' markets. It's unfortunate that the time of year when people are least likely to drive to Hood Canal (the dead of winter) coincides with when oysters taste their finest, said Lissa James, a fifth-generation oysterwoman.

For generations, Hood Canal tied much of its identity to logging, then lost some of its swagger as that industry faded. James hopes the local oyster industry will become a point of pride as it grows in stature.

Waterways: How We Live

Fifth-Generation Oysterwoman Lissa James

Lissa James considers herself a raw oyster evangelist. She grew up on Hood Canal, where she watched bald eagles soar; raced motorcycles and rode horses with her cousins; and, like her rural neighbors, ate local oysters grilled, fried, or chopped up.

She still remembers the surprise of eating them raw for the first time, cool and slippery.

"I had this sense of discovering something," she says, a sensation she recognizes on the faces of first-timers to this day. "One of our missions is to convince people who have never eaten a raw oyster that they should. And also, those who've never eaten them cooked, that they're really good cooked as well."

Getting the uninitiated to try oysters is good for the health of Hama Hama Oyster Company, the family business. She and her brother, Adam, are part of the fifth generation to help run the venerable oyster company that supplies such seafood hot spots as acclaimed Seattle oyster bar The Walrus and the Carpenter and Portland's Cabezon. She's a woman of power in an industry that, while still male-dominated, increasingly has more women calling the shots.

James has long found inspiration in nature.

"I've always just really loved the tideflats and I think they're really magical. The magic isn't lost by being around them more often," she said. "You're in this world that's underwater half the time, not a very friendly environment to humans. We haven't conquered it by any means. When the tide comes up, you've got to leave, or else put your snorkel on."

Port Angeles

Here's your gateway city to so much wonder: Hurricane Ridge, with Olympic Mountain peaks seemingly close enough to touch; Olympic National Park's rugged, rocky, and gorgeous beaches; and mossy, temperate rain

forests often so tranquil you will hear the water dripping from leaf to leaf. It's also home to the Black Ball ferry line, which connects the Olympic Peninsula with British Columbia via the Strait of Juan de Fuca. Be sure to hit legendary Swain's General Store (swains inc.com/store/home.html) to snag your clamming/crabbing license, clam guns, rain gear, and plenty of items you didn't know you needed: Fiesta Ware dishes, quirky Christmas lights, a new set of cast-iron skillets, and oodles more.

Kokopelli Grill, 203 Front St., Port Angeles, WA 98362; (360) 457-6040; kokopelli-grill.com. The dining room may be dark, but the flavors are vivid and bright. Come here for a delightful fusion of Southwest cuisine with fresh local seafood. Standouts include the smoked salmon chowder; New Orleans–style grilled oysters with garlic tequila butter and Parmesan cheese; the yellow- and blue-corn-crusted crab chile relleno; and the Kokopelli Kombo with sauteed prawns and large scallops served over house-roasted red tomatillo sauce and topped with *cotija* cheese. Be sure to try the prickly-pear salad.

Chef Michael McQuay's vibrant mix of flavors honed from his time living in Texas helped him take home a blue ribbon from the 2014 Ocean Shores razor clam festival. His recipe? *Moquecas*, or Brazilian fish stew, a mélange of fresh halibut, lobster, shrimp, scallops, salmon, razor clams, chorizo, garlic, wine, poblano peppers, coconut milk, and cilantro over coconut rice. Yum.

Michael's Fresh Northwest Seafood & Steakhouse, 117B E. 1st St., Port Angeles, WA 98362; (360) 417-6929; michaelsdining.com. It may not look like much from outside, but descend the shadowy stairs into the subterranean dining room and soon you'll be relaxing in a booth, cozy and comfortable, sipping a house cocktail, ready to dig into comforting takes on local seafood.

Don't miss the decadent Dungeness crab gnocchi; the Northwest bouillabaisse featuring clams, mussels, oysters, coho salmon, and Alaskan king crab legs with a garlic crouton; a delicious salmon sandwich; and bacon spinach oysters. Each spring, the restaurant hosts a clambake for the chance to feast on steamers, geoduck, razor clams, Manila, butters, and littlenecks; on Christmas Eve, they host a traditional Italian Feast of Seven Fishes.

Port Hadlock

In the 1800s, Port Hadlock's sawmill produced lumber that was shipped to San Francisco and as far away as Alaska and Hawaii. All these years later, restaurants and small businesses inhabit the historic buildings that remain, including the Ajax Cafe in the Galster House Building, the former home of the town's founder.

Ajax Cafe, 271 Water St., Port Hadlock, WA 98339; (360) 385-3450; ajaxcafe.com. The eclectic Ajax is becoming as well known for its food as it has been for its quirky hat collection for diners to wear as they gather just steps from the water. Pan-roasted wild salmon is delightful with a Chardonnay cream sauce, potato au gratin, and garden-fresh vegetables. Clam chowder comes with fresh clams in the shell. Warm up on overcast days with Northwest fisherman's stew, featuring clams, mussels, prawns, and fresh fish in a seafood bouillabaisse, or enjoy local oysters on the half shell or fried.

Port Ludlow

Often overshadowed by Port Townsend, its über charming neighbor, Port Ludlow offers gorgeous views and tranquility, tucked between the forest and Ludlow Bay on Puget Sound. Wander the waterfront and gaze upon sailboats, totem poles, mountains, and wildlife.

Fireside Restaurant, In the Port Ludlow Resort, 1 Heron Rd., Port Ludlow, WA 98365; (877) 805-0868; portludlowresort.com. Here's a prime spot to relax, unwind by the fire or a window seat overlooking the water, and savor the culinary bounty of the Olympia Peninsula, with organic produce harvested just up the road in Chimacum and salmon pulled hours earlier from Neah Bay, prepared to its best advantage. You also won't leave hungry from its robust happy hour, and its breakfasts are bountiful.

Port Orchard

Port Orchard had its start as a mill town, then a navy town (the Puget Sound Naval Shipyard is just across the way in Bremerton). Its revitalized downtown on the waterfront grows more charming by the year, especially with the introduction of the Port Orchard Public Market.

Port Orchard Public Market, 715 Bay St., Port Orchard, WA 98366; portorchardpublicmarket.com. This new collection of shops that mainly feature local food and drink includes Northwest Seafood & Wine, a fish market that features live Dungeness crab, fresh salmon from Neah Bay, and other local treasures. If you can't wait to get home to your grill, stop by Central Dock restaurant for that same seafood ready to enjoy.

Port Townsend

On a still, misty evening, this picturesque town with its Victorian-era business district seems frozen in time—you almost expect horse-drawn carriages to turn the corner over the cobblestone. On a sparkling afternoon, however, it bustles with energy from music festivals, a brisk tourist trade, congregations of boat lovers at the Northwest Maritime Center, and conventioneers from nearby Fort Flagler State Park.

Alchemy Bistro & Wine Bar, 842 Washington St., Port Townsend, WA 98368; (360) 385-5225; alchemybistroandwinebar.com. Alchemy is a celebration of the food and wine of the Mediterranean and offers that quiet, intimate date-night setting to which many restaurants aspire, complete with white tablecloths and a varied menu for repeat visits with your fellow canoodler, with a pocket park and fountain conveniently located just outside.

Seafood paella offers wild salmon, prawns, and local seasonal shellfish, combined with spicy chorizo and paella rice in a saffron broth. It's matched in abundance only by a cioppino that's thick with fresh mussels, clams, wild salmon, and prawns with a hint of spice and orange zest. The divine oyster stew is prepared with fresh local oysters and ginger. The salad niçoise is vibrant with rich hunks of Cape Cleare tuna, seared to order for truly fresh flavor. Wild Alaskan king salmon, also caught by Port Townsend's own Cape Cleare Fishery, is served with a roasted beet and horseradish cream sauce and a simple risotto. Date night and a seafood fix. This is winning.

Key City Fish Co., 307 10th St., Port Townsend, WA 98368; (360) 379-5516; keycityfish.com. If you crave it, there's a good chance Key City carries it, from fresh, wild Columbia River sturgeon and wild Alaskan spot prawns to vibrant ahi tuna flown direct from the waters off Hawaii, Washington sardines caught off Westport, and shimmering whole albacore tuna. And live Washington crawfish. And fresh lingcod from the coastal town of La Push and halibut from Neah Bay. How will you ever choose?

The shop smokes its own king, coho, sockeye, and chum salmon over alder chips. Soups are made from scratch, such as the Key City seafood chowder. There's also a variety of other treasures, including regional brews and ciders, locally made Mt. Townsend Creamery cheese (don't miss the Seastack), Mystery Bay Farm chèvre, and top-quality specialty meats and poultry from throughout the region.

One reason Key City is able to offer such diverse treasures: It partners with fishermen from coastal tribes. If you're a frequent fish buyer, be sure to join their loyalty club for discounts. And if you can't wait to eat until you get home, visit the market's taco stand, Key City Tacos To-Go, with a rotating list of featured ingredients (including calamari, mahimahi, shrimp, and a variety of meats).

Poulsbo

Think Poulsbo and many locals think Vikings. This "Little Norway" was settled in 1892 by Norwegian loggers, farmers, and fishermen who found the fjord-carved landscape reminded them of home. Its walkable downtown is heavenly on a crisp autumn day, Liberty Bay sparkling in the sun.

Central Market, (additional Seattle-area locations in Shoreline and Mill Creek), 20148 10th Ave. NE, Poulsbo, WA 98370; (360) 779-1881; poulsbo.central-market.com. Widely considered the best grocery store in Kitsap County, Central Market offers remarkably fresh organic produce; high-end, quality meats; lovely baked goods from their own ovens and top local bakeries; a wealth of ready-to-eat options including sushi, pizza, and a crisp salad bar; a huge bulk foods section; specialty ingredients from around the globe and for special diets; and an expansive seafood counter. It's a terrific spot to enjoy a tasty, healthy meal after a weekend eating over a campfire, or to load up on fresh ingredients for your first meal back in your own kitchen.

Central Market offers live tanks of local oysters, fresh spot prawns in season, local Dungeness crab, fresh king crab, and Kodiak Pacific cod in the winter. Wild salmon arrives by the season: fresh Alaskan from late spring to late summer, Copper River salmon in late May, Lummi Island reefnet-caught salmon July to October, and frozen-at-sea salmon year-round.

Molly Ward Gardens, 27462 Big Valley Rd., Poulsbo, WA 98370; (360) 779-4471; mollywardgardens.com. This secret local's spot tucked in a lush rural valley north of downtown serves farm-to-table dinners in farmhouse-style dining room. The seafood portion of the menu changes with the seasons, but has featured Dungeness Crab Louis, pan-fried Dabob Bay oysters, crab-packed Dungeness crab cakes, and seared rosemary weathervane scallops with mango sauce. Fans also rave about the kitchen's deft handling of beef, pork, and lamb. The gardens just outside this hidden gem are perfect for a post-meal stroll . . . or, for your next garden party.

Quilcene

This tiny community along north Hood Canal is famous for the world-renowned classical musicians who frolic at its annual Olympic Music Festival in a turn-of-the-last-century dairy farm, its National Fish Hatchery (in operation since 1911), and for its oysters, with their clean, mild taste.

PHOTO COURTESY OF OLYMPIC PENINSULA VISITORS BUREAU; PHOTO BY JOY BAISCH

The Olympic Timberhouse Restaurant, 295534 US 101, Quilcene, WA 98376; (360) 764-0129; olympictimberhouse.com. Don't you love it when you discover something unexpectedly good? Especially in the proverbial middle of nowhere, or in this case, the north Hood Canal. Here's where you can enjoy Hama Hama oysters in a restaurant setting either on the half shell or lightly breaded and fried. Dig into a generous platter of crispy fish-and-chips or taste wild salmon cedar planked with beurre blanc or seasoned and char-grilled with citrus butter and blackberry puree.

Sequim

The quaint town of Sequim (say skwim) sits in a rain shadow and thus enjoys many more days of sunshine than most of the Olympia Peninsula, which is home to the Hoh and Quinault rain forests. Enough lavender farms blanket the area to prompt hourlong backups during each summer's lavender festival. Dungeness Spit, whose 5½-mile sandy length makes it the longest of its kind in the nation, is another big draw, offering breathtaking views of the Strait of Juan de Fuca and good hiking. Check out the Red Rooster Grocery (theredroostergrocery.com) for locally caught smoked salmon and black cod. For an adventure, hire the Water Limousine for a cruise of area lighthouses and wildlife (puffins, auklets, bald eagles, orcas, porpoises, and more; thewaterlimousine.com).

Dock & Dine: Where to Eat While on the Water

You're on a boat? We're jealous. Here's a sampling of eateries that offer moorage while dining. Call ahead on sunny days to ensure a spot.

Bremerton

Boat Shed Restaurant (360-377-2600; facebook.com/boatshed restaurant) offers a killer deck that gets swarmed whenever the sun is shining over the gateway to Dyes Inlet.

Gig Harbor

Tides Tavern (253-858-3982; tidestavern.com) has plenty of window seats and a deck for warmer weather, perfect to watch the parade of vessels cruising through Gig Harbor's shallow entrance.

Seattle

Anthony's HomePort Edmonds (anthonys.com) offers guest moorage through the Port of Edmonds Marina while dining. Contact the marina office on VHF Channel 69.

Chinook's at Salmon Bay looks out at the North Pacific Fishing Fleet. Tie up your boat, then enjoy hot scones at brunch or happy hour oyster shooters and shrimp cocktail. Contact the Fishermen's Terminal office at (206) 787-3395 or VHF Channel 17.

Palisade (palisaderestaurant.com) is located in the main building overlooking Elliott Bay Marina. Call the marina for moorage information: (206) 285-4817. Then savor a cocktail or decadent meal.

Ray's Boathouse, Cafe & Catering (rays.com) is located just a few blocks south of Shilshole Bay Marina. Call (206) 789-3770 for moorage information and enjoy the postcard view from the cafe's deck or at the Boathouse's bar.

Westward (westwardseattle.com): Pop by this charming spot on Lake Union for fresh oysters on the half shell and gourmet picnic supplies from Little Gull Grocery or a full menu in Westward's dining room (or beside the bonfire).

Sequim

Dockside Grill (docksidegrill-sequim.com) is adjacent to the John Wayne Marina on Sequim Bay, about 18 miles east of Port Angeles, and is easily accessible from Seattle, the San Juan Islands, and Canada.

Tacoma

Johnny's Dock Restaurant & Marina (253-627-3186; johnnys dock.com) is perched along the Thea Foss Waterway directly across from the Museum of Glass. Stay for a drink, stay for dinner, or stay the night and enjoy the revitalized Tacoma waterfront.

Alder Wood Bistro, 139 W. Alder St., Sequim, WA 98382; (360) 683-4321; alderwoodbistro.com. Wood-fired Northwest cuisine at Alder Wood means planked local fish with seasonal vegetables and local Plowsong potatoes, artfully arranged; fragrant pizzas that feature intriguing combinations of locally produced chorizo, salami, spinach, organic feta, duck eggs, and oyster mushrooms; and meaty wood-fired mussels. When the weather's fine, their lush garden of a patio can't be beat.

Alder Wood prides itself on using local and seasonal ingredients, taking care to identify items on the menu produced in the surrounding Sequim-Dungeness Valley or within a 100-mile radius. For seafood lovers, the calamari salad—crispy fried calamari with local favorite Mama Lil's pickled peppers atop Spring Rain Farms mixed greens and a kaffir-lime vinaigrette—is a good bet, as well as the panfried local oysters with spicy roasted red pepper remoulade. Note: Seating is limited, so be sure to make a reservation.

Dockside Grill, 2577 W. Sequim Bay Rd., John Wayne Marina, Sequim, WA 98282; (360) 683-7510; docksidegrill-sequim.com. Take in views of Sequim Bay at this waterfront restaurant, the scene of many happy occasions in a casually elegant atmosphere as sailboats, otters, and even the occasional submarine from nearby Naval Base Kitsap slip past just outside your window.

Seafood standouts include the dry-rubbed cedar-planked salmon topped with Dungeness crab and triple citrus Riesling butter (behold, there's a rib-eye steak version as well!), the shrimp and lobster agnolotti, surf and turf poutine (fried shrimp and beef tips atop crispy fries with four cheeses and a Cabernet demi-glace), and tiger prawns grilled in ancho chipotle *crema*.

Local oysters on the half shell arrive with mignonette, cocktail sauce, and creamy horseradish; or enjoy them baked with bacon, spinach, Parmesan, and Pernod cream in a luscious oysters Rockefeller. Kick back after dinner with a cocktail from the Dockside's lounge, the Pelican Room.

Suquamish

Located along Agate Passage, Suquamish offers a breathtaking spectacle across the Puget Sound of Seattle, the Cascade Mountains, and Mount Rainier. Chief Seattle, one of the most influential leaders in the Northwest, is buried at Suquamish National Cemetery behind St. Peter's Mission.

Salmon-Watching & Habitat Tours

Kitsap County's network of readily accessible salmon streams makes it easy to witness the return of various runs each fall. The *Kitsap Sun* newspaper created an interactive website that offers video clips that show each waterway, describe the best times to see the spawning fish, and often mention where to park your car (data.kitsapsun.com/salmon-map). When in doubt, keep your eyes peeled for the brown-and-white signs that indicate a salmon stream. Hint: Chico Creek in Central Kitsap County, it turns out, is the most productive chum salmon stream on the entire Kitsap Peninsula.

For a fresh perspective, join a kayak or stand-up paddleboard tour of these waterways, organized by **Olympic Outdoor Center** (olympicoutdoorcenter.com) of Port Gamble. Some are led by biologist Paul Dorn, who manages the Suquamish Tribe Grover Creek Fish Hatchery. Tour a salmon hatchery, have a wild-caught, locally smoked salmon snack, and paddle up a stream filled with jumping salmon. You'll also likely spy bald eagles, osprey, and great blue herons.

Agate Pass Cafe, 7220 NE Parkway St., Suquamish, WA 98392; agatepasscafe.com. Simple, clean ingredients combine to create standout dishes under the hand of Chef Marty Bracken and sous chef Isaac Rehfield. The fish of the day arrives pan-seared atop a lively yam-ginger mash, vivid with blood orange beurre blanc and crisp apple slaw. Steamed local Manila clams are matched with chorizo, jalapeño, onion, and wine, with plenty of grilled bread to sop up the goodness. Most all ingredients are local, including the Pacific Northwest–based wine list. There's so much to like, including a menu that's friendly to those in your party who may not be seafood fans, all in a warm, friendly ambience. Note: Reservations are available for parties of five or larger, though smaller groups are encouraged to call ahead to be placed on the waiting list when en route.

Union

Alderbrook Resort & Spa, 10 E. Alderbrook Dr., Union, WA 98592; (360) 898-2200; alderbrookresort.com.

Whether you glide up to the dock in your boat, splash down by seaplane, or go over the Sound and through the woods by ferry and car from Seattle, you're bound for a fun and relaxing time. The Alderbrook resembles an upscale fantasy summer camp, complete with a fire pit, a cruise boat with a bar, organized outdoor activities, and plenty of hands-on (seafood-centric) classes—but with luxurious beds and panoramic windows that look on Hood Canal in the lodge rather than rickety bunks or a leaking tent. If hotels gave out merit badges, this one could create vests for frequent guests, based on how much they can learn and experience on a given weekend.

Their culinary events kick off with April oyster month, with oyster shucking classes, happy hour oyster specials in the bar and restaurant all month long, a weekly oyster barbecue with cooking tips, and informative beach tours with a focus on oyster education. May celebrates spot prawns with

a weekly cookout and cooking class on the lawn; in June, it's Dungeness crab, with the chance to catch a crab off the Alderbrook dock, learn how to properly bait and drop a crab pot, and observe how to tell if your catch is a keeper. July, it's mussels. August, a West Coast clambake. When September rolls around, it's time to celebrate salmon. In October, it's time to enjoy local mushrooms.

The restaurant offers a variety of local oysters on the half shell from Hama Hama Oyster Company and Taylor Shellfish Farms, served with cocktail sauce and a yuzu ginger mignonette, as well as steamed Hood Canal clams with white wine butter sauce and fresh lemons, and grilled local oysters with a saffron barbecue sauce. A sampling of fresh seafood on the menu that changes throughout the season: Columbia River steelhead with farro, black rice, and butternut squash hash; poached Dover sole with smoked baby carrots and roasted garlic marble potatoes; and Hood Canal panfried oysters with mushroom and gruyère bread pudding.

Top Tips for Hosting a West Coast Clambake

Alderbrook Resort Executive Chef Lucas Sautter hosts clambakes on the shores of Hood Canal and shared these tips for those who'd like to re-create the experience at home. East Coast clambakes focus more on lobster, while this version keeps the spotlight squarely on the bivalves.

- You will need a large propane burner that works outside (to enjoy the beautiful weather) and a large heavy-bottomed rondo or Dutch oven.
- Go to your favorite beach early and set crab pots to catch Dungeness crab. Then dig clams from the beach and pick some medium-size oysters or mussels. No beach? Call ahead to your favorite fish market or shellfish shop to place your order.
- Keep your crabs and mussels cold and the clams in saltwater so they can spit out excess dirt.
- Head to your local farmers' market and pick up sweet onions, corn, baby red potatoes, garlic, fresh herbs such as thyme, basil, dill, and chives.
- Invite your closest friends.
- Make sure you have a lighter, oyster shucker, large steamer, and a big bowl.
- Get a nice bottle of Sauvignon Blanc (it pairs best with shellfish). Actually make that two bottles: one for the shellfish, and one for you.
- Cut down the potatoes, corn, and onions into smaller pieces and put the herbs in a cheesecloth with the garlic. For extra flavor, put mirepoix (equal parts diced carrots, celery, onion) in the sachet, too.
- Get your burner going and put your hard veggies in the pot with wine, clam juice, and sachet (also heavily salt this solution).
- When the liquid comes to a simmer, first add the crab, then the clams and mussels. When the clams and mussels open up, your clambake is done (check the potatoes for hardness). Strain out the liquid and reserve. Put the shellfish and veggies in the bowl. Then reduce the poaching liquid and finish with butter (set aside for a sauce). Also melt some butter for dipping and cut some lemons for extra citrus. And enjoy!

Oyster Grilling Tips

- Scrub the outside of the oysters to make sure no debris gets inside.
- Always use the freshest oysters possible.
- Keep cold until use.
- Place on the hottest spots on the grill or fire.
- Place the oysters bottom-side down so they retain their liquor
- To avoid overcooking pull the oysters off the heat before they open up completely, but they should be expelling liquor. You can also tap the top of the oysters, listening for a hollow sound.
- Enjoy!

PHOTO COURTESY OF ALDERBROOK RESORT

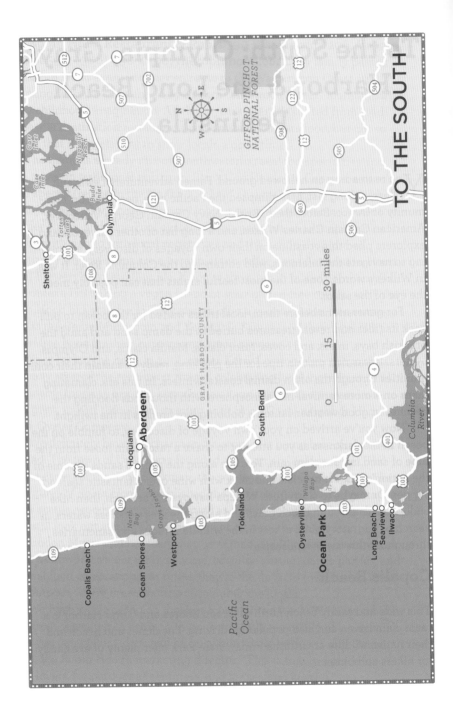

Coastal Razor Clamming

Unless you're a fan of cold weather coastal camping, finding a place to stay near the beach during clamming season (typically Oct through Apr) can be downright tricky (and even so with camping, as prime campsites can book up months in advance). These two rental properties offer contemporary amenities and fantastic beach access. Check our oystering advice in the "To the West" chapter for tips on what to wear, and head to the beach about 1 to 2 hours before low tide for optimal digging.

So, you've got your clamming permit (available at sporting goods stores and coastal gas stations). You've got your bucket to sit on and another bucket or mesh bag to hold those clams. Now, for the big question: shovel or clam gun? Either will do the job, says foraging expert and local author Langdon Cook. With a shovel, you dig slightly to the side of the show, the little dimple in the sand a clam leaves as its marker. With a clam gun—a hollow tube with handles you plunge into the sand and pull back up, hopefully with a clam inside the cylinder of sand—you center it directly over the show. Lest you think they're too easy, remember that razor clams can dig up to one inch per second in their efforts to evade you, so be quick!

Cook likes the democratic nature of foraging. "Anybody can go out and get a limit of clams or oysters and have a great meal." For tips on cleaning razor clams, search YouTube, or visit this this how-to guide created by the city of Westport, WA: westportwa .com/activities/razorclams/ cleaning.html. Then, try The Depot's recipe for Pacific Fried Razor Clams in the "In the Kitchen" chapter.

Iron Springs Resort, 3707 Hwy. 109, Copalis Beach, WA 98535; (360) 276-4230; ironspringsresort.com. Each of the 25 private cabins at this recently updated coastal resort is situated just-so on beachfront cliffs along more than 100 acres of coastal woodland to enhance privacy, creating the sense of being on a private ocean retreat. Iron Springs offers a guided clam dig for first timers or those who are rusty at spotting the clam's show at low tide. It includes a license and all the equipment you'll need to catch your limit on Copalis Beach: clam guns (a hollow tube with a handle at one end to yank cylinders of sand, hopefully with the clam inside, from the beach), shovels, clam bags to haul your loot, lanterns, and headlamps.

Groups are capped at three people per outing and are greeted at the resort with wine or hot cocoa after the dig, followed by a clam-cleaning tutorial and tools at the resort's clam-cleaning station. Then, head to your cabin armed with your bucket of cleaned clams and a recipe to make for dinner.

PHOTO COURTESY OF IRON SPRINGS RESORT

Seabrook Cottage Rentals

24 Front St., Pacific Beach, WA 98571; seabrookcottagerentals
.com. This stylized beach town is a collection of luxury ocean-front homes laid out like a friendly neighborhood, complete with stables, a town hall, a general store, and a restaurant. The streets are for bikes only, which generates a certain cama-raderie. "Cottages" sleep anywhere from 1 to 6 to 18-plus guests, making them ideal for large groups wanting to cook and dine and relax together. Wander down the staircase to the Mocrocks Beach and you're smack in the middle of a prime razor clamming site. Licenses, shovels, clam guns, and clam bags are available at Lil's Pantry and there's a razor clam cleaning station on site.

The Bainbridge Island Parks and Recreation department (biparks.com) and master forager Langdon Cook offer an annual razor clamming weekend at Seabrook that includes lodging, instruction, wine tasting, and a cooking class. Alums have been known to drag all their friends out to the coast soon after to show off their newfound skills.

Grays Harbor

True to its name, Grays Harbor can be rather bleak, both in atmosphere and weather. But those gray days make it even better for cozying up around a fire after a day spent digging clams, or to savor a perfectly grilled salmon fillet from the fish you just caught with the charter crew.

Bennett's Fish Shack, (also in Grayland and Westport), 105 W. Chance A La Mer NE, Ocean Shores, WA 98547; (360) 289-2847; bennettsdining.com. This small collection of coastal restaurants is inde-pendently owned and family operated. The Ocean Shores location offers both indoor and covered outdoor seating, plus a full-service bar and beer on tap. Ingredients are prepared fresh each day. Favorites include the fried crab (talk about decadent), grilled crab and cheese sandwich, charbroiled wild salmon, the hefty portions of beer-battered cod-and-chips, and meaty crab cakes. Its oysters hail from Brady's Oysters in nearby Westport.

Brady's Oysters, 3714 Oyster Pl., Aberdeen, WA 98520; (800) 572-3252; bradysoysters.com. Campers en route to Grayland beach cottages or Twin Harbors State Parks call this quaint little spot that straddles the line between Aberdeen and Westport the perfect location to supply bivalves for beach fire grilling. Tartar sauce, breading, and fresh lemons all are available in case you forgot them at home, along with fresh and smoked fish and freshly cooked crab.

Brady's made its mark on the oyster world in the early 1970s with Brady Engvall's suspended-culture method of raising oysters (it keeps them out of the mud and yields a better-tasting oyster, fans say). Brady's remains family owned and operated and now spans four generations.

Grays Harbor Public Market, 1956 Riverside Ave., Hoquiam, WA 98550; (360) 538-9747; ghpublicmarket.com. This quaint, historic, indoor market is open daily and offers several seafood options, including meaty and delicious Quinault Pride canned tuna, fresh razor clam sausage, and vacuum-packed smoked salmon from Briney Sea. You'll also find fresh salad dressings made with local herbs and berries by Fosse Farms; raw, local honey from Wakera Farms; and freshly baked blackberry pie and preserves from Nancy's Bakery. Browse arts and crafts, or take home plant starts, locally foraged mushrooms, and fresh flowers.

Lytle Seafoods Oyster Shack, 1 Rock View Ln., Hoquiam, WA 98550; (360) 538-2654. Swing by on your way home from a razor clamming adventure and pick up fresh oysters to slurp or grill, steamer clams, shrimp cocktail, oyster shooters, fresh Dungeness crab (in season), and smoked seafood from the friendly crew.

Westport

Westport is home to the new Salmon Tales Festival, which celebrates the community's long history as a charter fishing destination with a smoked salmon derby, charter boat bingo, live music, and family-friendly fun. It takes place each September, when ocean fishing comes to a close, river fishing is beginning, and coho are returning to the Westport Marina.

Memorable Spots to Rest Your Head

Sure, you can stay in a hotel. But the Northwest is rife with quirky spots to rest your head. These fun options in Washington, Oregon, and British Columbia add yet another dimension to your adventure.

Yurts: The sweet spot between a tent and a cabin, yurts are an affordable overnight option near many of the region's key waterways. Book quickly, because these popular accommodations go fast, especially for summer dates. Rustic yurts offer heat. Deluxe yurts offer kitchens, porches, and sometimes even TV. Search oregonstateparks.org, http://www.env.gov.bc.ca/bcparks, and parks.wa.gov for details.

Lighthouses: Drift asleep and drift awake to the sounds of the surf. Imagine the lonely vigil of watching and listening for distressed ships in the darkness. Then climb out of bed and rejoin the 21st century. Heceta Head Lighthouse (1894) in Yachats along the Oregon coast offers six rooms that come with a seven-course breakfast and a breathtaking view of rocky coastline. Point No Point Lighthouse near Hansville on the Kitsap Peninsula, built in 1879 on Puget Sound, offers views of Mount Baker and Whidbey Island, salmon fishing, miles of beach to roam, and bald eagles to watch. Find out more at uslhs.org.

Historic Beach Bungalows: Cama Beach State Park on Washington's Camano Island offers historic cedar beachfront cabins and bungalows along Saratoga Passage that offer a chance to step back in time to a 1930s-era Puget Sound fishing resort, refurbished with modern conveniences. Visit parks.wa.gov for more information.

Tree Houses: Spend the night in a gently swaying wooden or fiberglass sphere suspended from trees in the pristine Vancouver Island wilderness at Free Spirit Spheres (freespiritspheres.com). It's near Qualicum Bay along the Strait of Georgia, home to endless peaceful beaches and abundant clams and oysters.

Igloos: Overwhelmed by the hubbub in Vancouver, British Columbia? Make for the snowy mountains outside the city and learn to build your very own igloo. Enjoy dinner cooked in your "snow kitchen" and then curl up for bed. Go to westcoast-adventures.com for more details.

Historic Lodges: The Northwest is rife with lodges—both rustic and grand—tucked into spaces of overwhelming beauty. Washington's Olympic National Park is home to two near the Pacific: cozy and quaint former 1916 fishing retreat Lake Crescent Lodge, and sprawling 1926 wilderness retreat Lake Quinault Lodge. Along the southern Oregon Coast, the intimate and stylish Tu Tu' Tun Lodge (1970) beckons at Gold Beach, Oregon, where the Rogue River empties into the Pacific. In British Columbia, the historic Tweedsmuir Park Lodge (1929) sits on 60 acres of private wilderness land within the largest protected park in the province in pastoral Bella Coola. It offers salmon fishing and grizzly bear viewing near the base of the aptly named Mt. Stupendous (no, I'm not making this up). More details at tweedsmuirparklodge.com.

Natural Hot Springs: Shake off a cold, wet day with a hot, steamy soak in natural hot springs tucked amid mountain ranges, mossy rain forests, and river gorges throughout the Northwest. Sol Duc Hot Springs (olympicnationalparks.com) in Olympic National Park offers a rustic respite as you circle the Olympic Peninsula. Bonneville Hot Springs Resort and Spa (bonnevilleresort.com) in the Columbia River Gorge east of Portland offers luxurious accommodations. Both offer thermal mineral water soaks. Harrison Hot Springs (harrisonresort.com) outside of Vancouver in British Columbia offers a family-friendly experience and spa.

Merino's Seafood Market, 301 E. Harbor St., Westport, WA 98595; (360) 368-5009; merinoseafoods.com. A fresh, clean market that sells its own incredible canned tuna, smoked salmon, and clam chowder, as well as local fish and shellfish. If you're one of the many anglers heading out charter fishing, Merino's also packs and ships seafood so you can get it home easily.

Mike's Seafood, 830 Point Brown Ave. NE, Ocean Shores, WA 98569; (360) 289-0532; oceanshoresseafood.com. Locals recommend Mike's for the fresh fish, clams, and oysters from its counter and plenty of seafood favorites from its small casual restaurant. The menu ranges from linguine with crab and shrimp to razor clams and clam chowder.

Rediviva, 118 E. Wishkah St., Aberdeen, WA 98520; (360) 637-9259; redivivarestaurant.com. Almost universally, the regional response to this fine dining restaurant's 2013 opening was surprise and pleasure. Aberdeen has been in an extended economic slide for decades following the decline of logging, rendering it a town en route to the beach rather than a destination. Rediviva, an urbane, contemporary restaurant with the warm service of a small-town eatery, offers a sign that all that might change, right down to its name, which means "renewal" and harkens to the famous ship *Columbia Rediviva* that Captain Robert Gray sailed into Grays Harbor in the 18th century.

Chef-Owner Andy Bickar grew up in the area and launched his career at the Ocean Crest Resort in nearby Moclips until it burned to the ground. His menu features a wide variety of seasonal ingredients from the Olympic Peninsula and Washington coast, from seared steelhead and fresh oysters on the half shell to local lingcod roasted with a romesco crust and pasta with Dungeness crab. Smoked mussels come with fennel, salt pork, and cream and the clam chowder features local littleneck clams. The bar serves proper Moscow Mules in copper mugs and a multitude of Northwest wines.

Ilwaco

This fishing village at the mouth of the Columbia River was settled in 1851. It connected the succulent oysters of Willapa Bay with hungry 49ers in Gold Rush–era San Francisco, and was an arrival point for tourists arriving each summer from Portland to spend months in the ocean air and fish in "the salmon fishing capital of the world." These days, Ilwaco remains an exporter of Dungeness crab and albacore tuna but is better known for its proximity to major points along Lewis and Clark's journey west, including Cape Disappointment, and the Lewis and Clark Interpretive Center.

The first weekend of each December, its harbor gleams with lighted crab pots at the base of street lamps, a Christmas "tree" made of stacked crab pots, a lighted boat parade, and crabby Christmas carols. July brings

Clamshell Railroad Days (clamshellrailroad.org), with train songs, a railroad car to tour and more at Ilwaco's wee Columbia Pacific Heritage Museum.

OleBob's Galley Cafe & Seafood Market, 151 Howerton Way, Ilwaco, WA 98624; (360) 642-4332; olebobs.com.

Your first glimpse of OleBob's (pronounced Oly-Bob's) may well be through steam: A crowd likely has gathered around the cooker out front, awaiting fresh, whole Dungeness crab ready for cracking.

Since 2003, this family-owned, casual waterfront seafood market sends customers home with fresh, local Dungeness crab, crab cakes and dough, Willapa Bay oysters and steamer clams, plus wild Chinook salmon when in season. Its kitchen serves halibut tacos with homemade salsa; deep-fried oysters; baked oysters on the half shell with garlic and Parmesan cheese; hot crab cakes; homemade clam chowder; and cod, salmon, or halibut fish-and-chips. Savor a freshly steamed, whole Dungeness crab plate complete with melted garlic butter, cocktail sauce, and coleslaw. Still hungry? The market keeps a live tank of crabs, oysters, and Willapa Bay Manila steamer clams almost year-round for a fresh supply, says Roberta Muehlberg, one of the siblings who helps run the market.

OleBob's also offers its own canned local seafood, including wild Pacific salmon, solid white albacore tuna, and smoked wild salmon. It's named after Bob Hagerup (father of owner Bill Hagerup) and his best friend and fishing buddy Alan "Ole" Olson. Schoolteachers by trade, the two men also gillnet-fished along the lower Columbia River. On their cherished annual fishing trips to Alaska, they'd convert an old sailing vessel into a bowpicker and call it the *OleBob*. You'll find pictures of them and their adventures throughout the market. Also see their recipe for Baked Willapa Bay Oysters on the Half Shell in the "In the Kitchen" chapter.

PHOTOS COURTESY OF OLEBOB'S GALLERY CAFE

Pelicano Restaurant, 177 Howerton Ave. SE, Ilwaco, WA 98624; (360) 642-4034; pelicanorestaurant.com. Its surroundings may appear bleak, especially on a cloudy day, but step inside Pelicano and this hidden gem sparkles with warmth, fine food, and a fresh perspective on this fishing village's waterfront. Chef Jeff McMahon left Portland's acclaimed Saucebox restaurant for the peninsula to be closer to nature. He helmed the restaurant at the historic Moby Dick Hotel in Nahcotta, then opened Pelicano with his wife in 2008.

The monthly menu is small but mighty, with dishes inspired by the food traditions of Italy, France, and Spain and featuring an abundance of local fish and shellfish. Depending on the season, you might savor panfried oysters nestled with creamed spinach and pancetta; seafood chowder that boasts plenty of delicious morsels in a broth thickened with pureed potato and sweet corn; crab cakes full to bursting with sweet Dungeness; and a heavenly rockfish fillet.

The expertly mixed cocktails and bliss-inducing desserts (Belgian chocolate *pots de crème*, anyone?) also win raves, as does the wine list, featuring small local producers such as Columbia Gorge star Syncline Wine Cellars and many other treasures.

Long Beach

The namesake of the Long Beach Peninsula resides at a central point along the nation's longest contiguous beach (about 28 miles, give or take). In a story so familiar along the coast, Long Beach began as a summer playground for the well-to-do from Portland, before roads enabled easier access for anyone not near a steamboat terminal or train depot. These days, its main drag is weathered but imbued with a fresh energy as chefs and other business owners fleeing big cities team with homegrown town boosters to play up its history, refresh its main street, and appeal to the next generation of vacationers. Kitschy fun still abounds, from the oddities at Marsh's Free Museum to the overwhelming array of housewares, sporting goods, hardware, decor, toys, and more at Dennis Company. On a razor clamming weekend, celebratory signs everywhere leave no doubt as to how welcome you are.

The Pickled Fish, 409 Sid Snyder Dr., Long Beach, WA 98631; (360) 642-2344; adrifthotel.com. Perched atop the fresh and modern Adrift Hotel, this contemporary beach bar offers sweeping views of the waves and sunset, a fun atmosphere often infused with live music, and a vast array of local produce, meats, and seafood. The wood-fired oven produces pizza but also baked and fragrant Dabob Bay oysters lounging with spinach, a garlic cream sauce, and Parmesan. Willapa Bay oysters star in the semolina-crusted fish-and-chips, served with remoulade. Pan-seared cod arrives with seasonal farm vegetables and Station House Company steamer clams get the white wine and garlic treatment. The bar serves well-crafted of-the-moment cocktails (Moscow Mule, Corpse Reviver, Pisco Sour, etc.) as well as plenty of wines from Washington and Oregon.

Long Beach Peninsula

This peninsula is embraced by the Pacific Ocean to the west, the Columbia River to the south, and Willapa Bay to the east. Each offers its own bounty, with steamers and oysters from the bay, razor clams from the ocean's beaches, and salmon and sturgeon from the Columbia.

Eateries in this area are mostly of a touristy lot, offering plenty of clam chowder, seafood boils, and fish-and-chips in venues that mostly date back to the middle of the last century. But the past two decades have seen the arrival of intimate, seasonally focused, finer dining, largely because of chefs and restaurateurs resettling from Portland and other metro areas to start something new, march to their own drums, and be closer to nature.

Perhaps most famously, the late Chef Jimella Lucas and her partner, Nanci Sofia Main, brought national attention to the peninsula's culinary bounty and local, seasonal cooking at their critically acclaimed restaurant, The Ark, and after its sale, at Nanci & Jimella's Cafe and Cocktails in Ocean Park near Klipsan Beach. Now, restaurants such as Pelicano, The Depot, Pickled Fish, and 42nd St. Cafe & Bistro are treating the local catch with reverence and infusing dishes with flavors, cooking techniques, and influences from around the globe.

The main highway along the peninsula, SR 103, follows the path of the old Clamshell Railroad, which ferried wealthy Portland tourists, local schoolchildren, crates of oysters bound for San Francisco, fresh cranberries, and all manner of other freight along the peninsula.

Ocean Park

This tight-knit retirement community has many fans who visit and camp, fish, hunt, and dine on this narrow strip of land between the Pacific and Willapa Bay. Don't miss Jack's Country Store, offering a stylishly eclectic collection of practical, beautiful, and whimsical housewares, lamps, remedies, dry goods, toys, sporting goods, lawn furniture, and other merchandise since 1885. Another must-try: the Thunder Buns (a phenomenal sticky roll) from Bailey's Bakery in nearby Nahcotta.

Nanci & Jimella's Cafe & Cocktails, 21742 Pacific Way, Ocean Park, WA 98640; (360) 665-4847; jimellaandnancis.com. Before Pelicano, The Depot, and Pickled Fish helped create a small but thriving food scene along the Long Beach Peninsula, before the farm-to-table movement and eating local really took hold of the imagination of diners, Jimella Lucas and Nanci Main offered something different and changed what diners expected from coastal restaurants, one dish at a time.

For more than two decades beginning in 1981, the duo many chefs credit with helping to create what's now known as Northwest cuisine ran the famed Ark restaurant in nearby Nahcotta, a local darling of an eatery that earned national attention and accolades after ultimate foodie James Beard himself gave their impossibly fresh, flavorful, local-ingredient-based creations his seal of approval. This fine dining establishment, seemingly in the middle of nowhere, shifted the conversation toward cooking with local, organic, sustainable, and seasonal ingredients, with what was ripe locally, toward creating a true sense of place in each dish. And, lucky for them, the Northwest is filled with options: pure Willapa Bay oysters, sweet Dungeness crab, wild mushrooms from the nearby hills, high-quality meats, wild salmon returning home to the Columbia, cranberries from local bogs, wild game, and fresh herbs from kitchen gardens.

PHOTO COURTESY OF LONG BEACH PENINSULA VISITORS BUREAU

After selling the Ark, the pair opened their eponymous bistro-style cafe in woodsy Ocean Park/Klipsan Beach. Jimella and Nanci's is where you go to savor panfried oysters, devour Dungeness crab cakes served with Thai coleslaw, sip Jimella's secret clam chowder recipe, behold a piquant fisherman's stew packed with clams, prawns, calamari, and halibut, dig into crab mac and cheese, or pause with happiness midway through the grilled fish of the day, paired with organic braised vegetables. It's where you somehow make room in your belly for dessert. Sadly, Lucas passed away in late 2013 after a long illness. But her spirit (and her recipes and love for cooking) carries on.

Willapa Bay Oyster House Interpretive Center, 3311 275th St., Ocean Park, WA 98640; (360) 665-4547; portofpeninsula.org/oysterhouse.html. Located on the south side of the Port of Peninsula breakwater, this is a replica of a typical residence of oystermen and their families where you can learn what it was like to live in a home built on pilings over the water. The story of this historic industry on Washington State's southwesternmost bay is told in an 8½-minute video, and there are also historic photographs and tools of the oystering trade. Open from Memorial Day weekend through Labor Day weekend; tours and school groups welcome on weekdays by appointment.

Olympia

Dockside Bistro & Wine Bar, 501 Columbia St. NW, Olympia, WA 98501; (360) 956-1928; docksidebistro.com. This charming eatery owned by Chef Laurie Nguyen offers contemporary seasonal fare, a serene setting, and an extensive wine selection. Seafood, meats, and produce arrive from a bounty of local growers, including fresh clams and oysters from nearby Eld Inlet. Several seafood dishes stand out, including the salmon BLT with thick, crunchy bacon, slathered with pesto spread and served with Parmesan-seasoned fries. Other good bets: the seafood cocktail, the scallops seared with honey, and the salmon with duck mousse. Beyond seafood, the contemporary menu is a carnivore's delight with lamb, elk, Wagyu beef; and it's a good spot to savor a glass of wine or nurse a cocktail.

Olympia Farmers' Market, 700 N. Capitol Way, Olympia, WA 98512; (360) 352-9096; olympiafarmersmarket.com. This iconic farmers' market is in its fourth decade and draws devoted crowds who savor its variety and quirks. Enjoy crab cakes from the Ricklick family at Dingey's Puget Sound Cuisine; shellfish from Sound Fresh Clams & Oysters, raised nearby where the Little Skookum and Totten Inlets merge; and fish caught locally by Sea Blossoms Seafood. Market vendors typically sell Thurs through Sun from Apr to Oct, then Sat and Sun only Nov to Mar.

Olympia Seafood Company, 411 Columbia St. NW, Olympia, WA 98501; (360) 570-8816; olympiaseafood.com. Tony and Kira DeRito's loyal customers—and they are many—rave about the seafood market's thick, meaty crab cakes, its wonderfully fresh ahi tuna (just right for making Basic Hawaiian Tuna Poke, recipe found in the "In the Kitchen" chapter), and its creamy, filling clam chowder. Counter service is friendly and professional, with plenty of cooking tips and recipe suggestions. There's even a cookbook nook for those who desire additional inspiration. Also try their recipe for Parmesan-Crusted Lingcod found in the "In the Kitchen" chapter.

The DeRitos founded Olympia Seafood in 1999, selling live crab out the back door. After a remodel, they officially opened their front door in 2000, selling local and exotic seafood and shellfish. Much of their local selection is supplied by family members, who count among them more than 40 years of commercial fishing experience. Often on hand: fresh, live Dungeness crab, smoked salmon, and shrimp cocktail for meals on the run.

The Oyster House, 320 4th Ave. W., Olympia, WA 98501; (360) 753-7000; theoysterhouseatolympia.com. You can't beat the location: perched on Budd Inlet, home to oysters aplenty slumbering in their beds below. For generations, the Oyster House has served up local bivalves with a view as one of the oldest—if not *the* oldest—seafood restaurants in the state. It found its start in 1924 as a state-of-the-art packing plant for wee, native Olympia oysters, with an oyster bar added over time. It was a full-fledged restaurant by the 1940s, when pollution from nearby lumber mills prompted a decline in the health of Olympia oysters and more and more of the industry shifted to farming Pacific oysters. Tragedy struck in summer of 2013, when a fire destroyed the Olympia waterfront icon. The owners pledged to reopen in 2014 and had begun construction when this book went to press. The menu item loyal customers miss most? The restaurant's creamy clam chowder.

Oysterville

The prim and pristine village of Oysterville, founded in 1854 on the inland side of the Long Beach Peninsula, is almost startling when you happen upon it during your coastal drive. Its clapboard buildings appear frozen in time, its neat yards forever waiting for 19th-century kids to race home from school in knickers and caps, or for wedding guests to spill joyfully from its pristine white church.

Weddings still do take place in that church, the mail is still delivered to the longest continuously operating post office in Washington State, and many of the town's finest old homes are preserved by descendants of their

builders: families that built a future toiling in the sea in all manner of weather to supply hungry California gold miners with top-quality Willapa Bay oysters, before there were even roads and consistent transportation on the Long Beach Peninsula. (Many of the surviving homes were constructed of Northern California redwood shipped in as oyster schooner ballast, paid for with gold.) Like all boomtowns, Oysterville eventually hit a bust. By the late 1800s the native Olympia oyster beds had nearly been plucked clean, the county seat moved across the bay to South Bend, and the population began to trickle away. The introduction of Pacific oysters helped revive the industry, but not to the frenzy of the mid 1800s. In 1976, 80 acres of the community were placed on the National Register of Historic Places. Be sure to stop and wander a spell. Find a walking tour of Oysterville at funbeach.com.

Oysterville Sea Farms, First and Clark Streets, Oysterville, WA 98640; (360) 665-6585; willabay.com/newindex.html. How fresh is fresh? At this charming oyster outpost, third-generation oysterman Dan Driscoll and his team sell oysters, clams, and crabs harvested the same day from its tideflats along Willapa Bay. The seafood market also sells smoked oysters, oyster shooters, shrimp cocktail, razor clams, squid salad, smoked salmon spread, cranberry salsa, baking mixes, fresh-baked cookies, and more. Learn how to shuck oysters, grab a glass of wine, then sip and slurp away on the deck as you watch the next batch being harvested on the low tide. Revenue from Willabay's oysters fuels restoration and preservation of Oysterville's last oyster buildings. Note: Lines can be long on busy weekends.

Know Your Oysters: An Oyster Primer

Perhaps more than any other foodstuff, oysters taste of where they're from. At the most basic level, West Coast oysters tend toward sweetness compared to their brinier East Coast brethren (the Atlantic has higher salinity than the Pacific). Oyster connoisseurs prefer a pinpoint to these broad brush generalities. They'll note how an oyster was raised (suspended on a line in open water, or lounging on a muddy tideflat?); the appellation where it was raised (Willapa Bay, Nootka Sound, or Yaquina Bay?); the mineral content of nearby bodies of water that feed into that inlet, bay, or cove; the time of year of harvest; and the influence of weather and temperature on flavor. Oysters filter dozens of gallons of water daily. A sudden rainstorm that sends a rush of water down a neighboring creek could dilute the flavor of oysters harvested that day, whereas a drought could intensify it.

But let's not get ahead of ourselves. Back to basics.

- **Popular oyster locales** in the Northwest include Washington's Willapa Bay and Oregon's Yaquina Bay, both plundered of their native oysters to satisfy hungry miners during the San Francisco Gold Rush; the many coves, inlets, and reaches along Hood Canal and Puget Sound; and BC's Nootka Sound, Baynes Sound, Barkley Sound, and Jervis Inlet.
- **When to eat oysters?** The saying goes to avoid them in months without an R (summer months), when oysters typically spawn. Oysters are at their best raw in the colder months. Most varieties spawn during the summer and put all their energy toward reproduction—that's the time to panfry them, says Langdon Cook, a Seattle-based author and forager who teaches foraging classes around the region. In the winter, they put weight back on and get plump and meaty.

This is to the chagrin of oyster growers, who face a hard sell getting oyster lovers to trudge out to the coast when it's bone-chillingly cold and windy. The development of so-called triploid oysters that do not spawn has made it possible for oyster bars to stock fat oysters year-round.

- **How they're grown:** Oysters naturally grow in estuaries and marshes, places with brackish water. Over the years, growers around the globe have developed methods to coax out admired traits, from specific flavor profiles to a more cup-shaped shell that in turn forms a denser, meatier oyster. Here in the Northwest, growers use Pacifics for most of their innovations. Look for Kusshis, Pacific oysters cultivated atop floating trays and tumbled aggressively in Deep Bay off Vancouver Island in British Columbia; Shigokus, Pacifics grown in floating bags tied to stationary lines in Washington's Willapa Bay so that they tumble twice daily with the tides; and Chelsea Gems, grown in Eld Inlet in bags attached to racks staked low on the beach so that they develop sturdy, deep-cupped shells. In Oregon, most Pacific oysters are "ground cultured," or grown right on the beach.

- **Common oyster varieties** on Northwest menus include the tiny, coppery-tasting Olympia oyster; dainty and creamy Kumamotos; and many variations on the meaty Pacific oyster, including the Kusshi, Shigoku, Blue Pools, and Chelsea Gems. Taylor Shellfish Farms also grows East Coast favorite Virginica oysters on Totten Inlet.

- **Common descriptors** for oyster flavor profiles include melon, smoke, seaweed, lettuce, cucumber, mineral, copper. Oyster farms such as Hama Hama on Washington's Hood Canal have begun offering shucking and tasting classes at Seattle cooking schools like the Pantry and Delancey and at cookbook shop Book Larder to discuss what influences an oyster's flavor. "We'll eat a couple different oysters and discuss why they taste the way they do," said Lissa James of Hama Hama. "It's hard to get into, it's kind of a foreign language. If someone helps you just a little bit, like with wine, it opens up a huge door. 'Oh yeah! It *does* taste like grapefruit.'"

- **What the heck is Hangtown Fry?** You'll see this menu item again and again along the West Coast. It's an omelet juicy-rich with oysters and bacon, a trifecta of three of the most expensive ingredients that a San Francisco 49er who had just struck gold could buy to celebrate back in the 1800s. Hangtown, known as Placerville today, was a supply base for miners, and earned its nickname due to series of hangings as a form of Gold Rush-era criminal justice.

Aw Shucks: How to Shuck an Oyster

You will need a real oyster knife, found in most hardware stores and fish markets. Gloves are advised, at least one on the hand that is holding the oyster, but a towel will work just as well. I have found it's best to put the oysters in the freezer for about 15 minutes before shucking.

If using a small towel, drape it in your hand over the oyster, flat side up, or place it on a firm surface. Make sure to hold the oyster firmly. Slip the point of the knife between the top and bottom shells between the hinge.

Using a twisting motion, pry the two shells apart, making sure not to lose any of the liquid inside.

Run the knife around the top shell until you get to the other side. This will sever the tendon on the top of the shell.

Slide the knife under the oyster to cut it free from its shell (it will be connected by a tough knob). Place the oyster on a bed of crushed ice and serve with your favorite topping.

ILLUSTRATIONS BY ROBERT PRINCE

Seaview

Seaview started out as a summer community for well-heeled Portlanders who desired a cool ocean air respite from the inland heat. These days, it's known for restaurants that celebrate local coastal ingredients and, of course, the Shellburne Inn, the 1896 bed-and-breakfast that's the oldest continuously operating hotel in the state of Washington.

The Depot, 1208 38th Pl., Seaview, WA 98644: (360) 642-7880; depotrestaurantdining.com. Years ago, The Depot truly was a depot, a stop along the so-called Clamshell Railroad that carried people, oysters, the US mail, and other goods along the Long Beach Peninsula from the 1880s through 1930. Now the depot houses a cozy restaurant with red walls that hint at the passion of its owners for bringing finer dining to a part of Washington more famous for clam digging, oystering, and kite festivals.

While his menu features a range of meats, Chef Michael Lalewicz includes a good variety of local fish and shellfish, from clams perched atop toothsome bucatini and savory broiled Willapa Bay oysters to Dungeness

PHOTOS COURTESY OF THE DEPOT RESTAURANT

crab mac and cheese and a seasonal fresh, local wild catch of the day. Diners go mad for his petrale sole, halibut (which Lalewicz says always sells out), and spring Chinook salmon from the nearby Columbia River or Youngs Bay in Oregon—a fish whose flavor Michael calls "the best thing in the world." The wilted spinach salad, rich with bacon and shallots, is also worth writing home about. Find their Petrale Sole Piccata with Tomato Concassé and Pacific Fried Razor Clams recipes in the "In the Kitchen" chapter.

The restaurant draws a crowd even on dark and chilly winter evenings, when the boom of the boisterous Pacific surf drifts through the trees from nearby Seaview Beach. In the summertime, the crowd spills onto an adjacent deck. The Depot celebrated its 10th anniversary in 2013 and is going strong, in part for its creative events. The restaurant hosts a Lewis and Clark dinner, featuring wild game, as well as a wild mushroom feast in celebration of the region's abundance.

The 42nd Street Cafe & Bistro, 4201 Pacific Way, Seaview, WA 98644; (360) 642-2323; 42ndstcafe.com. This cheerful eatery set along the main road into Long Beach offers the breakfast spread you might expect at the seafood-centric bed-and-breakfast of your dreams: hot Dungeness crab beignets, a traditional oven-baked Hangtown fry omelet rich with Willapa Bay oysters and bacon, and a house-smoked salmon scramble with spinach, mushrooms, and gruyère. But you'd be wise to save room for lunch and dinner, when the wood-fired oven heats up and out come delectable surprises, including pizza topped with that lovely house-smoked salmon.

This locally owned cafe aims to celebrate the region's seasonal delights and showcase the seafood of the pristine waters that surround the Long Beach Peninsula: the Columbia River, the Pacific Ocean, and Willapa Bay. And its menu reads like a love letter to the local land and seascape. Buttermilk-battered fried razor clams arrive hot and tender, teamed with thin-cut french fries and honey coleslaw. Try fresh Willapa Bay steamer clams or delicate panfried oysters. On the seafood sandwich front, choose from a red rockfish and shrimp cake sandwich; a flash-fried

oyster po' boy; or the West Coast albacore tuna salad sandwich, layered with potato chips for salty, crunchy happiness. For seafood pasta fans, try the spaghetti tossed with sautéed albacore, fried capers, and garlic, then topped with spicy bread crumbs. In gloomy weather, warm up with seafood stew.

Owners Blaine and Cheri Walker have called the coast their home for 30 years and delight in creating a restaurant that seems equally liked by locals and tourists. The menu's Cajun influence stems from their many visits to New Orleans.

The Shelburne Inn, 4415 Pacific Way, Seaview, WA 98644; (360) 642-2442; theshelburneinn.com. Step back in time. It was 1896, and the Long Beach Peninsula, an oyster empire, was a thriving destination for wealthy Portland, Oregon, residents hoping to spend summer by the sea, enjoying the salty breeze and a multitude of amusements: beach bonfires, skiffs for rent on Willapa Bay, razor clamming, and salmon fishing. Why not hit the Oregon coast, you ask? Trains and roads were just beginning to pierce the hills and forests to reach Seaside, Gearhart, and other future

resort towns. Even before the Clamshell Railroad carried tourists (and oysters, and schoolchildren, and farm equipment) up the peninsula, tourists made their way by steamship.

The Shelburne Inn opened its doors that year in the small town of Seaview, just east of the Pacific's thundering waves. Charles Beaver chose the name Shelburne after a grand hotel in Dublin, Ireland, and it became one of the main stops along the Clamshell Railroad, dropping summer residents and visitors off at the inn.

More than 100 years later, it's the oldest continuously operating hotel in the state of Washington, a fixture on the National Register of Historic Places, and has maintained a timeless charm that permeates every aspect of your visit. Even at breakfast, the dining room gleams with loving attention to detail; morning light filters through the Art Nouveau stained-glass windows, off the paneled wood, and makes the silverware shine. You

imagine visiting in an earlier time, dressed in more elaborate attire. Then, after your next bite of the luscious oven-baked Hangtown fry omelet, rich with oysters and just a hint of the sea, you thank your lucky stars that it's a different era and you have jeans to unbutton.

At lunch and dinner, depending on the season, grilled Chinook salmon with cranberry butter celebrates two hyperlocal ingredients. North Coast bouillabaisse is packed with prawns, mussels, salmon, cod, Willapa Bay oysters, and Dungeness crab in a red wine and saffron broth. Dungeness crab and Oregon bay shrimp cakes come with roasted red pepper chutney and baby arugula.

The Shelburne's Northwest-centric wine list won a *Wine Spectator* Award of Excellence in 2013. Now you'll never leave, especially when the evening pianist begins to tickle the ivories of Gloria, a grand piano crafted by Washington piano maker Fandrich & Sons and named for one of the Shelburne's longtime and beloved guests, Gloria Swisher, a music teacher.

Shelton

Shelton once was famous for timber and Christmas trees. These days, it's most known for its shellfish, due in large part to the work of the Taylor family, now in its fifth generation of farming clams, oysters, and mussels throughout Washington and British Columbia.

Squaxin Island Seafood Bar, (Inside Little Creek Casino Resort), 91 W. State Rte. 108, Shelton, WA 98584; little-creek.com. Casino dining is hit or miss in Washington State, but this petite seafood bar off the main floor of Little Creek Casino owned by the local Squaxin Island Tribe is a gem. Fans rave about the crab bisque, crab cocktail, and oysters shucked to order, all served in a casual setting. The menu features fresh Dungeness crab, native clams, mussels, shrimp, and more. Portions are generous, and the seafood is fresh. Note: Smoking is allowed in the casino, so plan accordingly. Second note: The seafood bar is open until 11 p.m. most nights for anyone who tried—and failed—at campfire cooking or is heading home after a long weekend hiking the Olympic foothills.

Taylor Shellfish Farms, Shelton Retail Store, 130 SE Lynch Rd., Shelton, WA 98584; (360) 432-3300; taylorshellfishfarms.com. Since its humble beginnings farming Olympia oysters in the 1890s, Taylor Shellfish Farms is now the largest producer of farmed shellfish in the United States, with a popular outpost along Samish Bay on Chuckanut Drive (complete with grills to BBQ oysters within view of the San Juan Islands) and shellfish hatchery and nursery facilities in Hawaii and California.

Already a mainstay on restaurant menus around the Northwest (and in major oyster bars around the country), Taylor recently expanded its presence in Seattle by opening a popular shellfish market and oyster bar (Taylor Melrose) on hipster haven Capitol Hill. Marco Pinchot, Taylor's community relations and sustainability manager, says they were surprised at the sense of community that sprang up and around the market, and

responded by creating more events and eating space. "It was supposed to be retail, but we quickly found out people wanted it to be a place to hang out. The place just took off, and it's busy all the time."

Based on that success, in 2014, Taylor will be opening additional oyster bars in bustling lower Queen Anne and in historic Pioneer Square, which is walking distance to the ferries, Safeco Field, and CenturyLink Stadium. On the menu: signature cocktails, wine and beer, Dungeness crab, a raw bar, baked oysters, steamed clams, and mussels.

Walrus & Carpenter Picnics

Taylor Shellfish launched these whimsical events to whisk city dwellers by bus out to its tideflats so they, too, could experience the magic (and, bone-chilling temperatures) of winter nights on Totten Inlet. The picnics take place by moonlight (or, if it's a typical cloudy evening, by lantern light) on a low minus tide in the middle of winter—ideal weather for plump, superb oysters. Picnickers get to slurp freshly shucked Olympia, Shigoku, Pacific, and Totten Inlet Virginica oysters paired with oyster-friendly wines that won the Pacific Coast Oyster Wine Competition.

When the tide begins to rise, the gaggle gathers around a bonfire to sip a cup of hot oyster stew prepared by Xinh Dwelley of Xinh's Clam and Oyster House before piling back on the bus and heading home to Seattle. Proceeds benefit the Puget Sound Restoration Fund, which helps keep Puget Sound healthy so sea life can continue to thrive.

"Assuming these next two oyster bars go as well as we expect, these won't be the last," Pinchot predicted. "It's this farm-to-table thing that people want. They want to know the farmer."

The Taylor retail store in Shelton is open daily (except for major holidays) and offers live shucked or smoked oysters; clams, mussels, geoduck, and frozen razor clam meat; smoked salmon; and wild Northwest salmon and halibut. In 2014 it will begin selling chowder, oyster stew, beer and wine, Pinchot said. Be on the lookout for specialty oysters such as Totten Inlet Virginicas and Shigokus, which both sell fast.

Xinh's Clam and Oyster House, 221 W. Railroad Ave., Shelton, WA 98584; (360) 427-8709; xinhsrestaurant.com. Simply put, Xinh Dwelley is a powerhouse. She's a five-time winner of the West Coast Oyster Shucking Championship. She won cooking competitions and widespread acclaim with her oyster stew and her now-legendary curried mussels, and holds her own on national television, even while holding a geoduck.

Her namesake restaurant hosts diners from around the world, drawn to her vivid flavor combinations. Fresh Pacific oysters are served fresh on the half shell; baked topped with bacon and hoisin sauce; sauteed with ginger, garlic, herbs, and vegetables in a black bean hoisin sauce; or panfried and served with tartar and cocktail sauces. Her famous mussels are shelled and sautéed in a Vietnamese-style curry, flavored with coconut milk, lemongrass, cayenne pepper, ground peanuts, and seafood sauce, served with jasmine rice. If you're new to geoduck, this is a good place to give it a try. She shares her recipe for Clams in Hoisin Sauce in the "In the Kitchen" chapter.

Dwelley hails from Vietnam, where she worked on her family's rice farm as a child. As a teenager, she began picking up odd jobs for the US Army, and before long found herself cooking American food for an entire battalion. After she moved to the states with her American husband and son in the 1970s, she took a job with Taylor Shellfish Farms shucking oysters. Before long, her knack for cooking earned notice again, and she shared her dream of opening her own restaurant someday. In 1996, someday arrived, and Xinh's Clam and Oyster House opened its doors, introducing many diners for the first time to the flavors of her homeland. Note: Open for dinner only. Reservations recommended.

South Bend

This town bills itself as the gateway to Willapa Bay, and has the oysters to prove it with a bustling shellfish industry and a blend of weathered eateries and contemporary offerings. Burn off your lunch with a canoe or kayak along the bay from the town's dock, or gaze at the Tiffany glass dome that crowns the local courthouse.

Eastpoint Fish & Chips, 313 E. Robert Bush Dr., Ste. A, South Bend, WA 98586; (360) 875-5419; facebook.com/EastPointFishAnd Chips. This food truck serves up piping hot breaded Alaskan cod with hand-cut fries and coleslaw. Take in the view of Willapa Bay as you await your prize, then pick up crab cocktail, smoked salmon, fresh fish, and chowder to go from the nearby fish market.

101 Public House, 1019 W. Robert Bush Dr. (Highway 101), South Bend, WA 98586; (360) 550-6273; 101publichouse.com/south -bend/101-public-house. This South Bend newcomer offers a surprisingly contemporary experience along Willapa Bay: a quirky and comfy boutique hotel with a restaurant that offers a playful take on food made with local and organic ingredients, and a shop featuring art and gifts

Willapa Bay

It's a tranquil place, Willapa Bay, where you can hear birds call out to one another across the seemingly still waters, separated from the thundering Pacific by the Long Beach Peninsula. As with most quiet places, there's plenty going on beneath the surface, where freshwater from outflowing rivers mingles with saltwater. This thriving estuary—the second largest on the Pacific Coast after San Francisco Bay and among the most pristine in the nation—is a National Wildlife Refuge, a key stop for clouds of migrating birds, which in turns draw crowds of birders to gawk at pelicans, bald eagles, marbled murrelets, and great blue herons. Several species of salmon ply its waters, which lap against grasslands, tideflats, marshes, and rain forests. Then there are the oysters: lightly salty, delicate, with a sweet hint of cucumber.

For millennia, the Chinook, Chehalis, and Kwalhioqua tribes lived and hunted in the area. Later, settlers got into oystering, which became the big gig in town, and the quaint community of Oysterville and its neighbors hummed with activity. The appetites of San Francisco gold prospectors nearly wiped out Washington's natural stocks as barges dredged bottom of the bay. Generations later, the oyster population is restored, but a new threat looms: rising acid levels in the ocean that weakens oyster shells and leaves the bivalves vulnerable to predators. Industry leaders are hard at work on solutions, as are environmental advocates. It's easy to forget all these concerns when you gaze upon its serenity, whether you gaze upon it from Highway 101 or from a vantage point in sprawling, ever-changing Leadbetter Park at the tippy top of the Peninsula on the ocean side. Breathe deep, for you're in a sacred space.

created around the Northwest. Sure bets on the menu include anything oyster (fried, grilled, in stew, on the half shell), the refreshing bay shrimp sandwich, and the fresh fish of the day. Much like the Olympic Peninsula to the north and its Culinary Loop, the 101 has created a Freedom Tour of quirky, interesting stops from Aberdeen on Grays Harbor to Astoria just across the Columbia River in Oregon: 101publichouse.com/freedom-map.

Tim's Chester Club & Oyster Bar, 1005 W. Robert Bush Dr., South Bend, WA 98586; (360) 875-5599; 101publichouse.com/south -bend/chester-oyster-club. Dive into this locals roadhouse for oyster shooters, oyster sandwiches, and fried oysters that many seafood fans call the best they've enjoyed anywhere.

Tokeland

This tiny town along Willapa Bay within view of the Pacific is named for a native chief and is home to the National Historic Landmark Tokeland Hotel, which serves a home-style, oven-roasted, slow-cooked cranberry pot roast for Sunday dinner with a view of the water.

Nelson Crab Inc., 3088 Kindred Ave., Tokeland, WA 98590; (360) 267-2911; seatreats.stores.yahoo.net. This historic crab cannery has been in operation since 1934 and is now run by the third generation of the Nelson family. Its seafood stand offers treats like crab cocktail, crabmeat to make crab cakes at home, local shellfish, and plenty of canned seafood.

Want to make someone's day? Overnight them fresh Dungeness, or the Nelson's Tuna Taster, a selection of top-quality canned albacore in six flavor varieties.

OREGON

When wagon after wagon of settlers flooded Oregon via its famous trail in the 1800s, they discovered what native tribes had enjoyed for millennia: acres of towering woods that teemed with wildlife, rivers choked with fat salmon, a temperate climate where berries and crops of all kinds flourish, and an ocean abundant with seafood and shellfish, from succulent Oregon albacore to Yaquina Bay oysters. The Portland-born beloved American epicurean James Beard, a direct descendant of those trailblazers, brought Oregon's many culinary delights to the national stage. He rhapsodized about picnic-filled summers spent at the Oregon Coast town of Gearhart, devouring sweet Dungeness crab, his mother's razor clam soufflé, and fresh local fish. His vivid recollections of the morel mushrooms his father gathered, the texture of perfectly cooked salmon, and so many other meals helped inspire the celebration of fresh, local ingredients that we nearly take for granted in restaurants around the country today.

Oregon keeps one foot in the past as it innovates. Portland is lampooned for its obsession with all things organic and artisanal, yet diners descend from around the nation precisely for its small-batch, homegrown, foraged delights. Oregon is home to one of the country's largest seafood companies (Pacific Seafood) and also a small fleet of dory fishermen who plunge their nimble boats through the coastal surf at Cape Kiwanda to land rockfish, cabezon, and salmon. The pioneering spirit lives on in Portland's vibrant food trucks, which congregate in such numbers to resemble a never-ending hipster state fair of amazing eats. Meanwhile, polished chefs like Gabriel Rucker of Le Pigeon win James Beard Awards and other culinary honors. On the coast, younger generations are continuing the legacy of family restaurants like Mo's, while classically trained chefs make a splash with creative cuisine.

Oregon shares the mighty Columbia River and its maritime heritage with Washington, its neighbor to the north. Tumbling, ethereal Multnomah Falls, an easy daytrip from downtown Portland, provides your first inkling that the Columbia River Gorge puts the "gorge" in "gorgeous." Farther up the river, Celilo Falls, a grand cascade and vital fishing hub for tribes from miles around, remains submerged beneath the Dalles Dam, its legendary roar living on only in the minds of those who can summon its memory. Like the razor clams at Sunset Beach, like Lewis and Clark's salt harvest at Seaside, like the gray whales that surface by Depoe Bay, so much of Oregon's fascinating history lies just beneath the surface, awaiting your discovery.

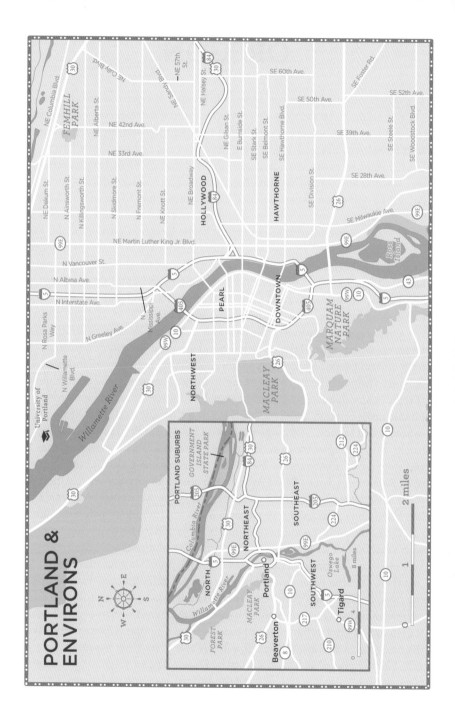

Portland & Environs

Dining in Portland is flat-out fun. Just when you think the creative minds of the city's ever-growing stable of innovative and playful chefs and restaurateurs have topped themselves, along comes a fresh take on Italian, Argentinian, Chinese, Peruvian, etc., delivered from the kitchen into dining spaces straight out of a Pinterest-worthy rustic and quirky-chic decorating fantasy (we're looking at you, Ned Ludd). Or the food will come from the back of a beat-up food truck that invites suspicion—until your first bite. Distilleries, coffee micro-roasteries, dueling artisanal doughnut shops, nomadic fish-and-chips spots, a killer brunch scene, happy hour that makes your city's seem sad: Portland's got it all, plus easy parking and a pack of James Beard Award–winning chefs (Naomi Pomeroy at Beast and Expatriate and Andy Ricker of famed Thai joint Pok Pok, to name a couple).

PHOTO COURTESY OF JOHN GAUDETTE

Seafood in the Rose City is an entertaining mix of weathered, longtime family-owned joints crammed with nostalgia; edgy new eateries helmed by tattooed, bespectacled and bearded, well-admired chefs who might spin their own vinyl on the turntable; and classic fish houses that serve dependable favorites with impeccable service. Then there's the food truck scene, into which seafood options are dropping anchor. What do they have in common? An almost lusty reverence for fresh and local ingredients and a need to celebrate anything Oregon and after that, anything authentically Northwest. Thus, no matter where you go, those Netarts Bay oysters, Oregon albacore, or Dory-caught rockfish likely will be solid. Your toughest decision will be deciding which neighborhood (sudden gourmet destination Southeast Division Street? The Pearl? Southwest?), which preparation (wood-fired oven? wok? back of a van?), and which culinary tradition to sample tonight (too many to list, along with some that likely haven't been invented . . . yet).

Andina, 1314 NW Glisan St., Portland, OR 97209; (503) 228-9535; andinarestaurant.com.

Year after year, Peruvian, family-run gem Andina is high atop the list of most-loved Portland restaurants. Its gloriously fresh cebiche and gorgeous, vibrant tapas keep many diners coming back for more. The warm welcome of the family's matriarch, Mama Doris, is another draw.

"Stop me if I talk too much," laughs Doris Rodriguez de Platt, who loves to regale the curious with the ancient culinary traditions of her homeland. Coastal fishermen long enjoyed fresh raw or lightly poached fish. The arrival of the Spanish in the 16th century introduced limes and other citrus,

PHOTOS COURTESY OF ANDINA; PHOTOS BY LINCOLN BARBOUR

Seafood Lover's Pacific Northwest

which helped cure the dish and add to its appeal. The arrival of a Japanese diaspora in later years introduced even more flavors to Peru's collection of tropical fruits and starches.

"Cebiche is our iconic dish. We pay lots of respect to variations of how to make it, just honoring the people and past generations." At Andina, this means starting with fresh, firm fish, taking care to cut it in even-sized cubes and salt it properly, taking care to squeeze the lime juice just so to avoid the bitterness of the peel. Taking care to remove the seeds and veins from the chiles, slicing the onion precisely, serving it all up with traditional corn and sweet potato for balance. Taking care.

Mama Doris advises diners to take a bit of corn and sweet potato with each bite of fish, so that the flavors can dance and sing and meld.

Another version combines shrimp, scallops, squid, and octopus. The Tuna Nikkei cebiche, a nod to the fishing traditions of Peru's Japanese population, adds ginger and soy sauce. Tiraditos, sashimi-style fresh fish, employ similar ingredients, methods, and flavors with thinly sliced fillets.

For those who prefer their seafood cooked, Andina comes through with seafood salads, grilled octopus kebabs with chimichurri, and crispy golden prawns studded with quinoa. And mussels cooked in white wine and served chilled with a tomato-corn salsa. And avocado stuffed with crab and topped with a poached prawn. And bay scallops baked with Grana Padano cheese and lime butter. Oh yes.

Note: Be sure to make a reservation if you heart is set on a particular evening.

Bamboo Sushi, Southeast: 310 SE 28th Ave., Portland, OR 97214; (503) 232-5255; and Northwest: 836 NW 23rd Ave., Portland, OR 97210; (971) 229-1925; bamboosushi.com. Bamboo proudly claims the title of world's first certified-sustainable sushi restaurant; its staff takes pleasure in demonstrating just how delicious marine stewardship can be. Best bets: the salmon flight (from leanest to fattiest cuts, when available), black cod, uni custard, tuna prosciutto, shrimp tempura, scallop sashimi, and albacore carpaccio.

Cabezon Restaurant & Fish Market, 5200 NE Sacramento St., Portland, OR 97213; (503) 284-6617; cabezonrestaurant.com. Portlanders can't get enough of Chef David Farrell's brothy vibrant cioppino, a heady combination of traditional cioppino and a bouillabaisse. It makes them smile. It makes them swear with reverence. It makes him happy to describe the steps that go into its creation, from the house-made fish stock to the saffron and tarragon.

"It's pretty darn good," he said. Portland's a soup-eating town. A batch is 3 or 4 gallons and when they're busy, his team prepares the cioppino five to six times each week. Some nights, they'll sell 25 to 30 bowls just of that. "We cook all the seafood in the broth to order. The crab is cooked, but the shrimp, the mussels, the clams, bits of fish. The calamari is last. We get really excited."

This farm-to-table (or is it sea-to-table?) neighborhood seafood bistro, tucked into two storefronts with stained-glass jellyfish on the ceiling, seems forever in motion. Farrell lists five options on the menu each day, with at least two being fish. Fresh oysters come from Hama Hama Oyster Company on Washington's Hood Canal and the Mediterranean blue mussels from Taylor Shellfish. He's served dory boat–caught black rockfish, lingcod, troll-caught king salmon, wild steelhead, petrale sole, Oregon albacore, and Columbia River sturgeon, of which he's a huge fan. "I smoke it and we grill it and it's an amazing fish."

Other favorites from the menu: truffled corn and Manila clam chowder, black cod with truffled risotto, leeks, chanterelles, romanesco and mussels, and Totten Inlet mussels with Spanish chorizo, borlotti beans, fries, and rouille.

Dan & Louis Oyster Bar, 208 SW Ankeny St., Portland, OR 97204; (503) 227-5906; danandlouis.com. This venerable and quirky oyster bar, now owned and managed by the fifth generation of the Wachsmuth family, offers a rotation of Northwest superstar oysters on the half shell that change daily, but have included sweet Quilcene Bay oysters from Washington's Hood Canal; local Tillamook Bay Kumamotos and Pacifics from Netarts Bay and Yaquina Bay; and Fanny Bay and Sinku from the waters of British Columbia. You also can get your oysters in a

Bloody Mary shooter, Cajun fried, or tucked into a creamy oyster stew. Step inside and the vintage nautical elements will make you feel like a stowaway.

EaT: An Oyster Bar, 3808 N. Williams Ave., Portland, OR 97227; (503) 281-1222; eatoysterbar.com. Go for the oysters. Stay for the live jazz, fried pickles and okra, and the build-your-own-Bloody-Mary station on weekends. Since 2008, this laid-back New Orleans–inspired joint offers fresh Northwest oysters (Chelsea Gems, Hama Hama, Netarts Bay, and the like) served on the half shell, as shooters, baked, or fried crisp and juicy, plus Cajun and Creole eats and classic NOLA cocktails in its stylish, industrial space. Top picks: the gumbo with its rich, flavorful roux, the spicy étouffée, and a collection of po' boys (including catfish, oyster, and shrimp). Downside: Uneven service and prep that might leave you stuck with an empty glass of sweet tea and overspiced or underseasoned vittles. But when it fires on all cylinders, it's magic.

The Fishwife, 5328 N. Lombard St., Portland, OR 97203; (503) 285-7150; thefishwife.com. Family-run for more than 20 years, this casual neighborhood eatery near the University of Portland with a diner-style dining room hits the spot with generous servings of fresh local seafood at a good value. Cioppino is loaded with salmon, scallops, and bay shrimp. The smoked salmon Alfredo often sells out, and you can enjoy cod, salmon, or halibut breaded and fried, grilled, poached, or blackened. Look for the sign with the mermaid.

The Frying Scotsman Fish & Chips, Food truck located on SW Ninth Avenue and SW Alder Street; (503) 706-3841; thefrying scotsmanpdx.com. Owner James King knew he wanted to become a professional chef all the way back at age 10, while growing up in a small town outside Glasgow, Scotland. A chance meeting with a Portlander visiting the UK spurred him to move to Oregon, where he's now calling the shots in the kitchen. He prepares his own tartar sauce and coleslaw daily, sources his fish through Pacific Seafood, buys his bangers (sausage) from Portland's Zenner's Sausage Company, and hand-cuts almost 100 pounds of local potatoes each morning. Seattle chef Ethan Stowell (Anchovies & Olives, Staple & Fancy) calls them the best fish and chips in Portland.

Unexpected Seafood Finds

Portland's proximity to the Pacific and the Columbia River means a steady stream of fresh fish and shellfish, transformed into delectable bites shared from the windows of food trucks and the kitchens of high-end dining rooms alike. Always ask about daily specials, as you never know what delights the fresh catch will offer.

Chitarra with Mussels & Almond Butter at Ava Gene's (Southeast/Richmond; avagenes.com): Among the innovative Italian offerings at this warm yet sophisticated spot is this dish, a soul-satisfying melding of sweet, savory, and carb. Don't miss the creative salads and fresh cannoli from Stumptown Coffee Roasters founder Duane Sorenson and his team.

Oyster Breakfasts at Bijou Cafe (Southwest; bijoucafepdx .com): Year after year, in a city that reveres breakfast and brunch, Bijou Cafe remains among its most adored spots for its creative approach to standards. Try fresh Northwest oysters baked with bacon and onion in a fluffy French-style omelet or as a hash dredged in cornmeal flour, sautéed with onions and potatoes and an over-easy egg.

Oregon Albacore Tuna Melt at Bunk (6 Portland locations and a truck; bunksandwiches.com): How local can a sandwich be? With meaty albacore fresh from coastal waters, ciabatta rolls baked in town, and Oregon cheese, this simple-yet-unforgettable concoction could well live up to its billing as the ultimate Oregon sandwich.

Fried Chowder Balls at The Bus Stop Cafe (Northeast; facebook.com/TheBusStopCafe): Deep-fried clam chowder? No matter on which side of the line you fall on this innovation, you can't deny the charm of enjoying fried chowder balls atop this Portland food truck, where the upper deck of a double-decker bus also serves as its kitchen.

Lobster Agnolotti at a Cena Ristorante (Sellwood; acenapdx .com): Creamy, rich, salty, unforgettable. We're talking the mini ravioli at this warm and inviting seafood-heavy Italian restaurant, where mascarpone raviolini are bundled with butter-poached Maine lobster for a mouthwatering treat.

Shrimp Toast at Expatriate (Northeast; expatriatepdx.com):
Combine one bartending star (Kyle Linden Webster) and one
Beast chef and veteran of *Top Chef Masters* (Naomi Pomeroy)
at this 30-seat bar with Asian-inspired bites, and it's small
wonder the result is dishes like this shrimp toast: beautiful,
deceptively simple, yet bursting with flavor. Also on the must-
list: crab Rangoon, Chinese sausage corn dogs, and any of the
expertly mixed cocktails.

Whole Roasted Trout at Ned Ludd (King; nedluddpdx.com):
Nearly every dish originates in Chef Jason French's wood-fired
oven at his whimsical American craft kitchen, including the
whole roasted trout with its crispy skin and smoky meat, bed-
ded in an ever-changing array of seasonal produce. Beyond
its top-quality food, Ned Ludd is worth a visit for the decor
alone, so well edited it resembles a Pinterest board for stylish,
rustic living come alive.

**Clam Chowder with Roasted Marrow Bone at Ox (Northeast;
oxpdx.com):** How can you improve upon the hearty goodness
of clam chowder? Top it with a roasted marrow bone crowned
with jalapeño slices. Scrape the marrow in, stir it up, and the
result is outrageously good at this Argentine-inspired meat-
fest of a restaurant.

**Crab, Noodle & Shrimp Meatball Soup at Smallwares
(Beaumont-Wilshire; smallwarespdx.com):** *Portland Monthly*
rhapsodizes about this soup, with its briny crab stock and its
shrimp meatballs that "throw sparks of chile and fish sauce." A
dimly lit open dining room full of interesting people-watching
makes it taste even better.

Jake's Famous Crawfish, 401 SW 12th Ave., Portland, OR 97205;
(503) 226-1419; mccormickandschmicks.com. This vivacious fish
house with its iconic neon sign has been going strong in various incarna-
tions since 1892, serving Northwest dishes as classic as the restaurant
itself: salmon roasted on a cedar plank, Oregon Dungeness crab, Chinook
salmon stuffed with crab, panfried Northwest oysters or petrale sole, succulent Alaskan halibut cheeks . . . you get the picture. The menu changes

daily to reflect the best seafood offerings available; the simplest preparations tend to be the best. Its tiled bar floor, cozy, high-back wooden booths, white tablecloths, and oftentimes raucous bar lend it an old-school aura, and help it bridge the gap between pleasing tourists and appealing to the nostalgia of locals. Tidbit: It was the first fish restaurant managed by partners Bill McCormick and Doug Schmick, spawning a seafood empire.

Pal's Shanty, 4630 NE Sandy Blvd., Portland, OR 97213; (503) 288-9732; palsshanty.com. This beloved dive bar/seafood joint closed in late 2013 after a major fire and is scheduled to reopen in 2014. Longtime fans—many of whom are second- or third-generation customers—can't wait to again taste Pal's exceptional clam chowder, panfried oysters, Crab Louie, and razor clam sandwiches, and other seafood favorites, which they consider the freshest and best in town. Pal's has been part of Portland since 1922. Note: Of the many treats you'll find here (full bar, local seafood, a small log cabin beer cooler that's homage to Pal the Dog's "shanty," the restaurant's namesake), you won't find a deep fryer. Get your fish-and-chips fix elsewhere.

The Parish, 231 NW 11th Ave., Portland, OR 97209; (503) 227-2421; theparishpdx.com. This open, warm, and fun restaurant is the second Southern-inspired spot from Tobias Hogan and Ethan Powell, the duo behind North Portland sister restaurant EaT: an Oyster Bar. A curved oyster bar of Oregon white oak anchors the room, flanked by antique captain's chairs for oyster admirers. Enjoy fresh Northwest oysters served up on the half shell, fried, or in a variety of oyster shooters (try the Kentucky, with chile-infused bourbon and lemon). Other good eats: the Parish burger topped with fried oysters; fried chicken; and the shrimp étouffée. Like its sister restaurant, The Parish can get a little too laid back when it comes to service and consistency.

Roe, Inside Block & Tackle, 3113 SE Division St., Portland, OR 97202; (503) 236-0205; blockandtacklepdx.com, roe-pdx.com. Like its namesake, Roe is a bit of a mystery, tucked discreetly within its boisterous sister eatery, Block & Tackle. Pass the peel-and-eat prawns, fried calamari, plates of fresh oysters, and grilled octopus salad, and you'll enter a relatively serene space that's akin to a seafood shrine to modernist cuisine.

The two-man team of Chef Trent Pierce and Sous Chef Patrick Schultz dazzles diners with vibrant, imaginative, 4- and 10-course menus that

change as consistently as the ebb and flow of the tide. Diners have been wowed by exquisite Dungeness crab in coconut milk, blissfully smooth sous-vide–cooked salmon, the caviar course, salmon skin chicharrones, the Roe Medley (lobster roe inside Parisian gnocchi, butter-poached lobster and golden char roe, topped with curls of salted, cured roe), and Alaskan spot prawn crudo with uni panna cotta, each plated with reverence.

Pierce, a third-generation restaurateur, was named visionary of the year by the *Oregonian* newspaper; *Willamette Week* named Roe its 2013 Restaurant of the Year. Plan accordingly if you're able to get a reservation: Ordering 10 courses, some diners have reported lingering in Roe for 3-plus hours.

Seasons & Regions Seafood Grill, 6660 SW Capitol Hwy., Portland, OR 97219; (503) 244-6400; seasonsandregions.com. It's not edgy, flashy, or trendy: Seasons & Regions is down-to-earth, with straightforward seafood dishes made with wonderfully fresh fish and local produce and served in generous portions. Devotees (many from the neighborhood) rave about the Dungeness crab wontons, the warm seafood salad, the smoked salmon quesadilla, and the honey ginger and lime salmon. Parking is notoriously tricky; head straight to the overflow lot at the nearby Jewish Community Center.

Veritable Quandary, 1220 SW 1st Ave., Portland, OR 97204; (503) 227-7342; veritablequandary.com. What keeps a restaurant open year after year when so many others come and go? In this case, gracious service, an elegant atmosphere, a view of the river, a splendid bar, and consistently outstanding food. Since 1971, this landmark restaurant with its window walls framed by cozy brick has served a litany of sumptuous dishes, including seafood specialties like halibut wrapped in prosciutto, wild Oregon Chinook salmon with cumin and coriander, and a rich seafood stew. Accompaniments and featured dishes change with the seasons. It also offers great people-watching, as nearly all types of Portlanders find their way here eventually, either on a date, brunching with out-of-towners, taking a business lunch, lounging on the patio with cocktails, or winding down after a night out. Make a reservation for the best seats.

Wong King's Seafood, 8733 SE Division St., No. 101, Portland, OR 97266; (503) 788-8883; wongsking.com. Dim sum is served until 3 p.m. daily at this popular seafood destination, and you'll do well to order

The Food Truck: A Portland Icon

Mention Portland's dining scene to anyone in the Northwest and food trucks are bound to come up. While other cities boast them as well, few come close to the sheer number, variety, and easy accessibility of Portland's ever-growing fleet. Here are three seafood-centric options.

Fishbox (Southeast; 4262 SE Belmont St.; Portland, OR 97215; 503-348-5244): It's a fish taco paradise parked at the Belmont Pod. Choose from tacos stuffed with Hawaiian-style ahi poke or with crispy-fried chile-lime salmon, each served with fresh tortillas, cabbage, and sauce. Vietnamese-style *banh mi* sandwiches come with smoked salmon and pickled veggies. Wild salmon appears again in Indonesia satay form. There's also clam chowder. Urp.

Sea Verdes (North; 3441 N. Vancouver Ave., Portland, OR 97227; 503-869-9901; seaverdes.blogspot.com): In a city that teems with food carts, this one still manages to stand out. Chef-Owner Elysa Watkins serves an energizing combination of fresh and fried seafood, antioxidant-rich smoothies, and hearty organic salads and pasta dishes. A seafood sampler: steamed mussels and shrimp served with rice; handmade salmon croquettes with wild Alaska salmon; delicately seasoned fried oysters with rice; shrimp and pasta with organic basil, tomatoes, spinach, garlic, olive oil, and lemon. Top any salad with shrimp, tilapia, or salmon.

Year of the Fish (Southeast; SE 50th Avenue and SE Division Street, Portland, OR 97215; letseat.at/yearofthefish): A rolling fish-and-chippery (and clam chowdery) with a penchant for sustainable seafood—and the option of gluten-free batter. Choose from wild-caught Alaskan cod, Pacific red snapper, halibut, wild-caught prawns, and clam strips. They also sling Willapa Bay oyster shooters. And anyone pining for the taste of RC Cola: You're in luck. It's on the menu.

the deep-fried shrimp balls, salt and pepper calamari, and delicate shrimp dumplings from the carts. Definitely make a reservation and bring your friends—the better to sample the extensive menu. If you come by at dinner, try the braised short ribs, roast duck, and honey walnut prawns.

Where to Buy in Portland

ABC Seafood, 6509 SE Powell Blvd., Portland, OR 97206; (503) 771-5802; abcseafood.org. This Asian grocery is packed with giant, bubbling live tanks filled with shellfish and live tilapia: Point out which fish you desire and they'll dispatch and clean it on the spot. A fresh selection and reasonable prices keep people coming back.

Flying Fish Company, 2310 SE Hawthorne Blvd., Portland, OR 97214; (503) 260-6552; flyingfishcompany.com. This tiny fish market owned by second-generation fishmonger Lyf Gildersleeve and his wife, Natalie, is attached to Kruger's Farm Market and next to a Grand Central Bakery, making it one-stop shopping when you're pulling together many a favorite meal. The cases hold a small but mighty fine selection of seafood mostly from Oregon, Washington, and Hawaii. You'll also find organic dairy and other organic products.

Mio Seafood Market, 1703 NW 16th Ave., Portland, OR 97209; (503) 219-9762; miosushi.com. Mio, the newest of the bunch, is a hidden gem many of its fans would prefer to stay a secret. It wins raves for its friendly customer service and an abundance of sushi-grade seafood for those of you who like to prepare sashimi, nigiri, and rolls at home (it's the seafood market for Portland-based sushi restaurant chain Mio, after all). Hungry? Pick up panko-crusted fish-and-chips made with whatever is in season (typically cod, salmon, or halibut), or a vibrant array of sashimi. You'll also find Asian and gourmet European products, a small produce selection, miso paste, fresh noodles, and other staples.

Newman's Fish Market, In City Market, Northwest; also in Eugene, OR; 745 NW 21st Ave., Portland, OR 97209; (503) 221-3007; newmansfish.com. Newman's has supplied fish to hungry Oregonians since 1890, when founder John Henry Newman peddled fish using a horse-drawn cart on the dirt roads of Eugene and Springfield. As it has changed hands and expanded over the years, Newman's has become a major supplier to Portland's burgeoning restaurant scene, from Le Pigeon and Cabezon to Ringside and the Zeus Cafe at Crystal Hotel. This fish market, neighboring a high-end deli, meat market, and specialty shops with fancy pasta and cheese, offers a huge selection of Oregon coastal favorites

in its glass cases, all cut to order, including smoked salmon, sturgeon, and escolar, homemade fish cakes and cocktail sauces, and seasonal seafood salads. Fresh tanks stand at the ready, filled with oysters, crab, and lobster.

New Seasons Market, With 13 Portland-area neighborhood locations; newseasonsmarket.com. This local favorite grocery chain carries only seafood that has been designated sustainable by Monterey Bay Aquarium and the Blue Ocean Institute, and buys directly and locally whenever possible. Preferred local suppliers include Reinholdt Fisheries (wild-caught hook-and-line salmon and tuna), Fishpeople of the Pacific Northwest (seafood pouch meals), Nisbet Oyster Co. (Willapa Bay oysters), Bristol Bay Salmon in Alaska, Iliamna Fish Company (wild salmon), and Linda Brand Crab (Dungeness).

Northwest Flavor, Right in Your Pantry

The Northwest prides itself on having a local, artisanal version of nearly every "basic" pantry item, from canned tuna to sea salt. They are wonderful pantry staples and also make delicious gifts for locals and visitors alike. When seeking just the right seafood gift, check with oyster farms and fish markets, many of which gladly will ship Dungeness, razor clams, smoked salmon, smoked oysters and more just about anywhere in the country. A few standouts: Bell Buoy of Seaside, Oregon; Seattle's Wild Salmon Seafood Market; and The Fishery on Salt Spring Island, BC.

Artisanal Sea Salt

Jacobsen Salt Co. (jacobsensalt.com) hand-harvests its sea salt from pristine Netarts Bay, Oregon. Available in pure flake or infused with Oregon Pinot Noir, Stumptown Coffee, and other regional delights.

San Juan Island Sea Salt (sanjuanislandseasalt.com) offers mineral-rich finishing salt (and its own San Juan Island honey) at farmers' markets throughout Washington. It's moist like a French *sel gris*, but a vivid white, and lovely in toffee and cookies.

Vancouver Island Salt Co. (visaltco.com) harvests sea salt by hand from the wild ocean side of the island and offers Canadian fleur de sel, plus salt in a variety of flavors (blue cheese, orange and lime, Spanish Paprika, and a version infused with wine from Canada's first aboriginal owned and operated winery, Nk'Mip Cellars).

Canned Local Tuna

Why settle for generic canned tuna you can buy anywhere in the country when you can support the efforts of your local fishing fleet? These cans are produced in small batches and crammed with luscious, meaty hunks of albacore, just the thing to top a salad or enjoy with a fork just as soon as you peel off the lid. The tuna's natural juices are rich in omega-3 fatty acids, the same ones you enjoy from salmon and other cold-water fish. Collect a variety of cans and present with capers, good mayonnaise, and other tuna salad accoutrements to fish-loving friends. Trust me, after a nervous giggle, they'll realize how lucky they are to know you. Many of these canned tunas are sold at farmers' markets, fish markets, fishing terminals, and right off the boats.

Chuck's Seafood (Charleston, OR; chucksseafood.com): Tender, mild, wild albacore tuna cut and packed by hand, then cooked in its own natural juices with just a pinch of sea salt for delectable flavor.

Estevan Tuna Co. (Courtenay, BC; bctuna.com): Wild BC troll-caught albacore, then hand-filleted and hand-packed. Fans send it by the case to loved ones for Christmas.

Fishing Vessel St. Jude (Bellevue, WA; tunatuna.com): Phenomenal tuna packed in flavors including smoked, garlic, dill, and Mediterranean.

Island Trollers (Whidbey Island, WA; islandtrollers.com): "Troll-caught in the North Pacific, one at a time" says it all. It sells unsalted wild albacore tuna packed with capers or habañeros, or just pure and simple.

Canned Wild Salmon

Seattle's Loki ("low-key") Fish Co. (lokifish.com) is a family-owned business that catches wild sockeye salmon by gillnet in Alaska, where it is bled immediately and chilled on board for premium quality, then flown to Seattle and processed with no artificial preservatives and colors.

Douglas Fir Jelly

Enjoy that fresh, green, hauntingly woodsy scent of Northwest forests in a jar. **Hama Hama Oyster Company (hamahama store.com)** in Lilliwaup, Washington, handpicks new growth from Douglas firs and boils the tender tips to make a tangy, citrus-and-mint flavored preserve. Spread it on toast, melt into a syrup for an evergreen cocktail, or use it to glaze seafood, chicken, and lamb.

Chinook Wines Long Live the Kings Blends

Pair a Yakima Valley red or white with your favorite Northwest seafood for the ultimate taste of place; the salmon restoration organization **Long Live the Kings** receives a portion of the proceeds from each bottle sold at area **PCC Natural Markets**. Longtime Washington winemakers Kay Simon and Clay Mackey say they hope these custom blends help to educate a few folks about the importance of wild salmon in our Pacific Northwest culture. For more information, visit lltk.org, pcc naturalmarkets.com, and chinookwines.com.

Tom Douglas Rub With Love

These spice rubs make it a cinch to season seafood, meat, and poultry before grilling, panfrying, or baking. Choose from protein-specific blends (seafood rub, pork rub, chicken rub, etc.) or global flavors (African peri peri rub, Bengal masala rub). The salmon rub, a combination of paprika, thyme, and brown sugar, is the same used at Etta's in Pike Place Market. Find the rubs at any **Tom Douglas** restaurant (tomdouglas.com), at the **Dahlia Bakery**, and at many Northwest groceries.

Pacific Northwest Best Fish Co., 24415 NE 10th Ave., Ridgefield, WA 98642; (360) 887-4268; pacificnwbest.com. This family-owned and -operated seafood store, smokehouse, and cafe are located near the Columbia River and Pacific for easy access to fresh, wild-caught seafood. All smokehouse products (sturgeon, salmon, black cod, albacore, and more) are smoked with traditional Northwest alderwood free of preservatives and artificial colors. If you got lucky fishing along the Columbia or other nearby waterways, this shop offers custom processing and smoking packages for your catch.

The cafe, housed in a cabin-style building with indoor and outdoor seating, specializes in down-home seafood, including hand-breaded halibut-and-chips, grilled mahimahi tacos, a calamari steak sandwich, and homemade clam chowder. Enjoy with a glass of local wine, or, call ahead and pick it up (they even offer curbside service).

HOOD RIVER

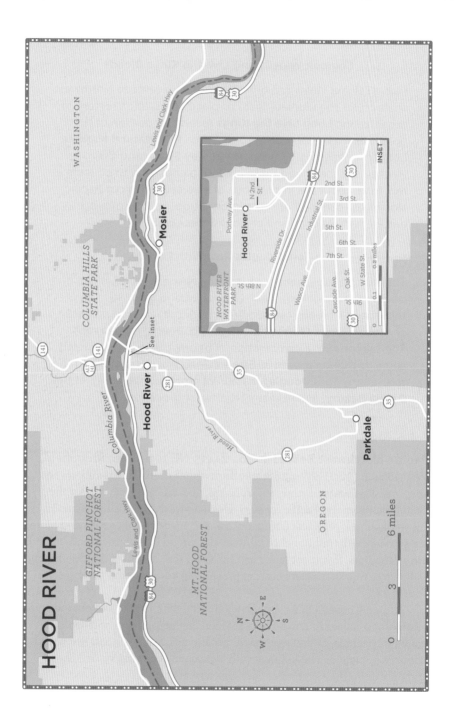

WASHINGTON

OREGON

GIFFORD PINCHOT
NATIONAL FOREST

COLUMBIA HILLS
STATE PARK

MT. HOOD
NATIONAL FOREST

Columbia River

Hood River

Lewis and Clark Hwy

Lewis and Clark Hwy

Mosier

Hood River

Parkdale

See inset

INSET

HOOD RIVER WATERFRONT PARK

Hood River

Portway Ave.
N 2nd St.
N 8th St.
Riverside Dr.
Industrial St.
2nd St.
3rd St.
5th St.
6th St.
7th St.
Wasco Ave.
Oak St.
Cascade Ave.
W State St.
9th St.

0   0.1   0.2 miles

N
W   E
S

0   3   6 miles

Hood River & the Columbia River Gorge

An hour or so outside of Portland, past the graceful majesty of Multnomah Falls in the sun-drenched Columbia River Gorge, Hood River feels a world away. This mostly walkable hillside town sits on and above the Columbia River and bustles with restaurants, cafes, coffee spots, art shops, a beloved ice cream stand, parks, and breweries. Tour one of the

PHOTO LICENSED BY SHUTTERSTOCK.COM

nearby wineries (Syncline is a rustic favorite), hike Post Canyon, wander the gardens of the nearby historic Columbia Gorge Hotel, windsurf on the river, or hit the Hood River County Fruit Loop, a self-guided tour of farm stands, U-pick farms, and darling towns. Breakfast on the deck at the local Best Western offers an unbeatable view. Across the river in Washington, White Salmon offers whitewater rafting, camping, and a growing collection of good places to eat, including lunchtime favorite Big Man's Rotisserie (406-579-9450). Head east along the Columbia, and you'll pass mighty hydroelectric dams (many of which offer tours and salmon-viewing areas) and fishing grounds that have nourished regional tribes for millennia. Tribal fishermen now supply many Northwest restaurants and farmers markets with a top-quality catch.

Brian's Pourhouse, 606 Oak Street, Hood River, OR 97031; (541) 387-4344; brianspourhouse.com. It's easy to be charmed by this restaurant, tucked into a cute gray house with a deck that's the place to be on

Confluence Project

Long before fur traders, British explorers, and Americans Lewis and Clark navigated the Columbia River Basin, indigenous people from throughout the Northwest gathered alongside its waters to fish and be nourished by its bounty. A public art installation effort known as Confluence Project seeks to lend context to the area's history and ecology. Designer and artist Maya Lin, best known as the designer of the Vietnam Veterans Memorial in Washington D.C., is collaborating with Pacific Northwest tribes, civic groups from Washington and Oregon, and additional artists, architects, and landscape designers. Key cultural sites along the Columbia will feature an art installation by Lin, artworks, restored habitat, and passages from Lewis and Clark's journals. Sites include Celilo Falls, a once-bustling, ancient center of regional trade and fishing. It was among the oldest continuously inhabited settlements in North America (10,000-plus years) until it was inundated by flooding from the Dalles Dam in 1957. Learn more at confluenceproject.org.

sunny days. You'll find many local ingredients in the dishes on the menu, including Columbia River salmon in various preparations throughout the year on the specials sheet. Salads, soups, steaks, cocktails: All are well-executed. Don't miss the fish tacos, stuffed with cornmeal-crusted tilapia, lime-cured cabbage, pico de gallo, and jalapeno remoulade. Whenever the menu features the butternut squash gnocchi, do not hesitate to order.

Henni's Kitchen & Bar, 120 E. Jewett Blvd., White Salmon, WA 98672; (509) 493-1555; henniskitchenandbar.com. A short jaunt across the river brings you to White Salmon, homebase for whitewater rafting tours and Henni's Kitchen and Bar, a new America-style eatery that specializes in tacos, curries, pastas, and burgers made from scratch.

Waterways: How We Live

Yakama Nation Commercial Fisherman
Pea Kea "Paul" Kuneki

Friends says Pea Kea "Paul" Kuneki can simply wave his hands to summon fish to his boat in the Columbia River. He scoffs at their flattery, but in truth, takes great pride in his talent, honed for more than 30 years since he was a wee tot and his mother brought him along with the family on their regular fishing trips.

"Most of it comes with learning through time," Kuneki says. And so it goes with preparing his abundant catch as well. After years of observing and helping his grandmother, mom, and aunts, Kuneki is skilled at drying salmon for winter-time snacking, for getting through occasional lean times, and for sharing at gatherings such as funerals and memorials.

As with most tribal fishermen, Kuneki has deep reverence for the first salmon caught in spring, which is celebrated with a special feast that marks the start of salmon fishing season. "You've got to honor that fish in the springtime. If we catch our first salmon on the Columbia ourselves, we will have our own little dinner, family time honoring that fish. It's just been like that for years."

Indonesian green curry features shrimp and pork awash in green chile and coconut milk. The pan-seared cod in the fish tacos is wrapped in handmade corn tortillas and served with toasted cumin slaw and *cotija* cheese. As with all Northwest spots, be sure to check the specials sheet for fresh seafood in season.

Nora's Table, 110 5th St., Hood River, OR 97031; (541) 387-4000; norastable.com. Step into this small (yet unexpectedly kid-friendly) venue for a sophisticated take on the best local ingredients. Seafood options vary with the seasons; in spring, the Canadian halibut arrives with toasted cous cous, sweet red pepper, and kale raab in a savory hazelnut-orange chocolate vinaigrette. The Goan seafood curry features Oregon petrale sole, mussels, and scallops with grilled naan. For meat-eaters, the juicy rib-eye from Columbia River Gorge neighbor Mountain Shadow Natural Meats is out of sight. And any restaurant that offers post-dessert hot beignets alongside coffee creme brulee is fine by me.

Sixth Street Bistro, 509 Cascade Ave., Hood River, OR 97031; (541) 386-5737; sixthstreetbistro.com. This laid-back spot, whose dining room sprawls throughout a breezy house, serves generous portions of down-home cooking made with ingredients sourced from throughout the region. At lunch, the grilled salmon wrap with blackened sockeye salmon, crisp red cabbage, and cilantro aioli truly satisfies. At dinner, look to the specials sheet for their hearty take on the day's fresh seafood.

Eugene

Nestled in a tree-fringed valley, Eugene is home to the University of Oregon, a thriving farmers' market, restaurants that cater to just about any eating lifestyle, and a variety of top-rate markets and co-ops (Market of Choice, Capella Market, Sundance Natural Foods, Kiva Grocery, etc.) that revel in supporting local farmers, fishermen, ranchers, and cheesemakers.

Alder Street Fish Co., 1239 Alder St., Eugene, OR, 97401; (541) 654-5109; facebook.com/AlderStreetFishCo. This cozy seafood market and dining space near the U of O campus offers tasty seafood baskets priced for college-student budgets. Popular on the menu: salmon Caesar salad, mahimahi fish tacos, clam chowder, and barbecued salmon. Fish-and-chip varieties rotate, and have included sockeye salmon, wild sturgeon, and coho salmon.

Fisherman's Market, 830 W. 7th St., Eugene, OR 97402; (877) 798-5988; eugenefishmarket.com. Yes, they have good fish-and-chips. But what makes Fisherman's Market special is its variety. A few highlights: the salmon burger featuring fresh-ground salmon on a toasted bun with waffle fries, the grilled teriyaki tuna sandwich, and the crab cocktail. The specials menu (also posted on the website) runs the gamut from Thai coconut peanut pasta with shrimp, scallops, and roasted veggies to a "Codfather"

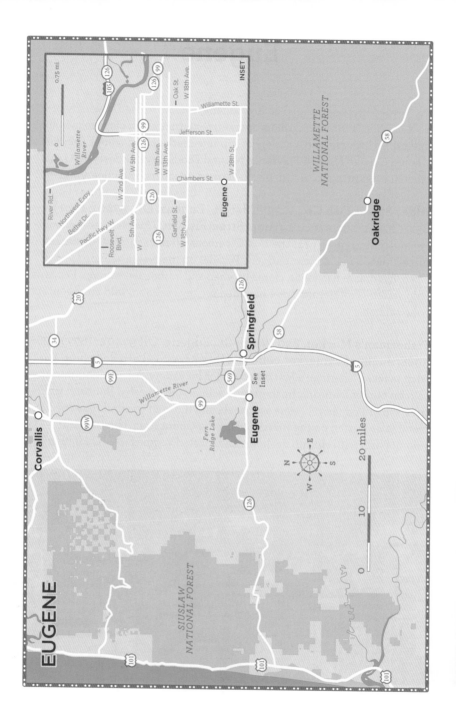

EUGENE

Corvallis

Eugene

Springfield

Oakridge

WILLAMETTE NATIONAL FOREST

SIUSLAW NATIONAL FOREST

Willamette River

Fern Ridge Lake

See Inset

N E S W

0   10   20 miles

INSET

0.75 mi

Willamette River

River Rd.

Northwest Expy.

Bethel Dr.

Pacific Hwy W

Roosevelt Blvd.

5th Ave.

W 2nd Ave.

W 5th Ave.

W 11th Ave.

W 13th Ave.

W

W 18th Ave.

Garfield St.

Chambers St.

Jefferson St.

Willamette St.

Oak St.

W 18th Ave.

W 28th St.

po' boy with chipotle mayo and waffle fries. Did we mention the variety of tartar sauces and coleslaws? There's plenty of fresh seafood and shellfish to take home as well, along with fresh crab. Ryan and Debbie Rogers, long-time Alaska fishermen, make sure of it.

Newman's Grotto, 485 Coburg Rd. at the Pavilion, Eugene, OR 97401; (541) 485-9292; newmansfish.com. This venerable Oregon fish market chain was founded in Eugene in the late 1800s then expanded to Portland, where it now supplies top restaurants. The Grotto offers fish-and-chips (choose from cod, halibut, salmon, shrimp, clams, or scallops), grilled fish served with rice and coleslaw, and prawn and fish rolls. Indoor seating is limited, but the patio is pleasant on a dry day and the take-out window makes ordering a breeze. Newman's main retail location on Willamette offers a more limited menu but a wide array of fresh, local seafood.

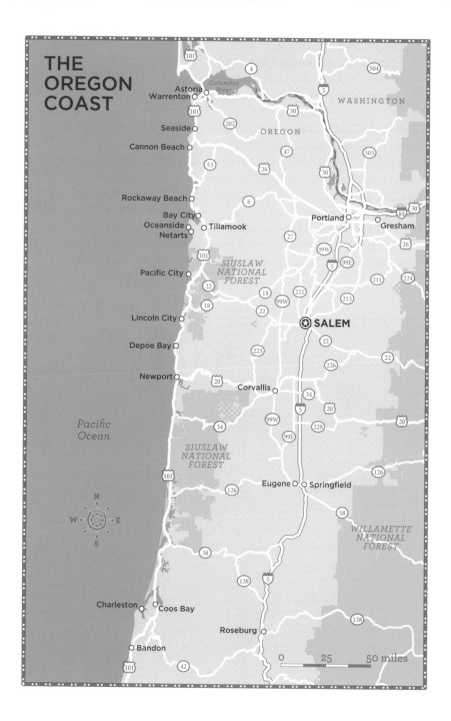

The Oregon Coast

It seems you can't drive 10 miles along the Oregon Coast without passing a state park. Or a seastack, or a smooth, sandy beach littered with agates, or a brackish, tree-ringed bay that teems with secrets (likely in the form of delicious oysters). Whether it's your first trip or your monthly trek with a cooler to stock up at your favorite fish market, the scenery demands that you reach for your camera, with gray whales, vibrant sunsets, and hypnotic vistas all vying for your attention. Thank goodness for all those drive-thru espresso stands to keep you going with a latte, biscuits and gravy, or a local Tillamook Ice Cream milk shake.

American food icon James Beard grew up here, launching his lifetime love affair with Dungeness crab. You'll find seafood at every culinary level; exquisite, modernist dining, down-home pub grub, and fresh, Pacific Rim–inspired bistro eats—and that's just in one town (Depoe Bay). If hunting and gathering is more your speed, stay at one of the privately owned combination marina/RV parks along the bays and rent all you need to go crabbing and clamming for the day. Most every coastal town has at least one good fish market, and each offers slightly different specialties.

Astoria

The approach to Astoria from the north, across the Columbia River, is most dramatic (and makes my bridge-averse husband white-knuckle the steering wheel). At first, you cruise near the surface of the mighty river. Then gradually, the bridge rises up, up, up toward the clouds. Suddenly, you're soaring, with the Pacific Ocean in view. Astoria, with its sea-weathered Victorians and towering column, awaits when you descend.

Astoria has several claims to fame. It's the oldest nonnative settlement west of the Rockies (1811 for those keeping track), named in reference to its namesake investor John Jacob Astor, who hoped to launch a fur-trading empire. It's home to one of the finest maritime museums on the West Coast and the storied FisherPoets Gathering (see festival listings). For 1980s movie buffs, this is where they filmed *The Goonies* and *Kindergarten Cop*. After several decades of hard times, Astoria's a city putting on a fresh face and rediscovering itself.

Bowpicker Fish & Chips, 1636 Duane St., Astoria, OR 97103; (503) 791-2942; bowpicker.com. In summer, you'll recognize it by the line of devotees, which often stretches down the block; in winter, by the steam wafting from the deep fryer. You'll spot the boat parked across the street from the Maritime Museum, a petite, curvy fishing vessel known locally as a bowpicker; the fisherman stands in the front of the hull to pluck his catch from the nets he hauls up. By the time you've made a return trip through the line to buy a second helping, you'll wish the boat were moving and that you were on it, so that you could take a little nap of contentment.

Many variations of fish-and-chips appear on menus throughout the Northwest; Ron and Linda Ford at the Bowpicker use fresh, white albacore tuna caught off the Oregon coast and serve it with steak fries. The fritters are hand-cut, meaty and succulent, breaded in a slightly piquant, barely there, beer-batter fish fry that's crisp and melts on the tongue, feathery and light.

The Bowpicker got its start years ago . . . in New Zealand. Ron Ford, a timber worker by trade, spent a year there thinning timber and eating fish-and-chips served from little huts. Later, on a trip to Alaska, he noticed a Chamber of Commerce housed in a fishing boat, which lingered in the back of his mind, says his wife, Linda.

"He was down in Astoria working and he had some really bad fish-and-chips somewhere, almost all batter and very little fish. He said 'You know there's got to be a different way.'"

A friend of his was retiring his bowpicker and asked if Ron had use for his boat. As a matter of fact, he did. After perfecting his beer-batter

recipe, Ron and Linda opened Bowpicker in 2000 with their daughter, Leah, and have watched its popularity grow ever since. Customers hail from as far as Australia, China, and Europe.

"We always say it just can't possibly get any busier, and then each year it seems to," Linda says. "We really don't ever advertise because we're so busy now that we don't want people to be disappointed that they had to wait so long."

Note: Cash-only and outdoor seating only, so if it's chilly or raining, prepare to eat in your car or huddled beneath an umbrella. It's worth it. Ben Jacobsen, owner of Jacobsen Salt Co. in Netarts, Oregon, calls Bowpicker one of his favorite spots on the Oregon Coast. "It's executed so simply and perfectly and it's just so good."

Columbia River Maritime Museum

Set aside at least an hour to enjoy this gem, and more if you have an interest in history, navigation, mapmaking, tribal culture, fishing, boating, or the Coast Guard (or, have a curious child in tow). This museum's interactive exhibits bring the Columbia River's storied history to light, with displays about the scores of shipwrecks along its infamous entryway, or bar; the numerous explorers who attempted to find it during the Age of Discovery; the immigrants who made its canneries hum, and how its catch contributed to the war effort. The museum is located at 1792 Marine Dr., Astoria, OR 97103. Call (503) 325-2323 or visit crmm.org for more information.

The Columbian Cafe, 1114 Marine Dr., Astoria, OR 97103; (503) 325-2233; columbianvoodoo.com/cafe/. Looks can be deceiving. The Columbian may masquerade as a greasy spoon, but its menu offers handmade pasta, a wealth of fresh, local seafood, and spicy vegetarian items that change by the season and often with each day's catch and produce delivery. A sampling: spring Chinook salmon poached with Champagne and asparagus and served on pasta with parsnip puree and blue cheese sauce; rockfish with lime, bell peppers, mushrooms, tomato, olives, and cilantro; and coconut lime prawn tacos. Note: This joint is cash-only.

Silver Salmon Grille, 1105 Commercial Ave., Astoria, OR 97103; (503) 338-6640; silversalmongrille.com. This comfortable spot offers hearty portions of halibut-and-chips, clam chowder, fresh-shucked Willapa Bay oysters, and generous desserts, plus salmon just about any way you like: baked; broiled; poached; stuffed with Dungeness crab, bay shrimp and Gouda; smoked; blackened in a hot cast iron pan; or broiled on an alder plank. Be sure to grab a drink at the antique bar in the lounge, constructed of Scottish cherry wood and shipped around Cape Horn to Astoria in the 1880s.

Bandon

Follow the Coquille River to where it meets the Pacific and you'll find the gorgeous seacoast town of Bandon, home to ruby-red cranberry bogs, towering offshore rock formations, a surprising variety of golf courses, and charming family-run restaurants.

Bandon Fish Market, 249 1st Street SE, Bandon, OR 97411; (541) 347-4282; bandonfishmarket.com. A consistent line out the door at a seafood joint means two things: good food, and fresh fish due to lots of turnover. Fans of this "small but mighty" spot rave about the juicy fried prawns, the salmon-and-chips, and the crab sandwich. If it's stormy out, beat feet for a chance at a table inside. If it's clear, battle the crowd for a picnic table outside, or, if all else fails, take your vittles to go and wander the boardwalk.

Tony's Crab Shack, 155 First St., Bandon, OR; (541) 347-2875; tonyscrabshack.com. This straightforward, clean, and cheerful little joint does fresh crab justice, serving freshly steamed Dungeness crab, killer crab cakes, crab louie, and luscious Bandon's Famous Crab Sandwiches, a sweet melody of fresh crab meat, Thousand Island dressing, and melted swiss on toasted sourdough. There are also meaty lobster rolls, fish tacos, fresh raw oysters, thick clam chowder, and teriyaki-sauced oysters. It's small, but has plenty of outdoor seating in nice weather.

Bay City

This quiet community is situated about 80 miles west of Portland and is across Tillamook Bay from the site of Bayocean, a planned resort community founded in 1906 on Tillamook Spit that was gradually swept away by the sea.

The Fish Peddler at Pacific Oyster, 5150 Hayes Oyster Dr., Bay City, OR 97107; (503) 377-2323; fishpeddler-baycity.com. Fans rave about the giant oyster po' boys, the "out-of-this-world" clam chowder in bread bowls, the decadent shrimp and crab melt sandwich, and, of course, the fresh oysters shucked at the oyster bar of this small, simple eatery tucked into the Pacific Oyster production facility.

In honor of the five rivers that stream into Tillamook Bay, the Peddler serves baked oysters in five styles: Wilson (sweetened with blue cheese), Trask (served with herb butter), Miami (topped with barbecue sauce), Tillamook (crowned with crisp bacon, diced red onion, and shredded Tillamook sharp cheddar), and Kilchis (basil pesto, Parmesan cheese, and a bit of hot sauce). Or you can enjoy them in a savory stew, as oysters-and-chips, or just on the half shell.

On Wednesday, enjoy all-you-can-eat oysters prepared as you like them. On Friday, all-you-can-eat fish. When you're done with your meal, watch the oyster shuckers in action and pick up seafood to enjoy later. Oregon seafood giant Pacific Seafood recently updated the menu here and also operates a sister Fish Peddler at its facility south along the coast in Newport.

Cannon Beach

Cannon Beach is fun-loving neighbor Seaside's artfully weathered, pedestrian-friendly coastal cousin, where small lots and the city's active design-review process have maintained a village atmosphere and preserved the mellow beauty of the town's oceanfront. Haystack Rock, the mesmerizing seastack along the beach, is among the most photographed tourist attractions in all of Oregon (the Heceta Head Lighthouse and Tillamook Cheese

factory also share this rarified air). It looks different from every angle, in every tide, at every time of day, silhouetted against a purple sky on a summer's night; dark and glowering in stormy weather, giant purple and orange starfish within the tidepools at its feet. Get a bird's eye view of the coastline from nearby Ecola State Park, where scenes from *Kindergarten Cop* (1990) and *The Goonies* (1985) were filmed.

Cannon Beach offers several seafood gems located on or near its tidy, charming main street. During the warmer months, don't miss the famous crab pizza at Pizza a'fetta, made with hand-tossed dough and the pizzeria's house-made Montrachet (cream) sauce (pizza-a-fetta.com).

Bill's Tavern & Brewhouse, 188 N. Hemlock St., Cannon Beach, OR 97110; (503) 436-2202; billstavernandbrewhouse.com. While not a seafood restaurant per se, Bill's has perfected several ocean staples along with its excellent typical pub fare, which makes it the perfect stop for a mixed carload of seafood lovers and landlubbers (they'll happily adjust dishes to make them vegan as well). The seafood stew is generous in its portions of halibut, cod, prawns, scallops, and bay shrimp and seasoned with saffron to a pleasing effect. The oysters in its oyster burger are huge and lightly breaded with a wonderful crispiness. Its clam chowder is thinner than most but packs a flavorful punch. Choose from cod or halibut for fish-and-chips; they're house-brew beer-battered and served with garlic bread and fries.

The atmosphere itself is crowded, loud, and welcoming, with sometimes chaotic self-seating, house-brewed beer and root beer on tap (don't miss the Blackberry Beauty, and Duck Dive pale ale), and easy access to Cannon Beach's shops and sand. Worn out from pondering how Haystack Rock landed on the beach? Order a beer sampler and linger.

Ecola Seafoods Restaurant & Market, 208 N. Spruce St., Cannon Beach, OR 97110; (503) 436-9130; ecolaseafoods.com.
This beloved, unassuming seafood counter and casual eatery named for the nearby state park offers fresh coastal seafood caught via hook and line by its own mini fishing fleet: the fishing vessels *Legacy* and *Legacy II*. This means the fish is remarkably fresh and high quality, which helps even the simplest preparations to shine.

Owners Jay and Cindy Beckman and their family have fished the Oregon Coast commercially since 1977. Their seafood counter and eatery housed in a weathered gray building off Cannon Beach's main drag offers specialties like fresh Oregon troll-caught king salmon, halibut, Dunge-

ness crabmeat and whole cooked crab, fresh Oregon shrimp, Willapa Bay oysters and steamer clams from Ekone Oyster Company, and breaded razor clams for easy cooking at home.

Ecola's galley menu ranges from simple and pleasing fresh seafood cocktails, an ever-popular smoked mussel appetizer, amazingly fresh calamari, fish-and-chips, whole crabs, clam chowder, and cod-and-chips. There's also beer on tap and a kids' menu. Enjoy your catch at the handful of tables inside or outdoors at picnic tables.

Charleston

This little fishing village on the entrance to Coos Bay is home to a commercial fishing fleet and plenty of charters for recreational angling. You can also angle a great view from nearby Sunset Bay State Park, Bastendorff Beach, and Shore Acres State Park. Shore Acres began as a private estate for timber and shipbuilding baron Louis J. Simpson and is the former home to sea lions and seals that bask on the reefs and islands just offshore, magnificent gardens, and a glorious holiday lights display each winter.

Chuck's Seafood, 91135 Cape Arago Hwy., Charleston, OR 97420; (541) 888-5525; chucksseafood.com. This custom cannery, smokehouse, and seafood market surrounded by fishing boats offers smoked oysters from its own oyster beds, a range of canned seafood caught by local fishermen, and all the Northwest fresh favorites, from steamer clams to albacore tuna. Loyal customers rave about the plump shrimp cocktail, the salmon sticks and oyster sticks, and the raw oysters.

Coos Bay

Coos Bay is the home of the Clamboree, launched in 2009 to celebrate the historic Empire district with clam specialties prepared by the Oregon Coast Culinary Institute, the Clam Scram 3-mile pet walk and run to benefit the local humane society, and the popular "Hollering Contest." That celebrates a local tribal tradition, when hollering across Coos Bay to the North Spit was a way of communication.

Fishermen's Seafood Market, 200 S. Bayshore Dr., Coos Bay, OR 97420; (541) 267-2722; fishermenseafoodmarket.com. This floating fish market's waterfront location on the Coos Bay Boardwalk can't be beat. Take home fresh, wild-caught seafood or enjoy the crisp delights from their deep-fryer. Hand-cut and breaded fish-and-chip options include fried halibut, oysters, Oregon clams, rock cod, snapper, or prawns, each served with crinkle-cut fries and coleslaw. Fans rave they are "melt-in-your-mouth" good, especially when enjoyed outside on a sunny day, watching the fishermen at work. Their clam chowder is made fresh daily with local Coos Bay butter clams and the smoked tuna salad sandwich is made with albacore. Yum. Note: There's no beer served here, so if you desire a brew to go with your fried favorites, get your food to go. Also, the clam chowder sells out quickly.

Salmon Homecoming Celebrations

Native tribes and communities throughout the Northwest hold a multitude of festivals to herald the return of salmon to local rivers and streams to spawn the next generation of fish. Some highlights:

Columbia Salmon Fest (Invermere, BC; columbiasalmonfest .ca): Before dams rose along the mighty Columbia River in 1942, salmon returned from the ocean more than 1,000 miles upriver to this community along British Columbia's border with Alberta in Canada's Rocky Mountains. Each September, this fresh festival aims to connect the next generation with its salmon heritage with a salmon feast, an intertribal powwow, and educational displays.

Issaquah Salmon Days (Issaquah, WA; salmondays.org): Each fall since 1970, this community in the Cascade foothills out-side Seattle has celebrated the return of spawning salmon up Issaquah Creek and the city's historic hatchery. In 2013, Salmon Days drew more 185,000 festivalgoers, hosted a grand parade with 100-plus floats, and served almost 2 tons of salmon barbecued by the local Kiwanis Club.

Mill-Luck Salmon Celebration (North Bend, OR; themillcasino .com/entertainment/salmon.cfm): What began in 2003 as a way to share the heritage, culture, and traditions of the Coquille Indian Tribe and neighboring tribes has grown into one of the largest Native American events in the region, known for its traditional salmon-bake dinner with the honored fish prepared in the Coquille open-pit manner, canoe races, drummers, and dancers. Every September.

Salmon Homecoming (Seattle, WA; salmonhomecoming .org): Every September since 1992, the Seattle Aquarium and Northwest Indian Fisheries Commission have gathered on the Seattle waterfront to promote stewardship of salmon habitat and welcome the salmon's return with a salmon bake, song and dance, and a canoe welcoming ceremony.

Salmon Homecoming at Oxbow Regional Park (Portland, OR): Each October, salmon lovers trek to this park along the Sandy River, one of the nation's designated wild and scenic

rivers, to talk with naturalists about habitat conservation and restoration and watch salmon surge through this 1,000-acre wilderness of old-growth forest, trails, and river beaches.
Wenatchee River Salmon Festival (Leavenworth, WA; salmon fest.org): Since 1991, this family-friendly September festival has drawn crowds to the Leavenworth National Fish Hatchery at the mouth of Icicle Canyon to celebrate the return of salmon to Northwest waterways with *gyotaku*, or Japanese fish rubbings; an intertribal village to learn more about native culture; salmon storytelling and songs; and plenty of outdoor activities.

Depoe Bay

A roiling Pacific is front and center in this coastal community that faces the ocean and offers a splendid vantage for whale-watching. Pull your car off Highway 101 and join the crowds that peer through telescopes and mar-

vel at the sea as it smashes and sloshes into the rocks below and bursts up from a spouting horn. Or, while away an hour at the town's whale-watching center, where docents share binoculars and tips to help you spot flukes and breaches amid the sparkling waves. If you're on a Memorial Day road trip, don't miss the annual Fleet of Flowers. Boats bedecked with blooms and greenery to honor of the area's dearly departed pass beneath the Highway 101 bridge and through Depoe Bay's self-proclaimed "world's smallest navigable harbor" as they

Oregon State Parks Whale-Watching Center

Gray whales migrate past the Oregon Coast twice each year but can be spotted almost all year-round, save for quiet times mid-November to mid-December and mid-January to mid-March. During peak times, whales come close to shore to dive, feed, and rub against rocks. It's surprisingly easy (and thrilling) to find them cavorting amid the waves.

Whale-watching tours abound for those who'd like to get up close. For landlubbers, pop into the white structure in a prime perch atop the city's sea wall, grab a pair of binoculars supplied along the window wall, and listen for guidance from the team of volunteer docents who have staffed the center during peak migration times since 1978. When you spy your first spout, breach, or fluke (a whale's tail), you'll be presented with an "I saw my first gray whale" sticker as evidence.

Depoe Bay offers a particularly good view, but swing by any Oregon State Park or other site along the coast with a "Whale-Watching Spoken Here" sign for a glimpse of the grays, typically from atop bluffs, hillsides, and lighthouses that stretch from Crescent City, California, on up to Ilwaco, Washington, at the southern tip of the Long Beach Peninsula.

have since 1945 to honor the memories of two fishermen who died at sea while attempting to rescue a fellow fisherman.

Gracie's Sea Hag Restaurant & Lounge, 58 N. Hwy. 101, Depoe Bay, OR 97341; (541) 765-2734 ; theseahag.com. Locals and tourists alike have frequented this Oregon Coast landmark since 1963, with its storm-weathered gray-shingled walls outside and kitschy nautical theme inside, including a captain's wheel, seafood-themed stained glass between booths, and lounge decor that likely hasn't been updated since the 1970s. Tucked into the tourist strip across from the city's sea wall in the heart of Depoe Bay, the Sea Hag offers live music, excellent clam chowder served in bread bowls, whole Dungeness crab, steamed butter clams, baked or grilled oysters, and a Friday-night seafood buffet. Like the decor, the home-style dinner recipes likely haven't changed over the decades. But the seafood is fresh and the ambience authentic.

Seafood sandwich options include the Sea Hag Crab and Shrimp, a fried oyster sandwich and the Sea Hag Shrimp Croissant. The deep fryer delivers three kinds of fish-and-chips (halibut, cod, or wild Chinook salmon in season) served with fries and garlic bread, as well as Sea Hag Boats featuring fries with large sea scallops, fresh Yaquina Bay oysters, clam strips, or gulf prawns. At breakfast the Hangtown Fry features Yaquina Bay oysters and you'll find local Oregon pink shrimp on the menu. The build your own omelet options include oysters, shrimp, and crab.

Restaurant Beck, 2345 S. Hwy. 101, Depoe Bay, OR 97341; (541) 765-3220; restaurantbeck.com. It's easy to miss Restaurant Beck, distracted as you likely are by the Pacific's pounding surf and the rugged coastal forest. Once you arrive, you'll wonder how you ever thought you could miss the unfettered view from its intimate dining room of Whale Cove, fringed by towering cliffs and coastal forest.

This fine-dining restaurant attached to the Whale Cove Inn south of central Depoe Bay offers the culinary expertise of Justin Wills, a James Beard Award semifinalist for Best Chef Northwest in 2012 and 2013, who presents each dish with an artist's eye for beauty, crafted from local foraged and farmed ingredients. Dining here is an event, with adventurous multi-course tasting menus, a varied wine list, and plenty of creativity at play; it's an ideal destination for those who live to eat rather than eat to live.

While not specifically a seafood restaurant, Restaurant Beck serves Oregon's coast treasures with skill and flair. Highlights from its ever-changing menu include pork belly with pickled sea beans and burnt hay ice cream; king salmon served rare with mustard-flower chimichurri, Meyer lemon roe, charcoal burner mushrooms, and fingerling potatoes; and albacore with heirloom tomatoes, garden herbs, Mexican sour gherkins, and jalapeño cucumber water. Whew.

Tidal Raves Seafood Grill, 279 US 101, Depoe Bay, OR 97341; (541) 765-2995; tidalraves.com. It's tough to find a coastal seafood spot with breathtaking views *and* a menu that features enough diversity of flavor and price to suit nearly any hungry carload of travelers who might pull up. Tidal Raves delivers, and has built a following since opening in 1990.

This contemporary restaurant owned by Jon and MaryLynne Hamlin serves straightforward options, such as panko-breaded fried razor clams, Manila clams steamed in Black Butte porter, and charbroiled wild salmon; hearty eats like smoked salmon chowder and a rich cioppino brimming

with clams, wild shrimp, crab, and fish in a tomato-herb broth; and dishes with global flavors, including a green curry replete with Pacific rockfish and large wild shrimp, Thai barbecued shrimp, and chilled udon noodles with seared sea scallops in a spicy peanut dressing. Specialties include char-grilled wild salmon with crab risotto and vodka sauce; spinach oyster bisque (which Hamlin claims will convert the oyster-averse); and herb-crusted Pacific snapper with shrimp caper sauce and smoked salmon potato cake. They shared their recipe for Smoked Shrimp—find it in the "In the Kitchen" chapter.

Don't miss the Seahawk bread, baguette toasted with smoked salmon, cream cheese, Havarti, shrimp, and onion. Hamlin also hopes you try his bread pudding with 100-proof sauce, a recipe he spent months developing.

Its prime location offers views from throughout the dining room of gray whales on the move, winter storms surging toward shore, sandstone cliffs, and lingering sunsets, just right with a cocktail or glass of Oregon Pinot Noir. "We've seen so many whales. It almost becomes 'Oh gosh, another one,'" Jon Hamlin said. "But the guests, they'll jump up and it's like you're in Safeco Field and someone just hit a home run and they'll run to the window. It's a lot of fun."

Lincoln City

As you cruise the Oregon Coast, Lincoln City seems to stretch for miles compared to other coastal cities. And small wonder: In the 1960s, five oceanside towns voted by a narrow margin to consolidate. Schoolchildren wanted to name the new community "Surfland," but Lincoln City won as the least controversial of nominated names.

Siletz Bay, shimmering along the south edge of town by the historic Taft District, is a prime spot for crabbing and clamming. Many restaurants feature fresh fish caught by the dory fleet to the north in Pacific City.

Barnacle Bill's Seafood Market, 2174 NE Highway 101, Lincoln City, OR 97367; (541) 994-3022; facebook.com/barnaclebills seafoodmarket. Barnacle Bill's dates back even further than the founding of Lincoln City proper. It opened in 1947 and has retained much of its unpretentious charm, earning lifelong customers with remarkable smoked salmon, shrimp cocktail, salmon jerky, fresh albacore, lingcod, rockfish, Dungeness crab, and more. Much of the seafood is caught along the Oregon Coast, including some by dory fleet at Cape Kiwanda that launches their small boats directly through the breakers into the ocean. Note: Cash or check only, so come prepared. Consider packing a cooler as well, so you can tote treasures home (or, to your home away from home) to enjoy later.

The Blackfish Cafe, 2733 NW Hwy. 101, Lincoln City, OR 97367; (541) 996-1007; blackfishcafe.com. Chef Rob Pounding first earned a reputation for swoon-worthy seafood on the Oregon Coast as the longtime executive chef at the nearby Salishan Lodge, which earned the top star accolades from AAA and Mobil during his tenure. Since 1999, he's been delighting diners at his own restaurant, the Blackfish Cafe.

Pounding's discerning eye for quality seafood is evident in the flavor and texture of each dish. Seared scallops are divine with mushroom risotto. Skilled roasted ocean trolled Chinook salmon is basted with fennel lime butter and served atop an Oregon blue cheese potato gratin. Crispy fried cornmeal oysters hail from Yaquina Bay. Fish-and-chips are prepared with rockfish or other local fish and battered with Deschutes Brewery Ale batter, fried crispy and served with homemade tartar sauce and napa cabbage slaw. Rockfish also appears in the satisfying fish sandwich. The pan-seared, bacon-wrapped Pacific albacore tuna arrives with new potato salad, pea shoots, braised greens. Heaven.

If you can, save room for house-made Ding Dongs with raspberry and cream sauce for dessert (or the peanut butter pie). Be sure to make reservations, as Blackfish books quickly. The only thing missing is an ocean view. Guess you'll just have to close your eyes and savor the last bite.

J's Fish & Chips, 1800 SE Hwy. 101, Lincoln City, OR 97367; (541) 994-4445. J's offers fish-and-chips, plain and simple, made with halibut, cod, and occasionally rockfish. The short menu also features baskets of clam strips and shrimp breaded plain or rolled in coconut, along with clam chowder and a fish sandwich. Lines can be long, parking can be tough, the wait can be long. Yet year after year, fans return for the family-friendly atmosphere, low prices, and what some have proclaimed the best fish-and-chips on the coast. Only one way to find out.

Netarts

For those who seek seclusion along the Oregon Coast, this is your town, safely tucked amid 2,500 acres of lush coastal rain forest along the Three Capes Scenic Route. Camp at Cape Lookout State Park and go hiking, beachcombing, and crabbing in and along Netarts Bay.

Jacobsen Salt Co., (503) 946-9573; jacobsensalt.com. Many chefs and food lovers will readily name salt as their most essential ingredient. Salt purveyor Ben Jacobsen came to appreciate good finishing salt while living in Scandinavia. When he returned home to the Northwest, he was struck by how much the culinary landscape had expanded, but noticed an element missing: regional salt.

"To me, it's the single most effective way to elevate every bite of food. Good salt can provide the salinity, but

Waterways: How We Live

The Finishing Touch: Ben Jacobsen

Oyster lovers can discern subtle differences in flavor between two oysters grown in different locales, so key is the water quality, temperature, mineral content, and salinity to how those bivalves ultimately will taste. And so it is with sea salt.

It took Ben Jacobsen 2½ years to determine which waterways offered just the right harmony of flavor, and to develop his harvesting process. The result is sea salt so admired it's now stocked at William-Sonoma and finer farmers' markets, and used by chefs of renown across the country.

"I tested more than 25 spots along the Oregon and Washington coast. I got 5 gallons of water from Hood Canal, from Cannon Beach, etc," Jacobsen said. "Some taste bitter and astringent and not good at all. And with salt, it all has to do with the water where you start."

Netarts Bay turned out to be far and away the best. "It's really special because it's an estuary; we have very few fresh-water inputs, which also means we have very little rain runoff, but also little pollutant and road runoff."

Given how much time he spends in or near the water, it's a good thing Jacobsen has a penchant for seafood. His advice? Cook shrimp, crab, clams, and other favorites in seawater.

"The stuff that's boiled in freshwater or even freshwater with salt added, it doesn't taste as good. When I was living in Norway, you could buy a kilo of shrimp off a boat in Oslo Harbor . . . fishermen would boil the shrimp they had just caught in saltwater. The salt permeates the meat and it is just so tasty and sweet."

PHOTOS COURTESY OF JACOBSEN SALT CO.; PHOTOS BY JEFF SCOTT SHAW

also heighten the sweetness of things, and also lend textural contrast. It's just an incredible way to really experience food."

Jacobsen Salt Co. harvests pure salt crystals from Netarts Bay, fed by streams that course through the coastal rain forest. They filter seawater, then boil it to remove the volume and the calcium that give a lot of salts a very bitter taste, then let what's left very slowly evaporate in shallow custom-made evaporation pans. Netarts Bay is remote and pristine, and Jacobsen would know. He tasted waters around the Northwest before he settled upon this off-the-beaten path stretch of the Oregon Coast along the Three Capes Scenic Route. (Note: You should definitely take this route, which also takes you past Cape Kiwanda, home to Oregon's historic dory boat fleet.)

The finishing salt is available in pure flake or infused with Oregon Pinot Noir, Stumptown Coffee, and other regional delights. (Kitchen note: He likes to use the coffee salt to finish acorn squash baked with brown sugar when it's hot from the oven for a caramelly, rich experience.)

A sprinkle of finishing salt can elevate enjoyment of even simple foods, such as a good baguette with good butter. Jacobsen says. "Say it's raining on a Tuesday night, and you don't know what to make, you don't have much time, so you buy a piece of meat or fish and you finish it with a good salt. There's no better way to elevate a rainy Tuesday night meal than using a good salt."

The Schooner, 2065 Netarts Bay Rd., Netarts, OR 97143; (503) 815-9900; theschooner.net. The Schooner is an Oregon Coast institution, shucking oysters and serving seafood on pristine Netarts Bay for more than 60 years. It underwent a significant remodel in 2009 that added a deck, outdoor mesquite grill, and wind-powered turbines to generate power. Add live music and house-infused liquors, and you've got yourself a party. A party fueled by enjoyable seafood.

The Schooner serves Netarts Bay oysters doused in cocktail sauce in a shooter, with a mignonette on the half shell, or "rockoyaki-style" (roasted in a wood-fired oven and topped with bacon, spinach, garlic, and sauce). Fish on the menu is wild-caught, such as the local panfried rockfish seared in rice flour and cumin and finished with a lemon herb whip, and often by the dorymen along the coast who fish with their distinctive dory boats at Cape Kiwanda.

Newport

Newport is a collection of all the best the Oregon Coast has to offer. Its laid-back bayfront teems with an active fishing fleet, the Oregon Coast Aquarium, the Rogue Ales Brewery, and restaurants that offer a taste of the past (the original Mo's chowder house from 1946) and the future (sustainability-focused Local Ocean). Newport's Yaquina (yuh-KWEN-uh) Bay is a thriving estuary that's home to brown pelicans, the northern

flicker, porcupines, and the state's largest oyster farm; twin historic lighthouses keep sentinel near its mouth, near a graceful landmark bridge built by the state's master bridge designer, Conde B. McCollough. The city is named for Newport, Rhode Island, the favorite town of Sam Case, who opened Newport, Oregon's first tourist resort, the Ocean House, in 1866.

On the ocean side of town, Newport's oceanfront Nye Beach neighborhood was the Oregon Coast's top tourist destination in the early 1900s with penny arcades, agate shops, and saltwater taffy shops galore. Its retro beach vibe today includes quaint shops and quirky lodgings including the Sylvia Beach Hotel, which bills itself as a hotel for book lovers (each room offers a different theme, from J.K. Rowling to Amy Tan to Ken Kesey). Some of Newport's beaches are sandy, some covered in round cobblestones, some scattered with agates. All offer picture-perfect Oregon Coast sunsets.

April's at Nye Beach, 749 NW 3rd St., Newport, OR 97365; (541) 265-6855; aprilsatnyebeach.com. This romantic and charming spot next door to the Sylvia Beach Hotel crafts seafood from sustainable sources and gathers its fresh, local produce from Buzzard Hill Farm in a Coast Range valley a few miles outside Newport. Chef April Wolcott and her husband, Kent, opened the restaurant in 1998 (she runs the kitchen; he runs the front) and have created an ambience that is warm and unpretentious.

The menu includes house-made ricotta cheese, sausage, and baguettes. The fresh catch of the day can vary from salmon with Thai curry sauce to simply grilled fresh salmon served atop seasonal vegetables. Steamed Northwest clams with spicy linguiça sausage, garlic, white wine, thyme, and Roma tomatoes. For the seafood averse, their duck breast wins raves. Dessert fiends: April's has its own pastry chef, so save room.

Local Ocean Seafoods, 213 SE Bay Blvd.; Newport, OR 97365; (541) 574-7959; localocean.net. Fresh. Clean. Local. Fair: This bright, casually sophisticated seafood haven embodies its oh-so-Northwest credo with gusto. Its open kitchen teems with sensational creations starring the fresh, local catch, supplied in large part by the local fishing fleet docked just across the street in Yaquina Bay. It supports fellow local businesses, lobbies for better management of fish populations, and prides itself on paying the 50 or so regular fishermen it works with fair prices for top quality. And this eatery/fish market could well steal the show on your coastal adventure. After all, that *is* its mission statement: to give people the best seafood experience of their lives.

Grab a seat at the neatly tiled counter that wraps around the kitchen and prepare to second-guess your initial order each time another lovely, fragrant dish comes together before your eyes. Snowy slabs of halibut and juicy wild prawns sizzle atop the grill, ready to lounge on beds of noodles and zesty salad greens. Dungeness crab lends its richness to yakisoba, to a haunting crab soup, to a creamy po' boy. Skillets of fragrant steamer clams in their shells clatter together as they're shaken and sauteed in a wading pool of Chardonnay, garlic, and butter. The Fishwives Stew offers succulent crab, shrimp, scallops, mussels, clams, and fin fish in garlic herb tomato broth. Or keep it simple with panko-breaded, panfried Yaquina Bay oysters, a grilled rockfish sandwich, a whole Dungeness crab, or Local Ocean's beloved fish tacos. Check out their recipe for Albacore Tuna Mignon in the "In the Kitchen" chapter.

The dining room's floor-to-ceiling windows, with roll-up glass for warmer months, overlook the bobbing boats of Newport's local fishing fleet; the graceful Yaquina Bay Bridge soars in the distance, and forested hillsides frame the whole scene. On a warm and sunny day, the view is magical and the connection to the sea unmistakable: especially with the new second floor added in spring 2014.

The tidy fish counter at the dining room's other end offers the menu's fresh catch with a side of data: where the crab, shellfish, or fin fish was caught, by which method (hook and line, long line, pots), and often, by which boat. Like most major fish markets, Local Ocean ships by next-day or second-day air.

Mo's Chowder, Six coastal locations: Cannon Beach, Florence, Lincoln City, Newport (the original and Newport Annex across the street), and Otter Rock at Devil's Punchbowl; moschowder.com. Folksy, friendly, fun: Mo's serves New England–style clam chowder, zesty Fish Tacos (recipe included in the "In the Kitchen" chapter), and plenty of nostalgia up and down the Oregon Coast. The chain of eateries is still going strong decades after the late Mohava "Mo" Niemi opened the original Freddie & Mo's along the Newport bayfront as a 24-hour diner for local loggers and fishermen back in 1946.

When business partner Freddie Kent became ill a few years later, Niemi bought out her partner's shares in the restaurant and gradually served more and more Northwest seafood. As a divorced mother of two, she also took a desk job at the local radio station to make ends meet, which led to a neighborhood talk show she hosted for nearly 30 years, further endearing her to the city. Over the years Niemi and her family added a clam chowder factory and partnered with an oyster farm to supply the restaurants. Now you can find Mo's clam chowder base for sale online and in grocery stores throughout the region for those times a coastal cruise just isn't on the agenda.

The familiar home-style food, the quirky stories, the decades of memorabilia on display, and feeling of taking part in a generations-long coastal tradition keep people coming back. When a customer mistakenly drove into the Newport location's dining room, Mo consoled her that the restaurant would just add a garage door so she could drive in anytime. Later, she added that garage door, complete with a mural depicting the incident. Now it opens in warm weather and transforms the packed space into an instant sidewalk cafe.

Coastal Geography

Don't know your coves from inlets? Read on.

What's an archipelago?

A collection of islands, such as the San Juan Islands or Gulf Islands.

What's the difference between a cape and a head?

Both are promontories, or tall points of land like sea cliffs that extend out into a body of water. Capes and headlands along the Northwest coast often are rocky or forested. Wind-lashed Cape Flattery is the northwesternmost point of the lower 48 states and marks where the Strait of Juan de Fuca tumbles into the Pacific. The lighthouse on Yaquina Head has guided ships along the Oregon Coast since 1873.

What do heads, bays, and peninsulas have in common?

The number three. Heads and capes, such as Oregon's Cape Lookout, are tall points of land surrounded by water on three sides. Bays are surrounded by land on three sides. Peninsulas are lengths of land surrounded by water on three sides (think Washington's Olympic Peninsula, surrounded by the Puget Sound, Strait of Juan de Fuca, and the Pacific Ocean).

What is a sound, and how is it different than a bay or a fjord?

Both are indentations in the shoreline along an ocean. Both are naturally protected harbors, and the terms often are used interchangeably. But for the most part, a sound is an ocean inlet substantially larger and deeper than a bay, and wider than a fjord. Puget Sound in Washington is famous for its oysters, salmon, and orca whales.

What are all those rock formations I see?

Seastacks. Some, like Haystack Rock in Cannon Beach, Oregon, and at Cape Kiwanda, Oregon, resemble their namesake. Others are tall and pillar-like, and sometimes wear an evergreen on top, like the seastacks along the Washington and BC coasts. They're also the namesake for a delightful cheese made by Mt. Townsend Creamery in Port Townsend, Washington.

How do spits form?

A spit is a long, sandy stretch of beach material that extends from the coastline out to sea, formed when the prevailing wind blows at an angle to the coastline. As spits grow over time, waves cannot get past them, causing mud flats or salt marshes to form on the protected side. Dungeness Spit along Washington's Strait of Juan de Fuca is the longest sand spit in the country.

Oregon Oyster Farms, 6878 Yaquina Bay Rd., Newport, OR 97365; (541) 265-5078; oregonoyster.com. Yaquina Bay oysters are still harvested daily here at Oregon's oldest oyster farm, founded in 1907 by the Wachsmuth family to supply what is today Dan & Louis Oyster Bar in Portland.

They offer Pacific and Kumamoto oysters in the shell, oyster cocktails, smoked oysters, steamer clams, and more. All orders are to-go, so pack your own forks and napkins and savor your creamy oysters and the farm's homemade cocktail sauce on a park bench overlooking the water. Bring a cooler to take extras with you. It's a beautiful drive from Toledo or Newport or Corvallis.

When discovered in 1852, Yaquina Bay's oyster beds helped feed San Francisco's voracious appetite for the bivalves, enriching many locals and prompting Newport's establishment as a coastal tourist destination. Soon enough, the native oysters were wiped out, with the rich oyster beds in Washington's Willapa Bay soon to follow. The introduction of the Pacific oyster decades later helped the industry return.

Oceanside

This cozy little town just off the Three Capes Scenic Route between Cape Meares and Netarts overlooks a lovely beach and the Three Arch National Wildlife Refuge. Ask the locals about the not-so-secret tunnel beneath Maxwell Point to access nearby beaches during low tides. Just be sure to return before the water does!

Roseanna's Oceanside Cafe, 1490 Pacific Ave. NW, Oceanside, OR 97134; (503) 842-7351; roseannascafe.com. A trip to Roseanna's, perched atop a hill with a killer view of the Pacific and nearby Three Arch Rocks National Wildlife Refuge, has been a coastal ritual for many who make the trek to tranquil Oceanside since the early 1980s. The decor may be a bit dated, but the warmth and charm of its staff and quality of the creative yet familiar seafood soon make that an afterthought.

You can't go wrong ordering one of the ever-changing specials, which have included locally caught sole stuffed with crab, artichoke, and spinach dip baked in a cream sauce; lingcod stuffed with smoked salmon, herbs, and cream cheese, and dusted in hazelnuts; and Arctic char with mango, cucumber, and shrimp salad. Be sure to save room for dessert. Note: Roseanna's does not take reservations. Also note: Those three arch rocks have names. The largest is Shag, the most westerly is Storm Rock, and the middle has two names: Finley Rock and Mid Rock.

Pacific City

This community along the Three Capes Scenic Byway is best known for its beautiful beach at Cape Kiwanda and the dorymen (and women) who eschew marinas; they'd rather rev up their dory boats and plunge from the beach straight through the surf toward their fishing grounds.

It's a scene that's been going on for 100-plus year now as the small boats range far offshore for albacore and within a 10-mile radius of Pacific City for salmon, halibut, rockfish, and Dungeness crab. A memorial wall along one end of the beach tells the history and serves as a memorial to those who did not return home from their time at sea—three members of the fleet over the past 100 years. That the number is so small is a point of pride for the Pacific City Dorymen's Association.

Pelican Pub & Brewery, 33180 Cape Kiwanda Dr., Pacific City, OR 97135; (503) 965-7007; yourlittlebeachtown.com/pelican. This grand, polished brew pub offers a lengthy bar at which to slake your thirst for Oregon microbrews and dramatic views of Cape Kiwanda and Pacific City's Haystack Rock. Hope you're thirsty, because this menu offers beer pairings with just about every item on it, the fruit of a constant collaboration between the executive chef and the brewmaster. There's even a brew named for the local fishermen: Doryman's Ale.

In warm weather, head to the patio to enjoy your seafood quesadilla (a slightly spicy mix of cod, rockfish, salmon, and Oregon pink shrimp with Tillamook pepperjack cheese), Parmesan panko-breaded panfried Netarts Bay oysters marinated in Kiwanda Cream Ale, or clams steamed in Kiwanda Cream Ale with fresh herbs and grilled house spent grain bread. Listen to

the breakers thunder to shore. Then work off your meal with a scramble up the nearby sand dune or a walk on the beach, keeping an eye out for dory boats heading out to sea through the surf. The pub has its own hotel attached in case you have a few too many ... or just can't bear to leave.

Waterways: How We Live

Dory Boat Fisherwoman: Jessica Jones

You never quite know where life will take you. Jessica Jones took up commercial fishing as a hobby after meeting her fiancé, who fishes with a small, nimble boat known as a dory, like so many fishermen in the Pacific City area (his is named *The Concubine*).

Several years later, the quality of her fresh catch has built a growing clientele in her hometown of Portland, including the popular seafood restaurant Cabezon.

"It's such an amazing feeling, it's almost surreal when you're out there on the ocean," Jones says. Due to the way they launch (through the surf), the window for dory fishing totally depends on the weather and the ocean, what is blowing, what the waves are. The ocean can be unforgiving, and she's been scared a few times.

But she relishes the pride she feels when she strides into a restaurant kitchen with her catch: bass, cod, halibut, salmon, cabezon, or sea trout greenlings.

"It's so empowering," says the fishmonger, who goes by Mrs.Monger on her business cards.

Rockaway Beach

This coastal town started out as a seaside resort in 1909 and still prides itself on its 7 miles of sandy beaches. It's also home to mammoth Western Red Cedars in its Old-Growth Cedar Wetlands Preserve.

Jetty Fishery Marina & RV Park, 27550 Hwy. 101 N., Rockaway Beach, OR 97136; (800) 821-7697; jettyfishery.com. If you're hankering to hunt and gather, this combination seafood market, campsite, RV park and crabbing/fishing/clamming hub is the way to go. Perched on the edge of Nehalem Bay, it's a pretty spot to pitch a tent or rent a cabin and listen to the sounds of the coast as you drift to sleep.

Catch your own dinner with a crab ring from the dock, or watch as Dungeness crabs are hauled from the ocean and steamed, salivating as

Oregon Treasure: Karla's Smokehouse

Hearts were broken throughout Oregon in 2013 when legendary fish smoker Karla Steinhauser announced she was closing up shop after nearly 50 years in business due to health challenges.

At 77, Steinhauser was still heading to her custom-built, propane gas–fired smokehouse throughout the week to produce remarkably good smoked oysters, tuna, salmon, and other specialties with her collection of homemade brines. She still chopped her maplewood chips by hand before soaking them. For years, her cheerful hand-lettered signs on her storefront greeted customers who couldn't get enough of her handiwork.

"I smoke small amounts of very high quality fish. We are not a factory. I am a craftsman," Steinhauser says, noting that she usually ran out of product daily due to demand. Just as she possesses an insatiable need to perfect her smoking techniques, she now hustles to share those techniques and recipes with anyone who has interest lest they be lost to history. She's bundled her knowledge into two thorough volumes, available at her website karlassmokehouse.com.

you imagine how great they'll taste with butter. Dig for clams along the Nehalem Bay Sand Spit—the Jetty rents clam guns, shovels, rakes, and buckets, along with shellfish licenses and all you'll need to clean your catch. Rent a boat to explore the deserted beaches of Nehalem Bay State Park as you wait for your crab traps to fill back at the dock. Wander along the beach to the nearby town of Manzanita. The Laviolette family has made it easy to dip your feet into coastal life for 30-plus years and counting.

Kelly's Brighton Marina, 29200 Hwy. 101 N., Rockaway Beach, OR 97136; (503) 368-5745; kellyscrabs.com. Kelly's is a combination marina, RV park, campsite, and prime fishing location on magnificent Nehalem Bay. If this sounds familiar in scope to Jetty Fishery up the way, it's because owner Kelly Laviolette used to run that with his mom, Shirley Laviolette, before buying Brighton Marina with his wife, Janice.

Rent all you need to go crabbing or clamming, or spend the day taking in the scenery and buy your crabs, clams, and oysters from the live saltwater tanks. Fans rave that they've made Kelly's an annual tradition in large part due to the upbeat crew and atmosphere.

Old Oregon Smokehouse, 120 Hwy. 101 S., Rockaway Beach, OR 97136; (503) 355-2817. This tiny shack with its hand-lettered sign produces mammoth-sized crab cakes that come with a creamy cashew dipping sauce, crab and cheese fondue in a bread bowl (!), smoked salmon and sturgeon, and salmon burgers, as well as fish-and-chips and oysters-and-chips. Fans praise its cleanliness and the variety of house-made sauces, plus an entire wall covered in different types of hot sauce if those weren't enough. Note: Only outdoor seating is available, so plan accordingly.

Seaside

Long before the arrival of saltwater taffy shops, arcades, and windsock sellers, explorers Lewis and Clark made their way to this sandy beach within view of Tillamook Head to harvest salt from the sea to cure wild game for their long journey home. They knew it to be a place of abundance; for generations, the native Clatsop people called it home and gathered berries, fished for salmon, and collected clams and mussels.

These days, come-as-you-are Seaside continues its long tradition (since 1850) as a touristy, carnival-like, summertime escape for Portlanders and others throughout the Northwest.

"We've got a very nice beach and people from outside the area are not accustomed to seeing a beach that's clean and if they're from the East Coast, there aren't very many beaches with access," said Randy Frank, owner of Norma's Seafood and Steaks, who grew up in Seaside and adores the Oregon Coast. He also enjoys the proximity to the fishing fleet. "You can actually walk on the beach and see the fishing boats out there, see the crabbers. You'll see people standing out there in the surf, fishing, you'll see people raking for crab or digging for razor clams. If you're in Astoria, you'll see the boats unloading and you'll think, 'Ah. That's going to be on someone's plate tonight.' I think it breeds anticipation."

Bell Buoy of Seaside, 1800 S. Roosevelt Dr., Seaside, OR 97138; (503) 738-2722; bellbuoyofseaside.com. This seafood specialty store and family-friendly eatery owned by the Hartill family beckons from the roadside with its iconic blue-and-red neon crab sign, just as it has for more than 50 years.

Brothers John and Terry Hartill do their own canning and smoking on the premises, make their own cocktail sauce, and ship a variety of seafood, including custom gifts packs, from their online store (one man in Florida calls himself the most popular guy in St. Petersburg when his shipment of fresh Dungeness and razor clams arrives each year as an annual tradition). Fans adore the cod-and-chips, the clam chowder, the freshly made crab cakes, and the crab and shrimp sandwiches.

Norma's Seafood & Steak, 20 N. Columbia St., Seaside, OR 97138; (503) 738-4331; normasoceandiner.com.
This beloved diner off Seaside's main strip has dished up fragrant clam chowder and creamy Oyster Stew (they shared their recipe—find it in the "In the Kitchen" chapter) since the 1960s. Owners Randy and Darleen Frank are longtime Oregonians and vow to serve only wild salmon, avoid MSG, go easy on the salt, and otherwise please the happy customers who have made a visit to Norma's an annual tradition.

"We have some people from out of state who send us pictures of their child in here eating and having a good time and saying it was the third generation growing up on Norma's food," Frank says. "It's very nice that people will offer up those things, and all the time since we've been here, people will offer up little stories and memories. They'll remember Norma sitting outside the kitchen smoking away back in the day."

The menu, jam-packed with various preparations of the local catch, crows about the clam chowder, and it's justified: It's rich and creamy, not too salty, generous with minced clams and small potatoes (and no pork, they like to point out). Frank says they had a day the summer of 2013 when they sold 56 gallons of it in one day. Norma's also offers a silky oyster stew made with fresh bivalves from nearby Willapa Bay; an assortment of seafood sandwiches; fried razor clams; and Northwest fish available just about any way you'd like. "A lot of our stuff is pretty simple, because we try not to cover up the flavor of what we're serving," Frank says.

Unlike many seafood joints of its ilk, Norma's offers an understated elegance. Its copper-topped tables quietly gleam, and its ocean colors soothe, part of discreet updates the Franks have made since they took the helm around the start of this century. Yes, there really was a Norma. Randy Frank knew her, just as he knows nearly everyone in Seaside. He grew up in the area (he graduated from high school with one of the brothers who owns Bell Buoy up the street), amid the invigorating winter storms and the packed sandy beaches of summer, and even met his wife here in the 1970s when they both worked at the late, great Crab Broiler restaurant. He keeps right on knowing everybody, too, because he's a hands-on owner.

"I'm here every day and I do the buying of the seafood," he said. "We're out there buying whatever's available locally. A smelt run came in last week and nobody expected it, but we had it on our menu. I like to do regional stuff that we have access to."

PHOTOS COURTESY OF NORMA'S SEAFOOD & STEAK

Tillamook

Yes, the cheese factory is there, and, yes, you should visit: It's actually Oregon's most-visited tourist attraction, in part for the range of ice cream flavors. Tillamook is also home to dairy farms galore and an air museum housed within a former World War II–era blimp hangar built from old-growth lumber.

Fresh Seafood Market, 3800 Hwy. 101 N., Tillamook, OR 97141. When you've had your fill of cheese and ice cream at the Tillamook Cheese Factory across the way, head to this unassuming seafood shack for super-fresh salmon or cod-and-chips, and top-notch clam chowder. The crab melt comes with generous amounts of freshly cooked Dungeness.

Warrenton

This homeport for commercial and charter fishing sits across Youngs Bay from Astoria near the mouth of the Columbia River, where it thunders out to meet the Pacific. It's minutes from Oregon's largest state park (Fort Stevens, complete with miles of trails, beaches, and even a shipwreck) and home to Clatsop County's smallest museum (the Warrenton Historical Society). Don't miss Fort Clatsop, the winter quarters of the famed Lewis and Clark expedition.

Warrenton Deep Sea Crab & Fish Market, 45 NE Harbor Pl., Warrenton, OR 97146; (503) 861-3911. Locals say they appreciate this waterfront market's cleanliness and consistently fresh, high-quality seafood, including live crabs, salmon jerky, shrimp cocktail, and an excellent selection of smoked options, including sensational smoked scallops.

BRITISH COLUMBIA

This westernmost Canadian province offers your best glimpse of a Northwest still untamed and wild at heart—yet admirably prim and proper when it wants to be (we're looking at you, Victoria!). Vancouver Island, named for the explorer who examined so much of the coastal Northwest, is home to temperate rain forests; white sand beaches; lighthouses that have witnessed legendary shipwrecks; and lakes, ocean, rivers, inlets, coves, water, water everywhere. Oysters everywhere, too: Aficionados exclaim at the sweetness, smoothness, and purity of bivalves that hail from the glacier-carved fjords along the Strait of Georgia, the hundred-mile inland sea that separates Vancouver Island from inland BC and Vancouver the city. Growers here have perfected the art of tumbling bags of youthful oysters with the tides, resulting in shells that could win beauty contests with deep cups that make for easier slurping.

Across the strait, the city of Vancouver trembles and thumps with energy, a thriving metropolis fringed by soaring mountains and forests. It hosted the 2010 winter Olympics with aplomb, this cosmopolitan, stylish-yet-sensible city easily absorbing and embracing visitors from the world over. Like its Northwest brethren to the south, most of the city's restaurants offer seafood specialties, given the abundance and easy access to high-quality fresh seafood. This diverse city's population demands and expects a lot from its restaurants, and they deliver: Thus, it's not unusual for diners to journey to Vancouver and nearby Asian cuisine–enclave Richmond from Seattle for sushi, dim sum, and other specialties BC seems to have perfected with otherworldly finesse. Note: US/Canada border crossings, by land, plane, train, or sea, require a valid passport.

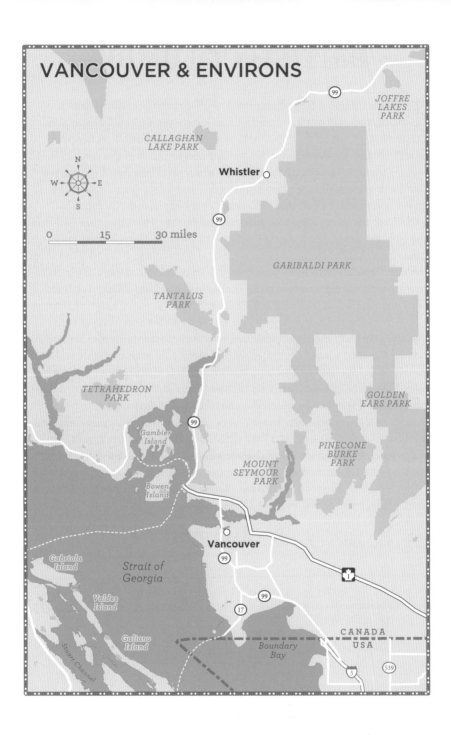

Vancouver & Environs

Few other cities in the world combine stunning scenery and urban living quite like Vancouver. Surrounded by water, forested mountains looming in the distance, skyscrapers and residential towers gleaming in the sun. Or shining in the mist, as this part of the world continues the watery traditions of its Northwest neighbors to the south. No wonder the city boasts its own old-growth forest within Stanley Park, prompting hikers to ask "Am I still in a city?"

It's a city that crackles with diversity. Mandarin and Cantonese are the first languages in more than one third of Vancouver's homes, and only San Francisco's Chinatown is bigger. It's a city that takes its food seriously, especially Asian cuisine and seafood: Whatever great meal you've enjoyed in Seattle or Portland, you can count on finding the same or even better version in their cosmopolitan northern neighbor.

Blue Water Cafe + Raw Bar, 1095 Hamilton St., Vancouver, BC V6B 5T4; (604) 688-8078; bluewatercafe.net. Expectations rise when a restaurant wins monikers like "Best Seafood" from multiple publications.

But Blue Water Cafe + Raw Bar just keeps right on delivering, thrilling diners with impeccable service and wild, sustainable seafood dishes from a variety of culinary traditions that are phenomenal in both pure flavor and presentation.

Executive Chef Frank Pabst hails from Michelin-starred restaurants throughout Germany and France, and sets the bar high. Tuna carpaccio seems to melt in your mouth. The miso sablefish is buttery and rich (see recipe in the "In the Kitchen" chapter). Char is cooked to perfection, with crispy skin and moist, flaky flesh, set to its best advantage by a delicate beurre blanc.

The list of oysters on ice sourced largely from BC waters numbers nearly two dozen. (Then there's the ceviche and seafood tower selections. And the caviar.) Live tanks have held Alaskan king crab, Dungeness, Atlantic lobster, spot prawns, sea urchin, and geoduck. Raw Bar Chef Yoshiya Maruyama aims for perfection with tuna *goma-ae* (albacore marinated with sesame seeds and soy) and myriad other plates, nigiri, sashimi, and rolls.

Finest at Sea Granville Island Smokery, 1805 Mast Tower Rd., Vancouver, BC V6H 3X7; (604) 684-4114; finestatsea.com. Finest at Sea operates its own fishing fleet and has been operating since 1977, which enables it to deliver on the promise of its name. The selection here is impressive: live or frozen BC spot prawns, live or cooked and cracked Dungeness crab, hot smoked salmon, cold smoked sablefish fillets, whole halibut (or fillets, cheeks, collars, or steaks), albacore tuna candy, Salt Spring Island mussels, fresh local oysters or sesame smoked oysters, and house-smoked BC sardines, just to get started. They excel at offering ready-to-eat seafood, from crab-stuffed mushrooms to BC Salmon Pot Pie. Canned seafood is abundant in a multitude of varieties, from canned spring salmon to canned smoked spring salmon to canned smoked albacore. You'll also find a Finest at Sea food cart on Robson Street and seafood boutiques in Vancouver's Kerrisdale neighborhood and in Victoria, where the company was founded.

Fisherman's Terrace Seafood Restaurant, 3580-4151 Hazelbridge Way, Richmond, BC V6X 4J7; (604) 303-9739. Perched high in the upscale Aberdeen Centre mall (next to Aberdeen Station), this always-packed, refined spot offers piping-hot dim sum that locals consider the perfect fuel before a day of shopping. No carts here: Order your selections from the menu, which may take awhile, as the options get overwhelming (try any of the delicately seasoned shrimp specialties, the spicy garlic squid, jellyfish cold plate, steamed pork *bao*, cilantro and beef *siu mai*, and various mushroom specialties).

Go Fish Ocean Emporium, 1505 W. 1st Ave., Vancouver, BC V6J 1E8; (604) 730-5040; gofishvancouver.com. This fish and chippery inside a shipping-container shack is just a short jaunt along the wharf outside the famous Granville Market, within view of False Creek and the gleaming downtown skyscrapers in the distance. The star is the oyster po' boy, filled with three juicy barbecued local oysters, crisp shredded iceberg lettuce, chipotle *crema*, sweet onion, and tartar sauce. Also try the Thai curry fish chowder and the salmon *tacones*—grilled salmon with cilantro-spiked salsa, chipotle *crema*, and slaw rolled into a white-flour tortilla cone. Fillets are coated in a crispy Granville Island beer batter for fish-and-chips. Enjoy your food along the wooden bar and tables outside, then hit the wharf to buy fresh salmon to take home for your next meal.

Minami, 1118 Mainland St., Vancouver, BC V6B 2T9; (604) 685-8080; minamirestaurant.com. Food is art at Minami, where dish after imaginative dish that crosses the sushi bar or arrives from the kitchen seems to glow with freshness and pure quality, in part because many quite literally glowed with flames from the kitchen's quick, flame-searing cooking method known as *aburi*.

Waterways: How We Live

Colene Chow's Spot Prawn Fest (SPF)

Steamed. Grilled. Panfried. Raw. Each spring, spot prawn fan Colene Chow daydreams how she'll savor the first catch of the season in May, scooped wild from the waters that separate Vancouver Island and the mainland. One year, Chow and her friends learned of the annual Spot Prawn Festival at Granville Island and felt inspired: Why not buy their own from the dock and hold their own festival at home? SPF was born.

The first year, they were a tad overzealous. They headed home with 15 pounds of delicate, sweet spot prawns, 6 pounds of mussels, and 2 pounds of scallops . . . for five friends. "We assumed each of us would be good to eat 2 to 3 pounds each," recalled Chow, a product marketing manager. "Our math was a little ambitious, but it really goes to show how much we love spot prawns!"

They spent the afternoon cleaning their catch, preparing spot prawn sashimi and ceviche, and then grilling, steaming, and panfrying the rest together.

Seasonal and regional ingredients and sustainable Ocean Wise program–approved seafood options unite to create stunning culinary masterpieces that are as lovely to behold as they are to eat, as the heat infuses the fish with the kitchen's signature sauces while also enhancing the natural flavors of the fish within.

Favorites here include hamachi with avocado sauce, scallops with cod-roe mayo, and salmon oshi sushi. Another highlight is fresh pressed BC

"It was great to have a variety to really show how diverse and delicious seafood is in all its forms," Chow said. Still, it turned out to be an embarrassment of riches. The following year, they focused on spot prawns alone, and skipped the grill in favor of their three favorite methods: panfried, and prepared as sashimi and ceviche.

Now, the group discusses the coming year's spot prawn cooking plan months in advance. And their numbers are growing: "One of the couples has a new baby, and they're looking into initiating their son into our SPF."

Tip Sheet: Throw Your Own Spot Prawn Fest

- For the freshest prawns, buy direct from fishermen at your local dock. No luck? Finer seafood counters often carry them frozen.
- Depending on what else you serve, Chow recommends 1 to 1½ pounds of spot prawns per person.
- Pair fresh, light side dishes with your prawns, such as grilled vegetables, garlic bread, or a salad.
- It helps to choose a kitchen with a good amount of counter space and a double sink (for de-heading the prawns).
- Have rubber gloves on hand to help the squeamish handle the prawns.
- Keep those prawn heads. Freeze them to flavor future seafood bisques and stews.
- If you grill your spot prawns, put someone on grill duty to avoid overcooking.

wild sockeye salmon, jalapeño, and *miku* sauce on a thin bed of rice. *Kaisen* soba peperoncino layers soba noodles with prawns, squid, scallops, sweet peppers, shiitake mushrooms, baby bok choy, jalapeño, crunchy tempura bits, and chile-garlic soy.

When you're not busy ogling the food, this space offers wonderful people-watching and eye-catching art, even better with a sample from the restaurant's extensive scotch selection.

Salmon n' Bannock Bistro, 1128 W. Broadway, Vancouver, BC V6H 1B5; (604) 568-8971; salmonandbannock.net. General awareness of First Nations or Native American cuisine often seems limited to fry bread and, perhaps in the Northwest, staked salmon roasted over a fire pit. Which is what makes the growing popularity of this restaurant that serves only foods inspired by local traditional cuisine so intriguing.

On the menu from Haida Chef Brodie Swanson: a wild sockeye salmon burger with fennel slaw; salmon soup; wild rice and oat mushroom risotto; featured game sausage; bison strip loin with sauteed BC prawns; elk soup; crispy Arctic musk ox; and a dish of spot prawns and poached beets with candied nuts and arugula. You'll also find Spirit Bear organic and fair trade coffee and jam made with Saskatoon berries.

All wild local fish, organic and free-range meats, bannock (a type of flat quick bread), and other culinary delights round out the menu. None contain preservatives or additives. Meats are not from factory farms and they avoid using genetically modified ingredients. So far, the most popular dishes are barbecued or smoked salmon, and deer shank with red wine gravy, paired with wines from Nk'Mip Cellars, a native-owned and -operated winery in the Okanagan Valley.

Yew Seafood & Bar, 791 W. Georgia St., Vancouver, BC V6C 2T4; (604) 689-9333; yewseafood.com. Ensconced in the Four Seasons Hotel Vancouver, casually elegant Yew is the very best kind of hotel restaurant: one that continues to innovate, excite, and delight despite a built-in audience. Fans obsess over the lobster mac and cheese, the Dungeness crab tacos, the West Coast seafood paella, Qualicum scallops, and the halibut with crispy Humboldt squid. There's an extensive high-end wine list, a grand vegan menu, and a three-course brunch. And if you can't decide, there's always Champagne and oysters.

Whistler

After so many adventures at sea level, Whistler offers a chance to enjoy the dramatic scenery of BC's Coast Mountains and forests at eye level. This walkable resort town teems with skiers and boarders in winter, hikers and mountain bikers in summer, and abounds with good places to eat. It hosted many alpine events during the 2010 Winter Olympics in nearby Vancouver.

Araxi Restaurant & Bar, 4222 Village Square RR4, Whistler, BC V0N 1B4; (604) 932-4540; araxi.com. Executive Chef James Walt was an early pioneer of the farm-to-table movement, and it's very evident in the freshness of his menu, which bursts with color and seasonality. He shares Araxi's recipe for Arctic Char with Salsify, Crosnes & Rutabaga with Lemon Butter in the "In the Kitchen" chapter.

PHOTO COURTESY OF ARAXI RESTAURANT; PHOTO BY STEVE LI

The marble-topped oyster bar offers up to a dozen varieties delivered fresh daily. The Dungeness crab roll in egg crepe is wrapped with cold-smoked wild salmon, watercress, and yuzu mayonnaise with avocado and tomatillo salsa verde. Wild BC sockeye salmon becomes glorious sashimi, with avocado and cucumber adding a green spark. The two-tier seafood tower is a stunning presentation of all the best the region has to offer, including Read Island mussels, seared tuna, seaweed salad, and a Dungeness crab roll.

Rimrock Cafe & Oyster Bar, 2117 Whistler Rd., Whistler, BC V0N 1B2 Canada; (604) 932-5565; rimrockcafe.com. Chef-Owner Rolf Gunther and his talented team craft memorable Northwest cuisine from wonderfully fresh ingredients that have transformed first-time diners into loyal fans of this restaurant just outside Whistler Village. Rimrock's handling of seafood is superb: rich lobster bisque with Armagnac cream; seared rare tuna and ahi poke in a sesame miso sauce; tender, fragrant baked salmon; oysters broiled Rimrock-style with salmon, béchamel, and gruyère cheese (and also available raw on the half shell). The mixed grill (grilled lamb, beef tenderloin, venison, and duck breast served with béarnaise sauce) is a must, as is the house spaetzle, a shout-out to the chef's time in Germany. Combine consistently outstanding food with gracious service and a dining room with character, and it's clear why Rimrock has remained a Whistler favorite all these years after its opening in 1988.

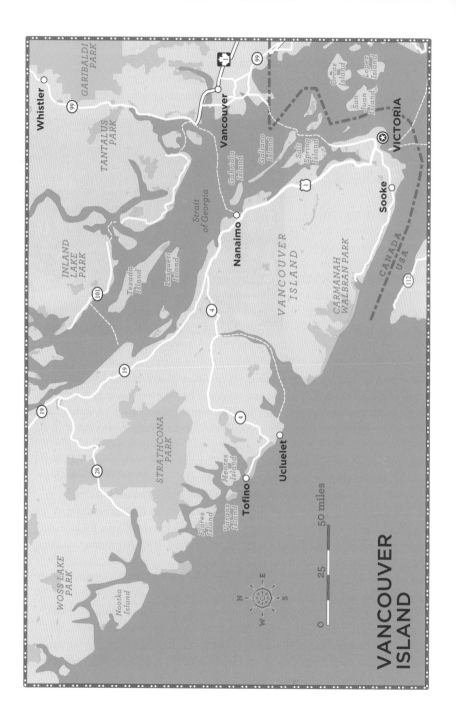

VANCOUVER
ISLAND

Vancouver Island

Prepare for adventure and contrasts on this island, the largest on North America's West Coast (similar in size to Jamaica), from prim and proper historic Victoria to wild and rustic Tofino on the Pacific Coast. First Nation tribes made their home here for centuries before Captain James Cook first set foot on the island in 1778 and George Vancouver surveyed it in 1792. With the exception of its faded fur trade and booming tourist trade, its main industries—timber, fishing, mining, and agriculture—have remained largely the same since then. Hikers, kayakers, and storm-watchers adore the remote, rugged landscape, which swings from wind-lashed coasts to tranquil sounds and bays, misty coastal rain forests to mountains thick with second-growth timber.

In recent years the island has grown into a food lover's paradise. High-quality ingredients abound from regional farms, creameries, cider-ies, and waters. Refined restaurants and casual joints alike have emerged that elevate the flavor of the meal to as high a draw as the majestic views. Get there by ferry from Vancouver; or from Washington, access the island via Port Angeles on the Black Ball Line or via Seattle aboard the *Victoria Clipper*.

Nanaimo

Perched along the sparkling Strait of Georgia across from the city of Vancouver, surrounded by forests and mountains is Nanaimo. One claim to fame is its namesake cookie, the chocolaty and creamy Nanaimo Bar. Another is its annual bathtub race during the city's Marine Festival, orga-nized by the inimitable Loyal Nanaimo Bathtub Society. Another is its seafood.

The Bold Knight, 1140 Trans-Canada Hwy., Nanaimo, BC V9R 6N6; (250) 754-6411; boldknight.ca. This unpretentious local spot bills itself as the "ultimate steak and seafood house" with a menu plentiful with well-prepared seafood from throughout the region, from Fanny Bay oysters Rockefeller and herb and panko-crusted BC halibut to broiled wild BC salmon fillet and baked tiger prawns with garlic butter. It's a favorite of local families for special occasions.

Hilltop Bistro, #102 5281 Rutherfod Rd., Nanaimo, BC V9T 5N9; (250) 585-5337; hilltopbistro.ca. There's a fine balance between offering a quality menu and attentive service without coming off as snooty or pretentious. Hilltop pulls this off by creating an intimate, charming space and taking pride in the cooking without taking itself too seriously.

The carefully edited menu is not seafood-focused, but each day presents several wonderful selections, from halibut croquettes to smoked black cod to Arctic char, each beautifully presented. Steaks are cooked sous-vide to achieve ideal doneness. Deciding which appealing dessert to choose prompts soul-searching. With such attention to detail, no wonder it won the 2013 People's Choice for best restaurant on Vancouver Island in *BC Living* magazine. Note: Now that you know this, make sure to call for reservations.

Sooke

This chill fishing village lies about 45 minutes by car outside Victoria on the southern tip of Vancouver Island at the end of scenic Highway 14, the Pacific Marine Circle Route, which offers breathtaking views of white sand beaches, the Olympic Mountains to the south, mossy and brooding coastal rain forests, and the Juan de Fuca Strait. On a bike? Take the woodsy Galloping Goose Trail (gallopinggoosetrail.com).

Smokin' Tuna Cafe, 241 Becher Bay Rd., Capital, BC V9Z 1B7; (250) 642-0332. This casual spot is a hidden gem, with friendly ambience, fresh and local ingredients, and a sweet water view. Seafood hits include salmon spring rolls, breaded and deep-fried tuna loin, and what many call the best calamari of their lives. It's just a short drive from the end of the coast trail in East Sooke Regional Park next to Aylard Farm with white sand beaches and hiking trails through more than 3,500 acres of ancient coastal rain forest.

Sooke Harbour House, 1528 Whiffen Spit Rd., Sooke, BC V9Z 0T4; (250) 642-3421; sookeharbourhouse.com. Before farm-to-table officially was a thing, the chefs at Sooke Harbour House, about an hour's drive west from Victoria on the scenic west coast of British Columbia, were infusing their dishes with the very best organic ingredients they could gather on Vancouver Island and beyond, creating a menu that changes nightly to reflect the harvest, including whatever's fresh in the kitchen garden.

For years, Sooke Harbour House was considered one of the best small inns in the world, and was showered with kudos and awards, including from *Wine Spectator* for its wine cellar. It has been up for sale since 2012, and by many accounts, has lost a bit of its trademark luster and hospitality. Hopes are high this venerable lodge will resume its high perch. Note: The restaurant is closed Tues and Wed.

Tofino

If you've made it all this way, congratulations! It takes some doing to get to Tofino, but once you reach its rugged, otherworldly beaches and forests, dine at its many memorable restaurants, and get to the know the people, you may never want to leave.

Big Daddy's Fish Fry, 411 Campbell St., Tofino, BC V0R 2Z0; (250) 725-4415. Post-surfing (or post-hiking, beachcombing, or kayaking) stop by this joint for fresh-cut fries and tempura-battered halibut, cod, salmon, or prawns with homemade tartar sauce. There's also popcorn shrimp, coconut prawns, burgers, chowder, fish tacos, and Dungeness crab. Enjoy at their outdoor tables, or wander to a nearby park and take in views of the harbor toward Meares Island. Soft-serve ice cream fans: Big Daddy's Sweet Tooth offers 25 different flavors. Note: Both of these ventures are cash only.

The Pointe Restaurant at Wickaninnish Inn, 500 Osprey Ln., Tofino, BC V0R 2Z0; (250) 725-3100; wickinn.com/restaurant .html. If you have a bucket list (or at least, a seafood-centric bucket list), make sure to add this landmark restaurant. You walk into a round room

with a copper fireplace in its middle and windows all around, offering breathtaking views of the surging Pacific as you select a few favorites, or indulge in a 3-hour, multiple-course tasting menu that highlights the very best of BC's seafood heritage.

Chefs Warren Barr and David Slider and their team make magic with seafood that's often fished from the waters within view of the dining room, including spring salmon and field cabbage with abalone mushroom and new potatoes; pan-roasted lingcod and charred octopus; and seared Tofino halibut with potato and leek ragout and wild mushrooms in buttermilk and leek oil. Desserts, bread, butter, and chocolate croissants all are house-made.

Note: The Pointe also offers a Champagne Sunday brunch. The evening dress code is smart-casual.

Wildside Grill, 1180 Pacific Rim Hwy., Tofino, BC V0R Canada; (250) 725-9453; wildsidegrill.com. Fish tacos, grilled salmon burgers, and seafood gumbo are the star attractions at this roadside surfer fish shack with outdoor seating just a short jaunt outside Tofino proper. Also on the menu: burgers featuring halibut, oysters, scallops, tuna, or shrimp. The main regret expressed by those who've had the good fortune to eat there is that they didn't visit more often during their Tofino getaway.

Ucluelet

This fishing village and resort town on the west coast of Vancouver Island offers wild, rocky, driftwood-strewn Pacific Ocean beaches, and kayaking along its sheltered waters. Ukee, as the locals call it, has also joined with Tofino to the north to form the Tofino Ucluelet Culinary Guild, a band of restaurants, farmers, and foragers united in drawing attention to and celebrating the array of high-quality foodstuffs and eating experiences in this achingly beautiful and remote part of the world.

Jiggers Fish & Chips, 1801 Bay St., Ucluelet, BC V0R 3A0; (250) 726-5400. If only all food trucks held such treasures. Fresh, light, and golden panko-breaded fish (halibut, cod, lingcod, and other species, depending on the season) and chips arrive in baskets with fries and coleslaw and tartar sauce, ready to enjoy at their outdoor tables (mind the weather when planning your visit). Prawns come on a skewer, crispy and light. The fish sandwich manages to be filling without becoming a gut bomb. Locals note this truck can keep unpredictable hours; so make a point to stop when you do see it.

Norwoods Restaurant, 1714 Peninsula Rd., Ucluelet, BC V0R 3A0; (250) 726-7001; norwoods.ca. Step inside this inconspicuous restaurant and marvel at your luck: Owner Richard Norwood, Chef de Cuisine Ryan Mclean, and their team offer a refined-yet-casual take on the local wonders of the Northwest, with culinary influences from around the globe, served in an intimate wine bar setting. As with most restaurants that celebrate what's locally fished and foraged, the menu changes by the day and throughout the day. Seafood favorites include the warm salad of grilled octopus and scallops, ceviche, coconut curry mussels, local oysters on the half shell, and seared black cod, all obtained from sustainable supplies per Canada's Ocean Wise program. A growing number of diners claim it to be among the best meals of their lives. Due to this, be sure to make a reservation if your heart is set on a particular time and date.

Offshore Seafood Restaurant, 2082 Peninsula Rd., Ucluelet, BC V0R 3A0; (250) 726-2111. Some fans return just for the salmon ravioli—giant Chinese-style dumplings plump with salmon and onion. Others go wild for tom yum soup with fresh seafood and rice noodles, super-fresh sushi rolls, and, of course, the boiled crab. The Asian culinary influences here elevate already superb coastal seafood and offer a nice break for those on lengthy trips to the area.

Victoria

This capital city of British Columbia wears its crown well, with the charming streets, lovely parks, and culture aplenty reflecting its Old World influences. It's also the cycling capital of Canada, and, thank goodness, so you can burn off all the food you'll be enjoying here.

Finest at Sea, 27 Erie St., Victoria, BC V8V 1P8; (250) 383-7760; finestatsea.com. Finest at Sea operates its own fishing fleet and has been in business since 1977, which enables it to deliver on the promise of its name. The selection here is impressive: live or frozen BC spot prawns, live or cooked and shucked Dungeness crab, hot smoked salmon, cold smoked sablefish fillets, whole halibut (or fillets, cheeks, collars, or steaks), albacore tuna candy, Salt Spring Island mussels, fresh local oysters or sesame smoked oysters, and house-smoked BC sardines, just to get started. They excel at offering ready-to-eat seafood, from crab-stuffed mushrooms to BC salmon potpie. Canned seafood is abundant in a multitude of varieties, from canned spring salmon to canned smoked spring salmon to canned smoked albacore. You'll also find a Finest at Sea food cart on Robson Street and seafood boutiques in Vancouver's Kerrisdale neighborhood and at Granville Island.

The Fish Store at Fisherman's Wharf, On Victoria's Inner Harbour (enter off St. Lawrence Street or Dallas Road); (250) 383-6462; floatingfishstore.com. This floating fish store wins raves for its fish-and-chips, oysters-and-chips, and flavorful fish tacos, considered by many to be the best on Fisherman's Wharf, and also serves steamed mussels and clams, seafood salads, salmon chowder, and local oysters on ice. Its proximity to the water pays off with a wonderful view of the working harbor, where sea otters and seals glide right past, and the ability for fishermen to tie up their boats and deliver their catch of halibut, snapper, spot prawns, or salmon in person. Not in the mood to walk, bike, or cab it? Hop aboard a Victoria Harbour water ferry (victoriaharbourferry.com) and tell the skipper you'd like to be dropped at Fisherman's Wharf.

Its fish counter offers live or steamed Dungeness crab (they like to point out that these crabs have not touched land until purchased by you); whole albacore tuna or in steaks, quarters, sashimi-grade loins, or smoked; and Vancouver Island mussels, oysters, and clams, typically from Victoria, Desolation Sound, and Clayoquot Sound. Their entire selection is certified Ocean Wise, or sustainable to the hilt. Tip: Stop by between 3 and 5 p.m. daily for buck a shuck—featured oysters for just $1 Canadian.

Red Fish, Blue Fish, 1006 Wharf St., Victoria, BC V8W 1T4; (250) 298-6877; redfish-bluefish.com. Don't wait until you're starving to head for this quirky seafood spot tucked into a charming upcycled cargo container on a wooden pier in Victoria's Inner Harbour. You'll most likely be waiting in line with everyone else who's pining for specialties like jerk fish poutine; the grilled Qualicum Bay scallop burger with tempura pickles, tuna-belly bacon, tangy tartar sauce, and lemon-pickled onions, served on a fresh-baked Irene's Bakery Portuguese bun; or the RFBF BLT (smoked albacore tuna belly bacon with romaine hearts, tomato, and tartar sauce).

Local seafood here is grilled, seared, or fried, and then placed on salads, tucked into sandwiches, or added to *tacones* (grilled flour tortillas with slaw, pea shoots, lemon pickled onions, and a variety of grilled or smoked seafood, such as wild salmon, Fanny Bay oysters, or albacore tuna). Wild Pacific fish-and-chips are tempura-battered and available with halibut, salmon, or cod and served with hand-cut, twice-fried Kennebec potato fries.

As an added bonus, Red Fish, Blue Fish only serves seafood from sustainable populations, making it 100 percent Ocean Wise—akin to serving only species with populations declared healthy and sustainable under Monterey Bay Aquarium's Seafood Watch program.

In the Kitchen

Appetizer & Small Plate Recipes

Soup, Salad & Sandwich Recipes

Main Dish Recipes

Cooking Tips

For additional cooking tips, please see Chef Lynne Vea's shellfish cookout tips in the "To the North" chapter and the clambake/barbecue oyster tips from Executive Chef Lucas Sautter at Alderbrook Inn in the Union section of the "To the West" chapter.

Appetizer & Small Plate Recipes

Baked Oysters
Recipe Courtesy of The Oyster Bar

(MAKES ABOUT 4 DOZEN OYSTERS)

Warm, rich, and creamy, just the dish to enjoy as you gaze out at the closest thing to Samish Bay in your neck of the woods. This recipe makes enough for a party; divide by four if you'd prefer a yield to serve a hearty dinner for two. Don't have a pot large enough to handle 16 cups of spinach? Cook this delightful concoction in batches.

1 cup sliced shallots
¼ cup bacon fat
½ cup Pernod
4 cups heavy cream
16 cups chopped spinach (Note: 1 pound of fresh spinach yields about 6 cups)
Dash of Tabasco
Salt and pepper to taste

4 dozen shucked oysters in the half shell
Rock salt
1 cup diced tomato
1 cup diced cooked bacon
Dried bread crumbs
Fresh minced chives
Lemon wedges

In a large saucepan, saute the shallots in the bacon fat until they brown.

Deglaze the pan with the Pernod and let the alcohol burn off.

Add the cream and reduce until thick bubbles form.

Take off the heat and add the chopped spinach and stir until it breaks down and wilts.

Season with Tabasco, salt and pepper to taste, then reserve.

Lay the oysters on a sheet tray with a layer of rock salt to help keep them upright. Put a tablespoon of the creamed spinach on each oyster to cover. Sprinkle the tomato and bacon on each of the oysters and then finally a generous sprinkle of bread crumbs.

Bake in a 400°F oven for 10–15 minutes until golden and bubbly. Top with fresh chives and serve with lemon.

Baked Willapa Bay Oysters on the Half Shell

Recipe Courtesy of OleBob's Galley Cafe & Seafood Market

(SERVES 2)

After a blustery day on land or sea, these oysters will help to warm you.

¼ cup butter
Minced garlic (if desired)
6 medium-size raw oysters
6 cleaned oyster shells
¼ cup grated Parmesan cheese

Melt the butter in a small saucepan over low heat (add minced garlic if desired).

Place a raw oyster on each oyster shell and put on a baking sheet.

Drizzle the melted butter over each oyster. Reserve excess for garnish.

Bake oysters at 450°F for 5 minutes.

Remove from oven and sprinkle each oyster with Parmesan cheese

Bake for another minute or so until cheese is melted.

Serve with melted garlic butter, cocktail sauce, coleslaw, and sourdough bread.

Mo's Fish Tacos

Recipe Courtesy of Mo's Chowder

(SERVES 4)

Gabrielle McEntee, one of Mo's grandchildren and part of the third generation to run the business, calls these fish tacos one of the most popular menu items . . . besides the clam chowder, of course.

Green Jalapeño Dressing and Slaw

  2 cups mayonnaise
  1 clove garlic
  ¼ cup chopped fresh cilantro
  2 tablespoons water
  2 tablespoons rice vinegar
  1 jalapeño seeded and finely chopped
  ¼ teaspoon ground black pepper
  ½ teaspoon salt
  1 tablespoon fresh lime juice
  3 cups shredded cabbage

Combine all ingredients in a blender except for the cabbage.

Toss dressing with cabbage to desired consistency (Note: This recipe will make more dressing than you may need for one meal).

For the Fish

  4 (6 ounce) fish fillets (lingcod, true cod, or snapper)
  ¼ teaspoon salt
  ¼ teaspoon pepper
  Panko bread crumbs (follow directions on package,
    which call for flour, eggs, and milk)
  Peanut oil
  4 corn tortillas
  Sour cream and salsa, for garnish

Salt and pepper fish fillets then coat fillets in panko breading. In a medium hot skillet add 2 tablespoons peanut oil and fry fish for about 3 minutes on each side.

Remove from pan and cut each fillet in half.

On a warm corn tortilla and add ¼ cup cabbage mixture and one half fish fillet. Top with sour cream and your favorite salsa.

Smoked Manila Clam Dip
Recipe Courtesy of Westward

(MAKES ABOUT 1¼ QUARTS)

Chef Antonitsas puts her wood-fired oven to wonderful use with this recipe. Use a smoker at home, or drop the lid on your grill. Serve this delight with potato chips and Champagne or really cold beer.

5 pounds live clams
⅛ cup white wine
1 clove garlic, sliced
Juice and zest of 1 lemon
1 teaspoon finely chopped shallot
1 cup aioli (available online or at finer markets)
1½ cups Greek yogurt
Pinch of sugar
1 teaspoon salt
½ teaspoon freshly ground black pepper
1 teaspoon chopped chives
1 teaspoon chopped dill
1 teaspoon chopped parsley
Aleppo chile (optional)

In a heavy-bottomed pot with a tight-fitting lid, steam clams in white wine and garlic over medium heat until the shells open.

Let cool, reserve the liquid, and remove clams from their shells. Toss any unopened clams and shells.

Return the pot to a simmer and reduce the reserved liquid by half. Pour over clams, then cold-smoke the clams in a wood oven or smoker at about 150°F for 2 hours.

Chop smoked clams finely, reserving their juice to add later for added flavor and consistency.

Combine with lemon juice, lemon zest, and shallot. Add aioli, Greek yogurt, sugar, salt, and pepper. Allow the flavors to meld, preferably overnight.

When ready to serve, mix in chives, dill, and parsley. Top with Aleppo chile, if desired.

Smoked Shrimp
Recipe Courtesy of Tidal Raves Seafood Grill

(SERVES 4 AS AN APPETIZER)

This appetizer is one of the most popular items on the menu at Tidal Raves.

16–20 count wild shrimp, shell on
1 tablespoon granulated sugar
1 tablespoon kosher salt
2 limes, juiced
1 cup alderwood chips

Rinse the shrimp well, then pull off the legs and split the back and clean out the vein. Leaving the split shell on aids in moisture retention but can be removed if preferred.

Toss the shrimp with the sugar, salt, and half the lime juice. Allow to marinate for 30 minutes but don't rinse them again prior to smoking.

Place shrimp on the rack of an electric smoker-cooker and set to about 225°F for about 45 minutes. Check to see if the shrimp are done through and no dark blue color remains. It's important to not overcook the shrimp but it's more important to cook them through (about 175°F internal temperature).

Note: If you don't have a smoker, set up a large, heavy-bottomed, oven-safe pot with a rack that fits in the bottom with the chips under the rack. Turn the stove heat on medium until the chips start to smoke, then cover the pot and turn the heat down to medium-low. Check the shrimp after about 20 minutes as this method of smoking usually produces higher heat than a smoker-cooker.

Note: If you use a sportsman's smoker, you might need to finish cooking them in an oven set at about 250°F until done, or smoke them longer as the heat source is usually less impactful.

Squeeze another lime or lemon over the shrimp and refrigerate until use.

Easy Vietnamese Dipping Sauce
    1 cup mayonnaise
    2 cloves garlic, minced
    1 tablespoon sriracha sauce
    1 lemon, juiced

Mix the mayonnaise, garlic, sriracha, and lemon juice together well and allow the flavors to "bloom" for at least 2 hours prior to serving. Use more sriracha or less according to your taste.

Totten Inlet Mediterranean Mussels Steamed in Sherry with Garlic & Smoked Paprika

Recipe Courtesy of Blueacre Seafood

(SERVES 2 AS AN APPETIZER, 1 AS AN ENTREE)

Totten Inlet, tucked between Olympia and Shelton, Washington, in south Puget Sound, is among the most famous growing regions for shellfish. Oysters and mussels quickly grow plump in the inlet's algae-rich waters. When you're not in Washington, use the freshest, best mussels at your disposal.

1 teaspoon whole fennel seeds
1 teaspoon whole white peppercorns
1 teaspoon whole coriander seeds
¼ cup blended oil (canola/olive preferred)
1 pound very fresh large mussels, debearded and washed (Taylor Shellfish Mediterranean mussels recommended)
5 ounces (about ⅔ cup) dry sherry
¼ cup sherry vinegar
1 tablespoon butter
2 teaspoons coarse kosher salt
2 ounces piquillo peppers, julienned (or roasted red peppers, peeled and seeded)
2 cloves garlic, peeled and minced
1 medium shallot, peeled and minced
½ tablespoon smoked paprika
1 tablespoon fresh oregano leaves
1 tablespoon crushed Marcona almonds
1 tablespoon finishing quality Spanish extra-virgin olive oil

Lightly toast fennel, white peppercorns, and coriander seeds in a medium sauté pan to release oils, then grind in spice grinder.

Preheat blended oil in a 12-inch heavy-gauge sauté pan over high heat.

In an identical pan place mussels, sherry, vinegar, butter, salt, and piquillo peppers.

When oil is hot, remove from heat, add garlic and shallots and sauté until edges start to brown lightly. Add paprika and mixture of ground coriander, white pepper, and fennel. Cook briefly.

Remove from heat and add the ingredients of the mussels pan. Invert pan to use as a lid.

Return to high heat. Steam on high for 3–4 minutes, and remove lid to check doneness. Mussels are cooked when they are open.

Replace lid and continue to cook until all of the mussels are open. Sprinkle with oregano leaves and cook briefly.

Plate mussels, spoon sauce over, and garnish with almonds and drizzle of olive oil.

PHOTO COURTESY OF BLUEACRE SEAFOOD

Welch Family Crab Cakes
Recipe Courtesy of Andrew Welch

(YIELD: ABOUT 8-10 CRAB CAKES)

When he's not out sharing his harvest, Andrew Welch likes to cook and shell the Dungeness crabs he hauls in with his daughters and make crab cakes, especially when his family entertains. "They are good and have no filler," he says of his recipe.

½ red bell pepper, cut fine
½ green bell pepper, cut fine
1 tablespoon chopped parsley
2 tablespoons mayonnaise
2 eggs
1 tablespoon baking powder
1 tablespoon Worcestershire sauce
2 teaspoons Old Bay seasoning
Squirt of hot sauce to taste
1 pound cooked crabmeat (about 2 crabs' worth)
Panko flakes (optional)
Parmesan cheese, grated (optional)

Combine all of the ingredients with the crab. If you like, roll each cake in panko flakes and Parmesan for a crispy, savory crust.

Heat a skillet over medium-high heat.

Panfry the cakes until they are golden brown, about 5–7 minutes per side.

Black Cod Heirloom Caprese
Recipe Courtesy of The Robin Hood
(SERVES 4)

Basil Oil
¼ cup fresh basil
1 cup extra-virgin olive oil

Beurre Rouge
1 cup red wine vinegar
1½ cups red table wine
2 tablespoons chopped shallots
½ teaspoon ground white pepper
½ pound unsalted butter

Bacon Aioli
2 strips bacon, fully cooked and finely chopped (reserve bacon grease)
1 tablespoon finely chopped shallots
½ teaspoon minced garlic
1 cup mayonnaise
½ teaspoon Dijon mustard
½ teaspoon brandy
¼ teaspoon salt
¼ tsp ground black pepper

PHOTO COURTESY OF THE ROBIN HOOD RESTAURANT

Balsamic Glaze
1 cup balsamic vinegar

Fingerling Chips
4 small fingerling potatoes
Oil for deep frying
Salt and pepper

Black Cod
4 tablespoons extra-virgin olive oil
Salt and pepper
4 (7-ounce) black cod fillets
4 small to medium heirloom tomatoes, sliced
4 tablespoons crumbled feta cheese

To make basil oil: Blanch basil in boiling water, remove and add to olive oil. Blend until smooth.

To make beurre rouge: Combine red wine vinegar, red table wine, shallots, and pepper. Bring to a boil, then simmer until reduced to a thick sauce. Slowly add ½ pound butter until the sauce has reached your desired consistency. Blend until smooth.

To make bacon aioli: Mix bacon, shallots, garlic, mayonnaise, mustard, brandy, salt, and pepper.

To make balsamic glaze: Bring balsamic vinegar to a boil, then reduce to simmer. Simmer until it is reduced by half.

To make fingerling chips: Thinly slice fingerling potatoes lengthwise. Deep fry in oil, salt and pepper to taste.

To prepare black cod: Heat extra-virgin olive oil or grapeseed oil on high heat. Carefully add fillets skin side down (they should sizzle as soon as they touch the oil). Add a pinch of salt and pepper to each fillet. Press each fillet flat to prevent curling. Cook for 5–7 minutes on one side until golden brown and crispy. Carefully flip and continue to cook for another 3–4 minutes.

To assemble: Spread a tablespoon or so of the bacon aioli where you will set the fish, then drizzle the plate with beurre rouge. Fan heirloom tomato slices across plate, gently set fillet alongside the tomatoes, then top with fingerling potato chips. Sprinkle feta cheese on and around the tomatoes, then drizzle with balsamic glaze and basil oil.

Dungeness Crab BLT
Cooking Guide to How to Build a Dungeness Crab BLT, Seatown Seabar-Style

Says Chef Tom Douglas: Dungeness crabs and crab cakes are featured at several of our Seattle restaurants. In particular, our little joint Seatown, in the Pike Place Market, is a prime place for grabbing a Dungeness crab cocktail, a whole steamed, chilled, and cracked Dungeness crab with drawn butter and mayo, or instead of the Dungy, some clusters of snow crab legs, or a couple of impressively large and spidery Alaskan king crab legs. But the best-selling crab dish of all at Seatown is the humble-sounding Dungeness Crab BLT.

To make a Dungeness Crab BLT, mix a few ounces of fresh Dungeness crabmeat with a few tablespoons of sriracha-spiced mayo. Toast the cut sides of a split baguette and fill it with the crab mixture, 3 slices of crisply cooked, thick-sliced bacon (preferably our favorite bacon, Bavarian Meats), 3 slices of green tomatoes that have been pickled in rice wine vinegar, sugar, and spices, and a leaf of romaine. We think you'll agree this makes the best damn BLT you ever tasted.

When we need picked crabmeat for a BLT or to make a crab cocktail or crab cakes, we most often use the region's local Dungeness, which is flavorful and sweet. But the most important thing when sourcing crab is to use what's available in your area, as fresh as possible.

Dungeness crabmeat tends to be wet. Drain your crabmeat in a sieve and, if it's wet, gently squeeze the crabmeat with your hands to remove excess liquid. Then again, you don't want your crabmeat to be stringy and dry, so don't get too energetic squeezing out all the flavor. While you're gently squeezing, you can feel around for any bits of cartilage or shell and remove them.

When you're mixing crabmeat with the spicy mayo—if you're making a BLT for example—mix gently so you don't smash up the precious lump meat. Also, Dungeness tends to be salty, so don't add additional salt until after you taste.

Grilled Washington Sardines with Wild Watercress Salad
Recipes Courtesy of Anchovies & Olives

(SERVES 4)

Fresh sardines are meaty and delicious, packed with virtuous, heart-healthy fats. Substitute tame supermarket watercress if you don't have access to the wild stuff.

> 8 sardines (or as many sardines as you can eat—I would recommend two
>   per person)
> ¼ cup extra-virgin olive oil, half for dressing the watercress and half for
>   brushing the sardines before you grill them
> Salt and pepper
> 4 handfuls of fresh, wild watercress
> 2 lemons, one for dressing the watercress and one for squeezing over
>   the grilled sardines

Preheat the grill on high. Brush the sardines with half the oil and season with salt and pepper.

Place the sardines on the hot grill and cook 3–4 minutes per side, or until the flesh pulls away from the bones easily and the skin is very crispy and golden brown. Divide the sardines among four dinner plates.

Toss the watercress with remaining olive oil and the juice from one lemon, and season to taste with salt and pepper. Divide the salad among the four plates.

Squeeze the other lemon over the hot sardines and serve right away. Enjoy with a warm, crusty baguette with butter and a nice glass of wine.

Norma's Oyster Stew
Recipe Courtesy of Norma's Seafood & Steak

(SERVES 1)

What makes this stew a real treat is that each bowl is prepared fresh to order, says Norma's owner and Seaside local Randy Frank. The key: Do not cook the oysters through before adding the half-and-half. "We're introducing the half-and-half in there so they cook in that milk and it seeps in there. Then, they're a little more tender. They're not chewy." Serve with fresh baked bread or garlic toast and you've got yourself a fine meal.

> 5 ounces fresh Willapa Bay oysters (or your region's best oysters)
> 1 tablespoon butter
> ½ teaspoon seasoning salt (like McCormick's)
> 4 dashes Worcestershire sauce
> 10–12 ounces half-and-half, to taste
> 1 dash Tabasco sauce
> Paprika for garnish

In a pot, heat oysters with a tablespoon of real butter over medium heat. Add seasoning salt and Worcestershire sauce. As the oysters warm (but before they're fully cooked), add desired amount of half-and-half and continue heating the pot until the mixture is steaming, but not boiling. Add Tabasco and combine. Ladle into a big bowl and garnish with paprika.

PHOTO COURTESY OF NORMA'S SEAFOOD & STEAK

Main Dish Recipes

Albacore Tuna Mignon
Recipe Courtesy of Local Ocean Seafoods

(SERVES 4)

First-timers—and regulars—at Local Ocean marvel at the flavor of this trademark dish. Bacon-wrapped albacore is grilled medium-rare and served atop a bed of pan-seared vegetables with frizzled onions. A fresh, decadent delight. Chef Charlie Branford breaks it down for us. There are a lot of steps, but it's worth it!

4 strips of the best bacon you can purchase
4 (6–7-ounce) portions of albacore tuna loin
1 tablespoon ground black pepper, plus extra for seasoning
2 teaspoons kosher salt, plus extra for seasoning
4 skewers

2 cups flour
Oil for frying and sautéing
2 yellow onions, shaved $\frac{1}{16}$–$\frac{1}{32}$-inch thick on a mandoline
2 cloves garlic, finely chopped
1 medium shallot, finely chopped
2 green onions, trimmed and cut into $\frac{3}{4}$-inch lengths on the diagonal
2 medium carrots, scrubbed and sliced $\frac{1}{4}$-inch thick on the diagonal
2 medium zucchini, sliced $\frac{1}{4}$-inch thick on the diagonal
1 large or 2 small red bell pepper(s), stemmed, quartered, seeded, and cut into $\frac{1}{2}$-inch chunks
1 bulb fennel, trimmed of discolored bits, quartered, cored, and sliced $\frac{1}{4}$-inch thick on the diagonal
8 ounces white or cremini mushrooms, woody ends trimmed, brushed clean, and quartered
1 cup vegetable stock, homemade is preferred.
Tomato Saffron Sauce (see recipe)

Heat the oven to 425°F.

Lay out the bacon on a lined sheet pan and cook in the oven for 14 minutes. Pull out, reserve the fat for some other dish, cool the bacon to room temp.

Season the tuna with salt and pepper and wrap with a slice of bacon. Use the skewer to keep the bacon on.

Light up the barbecue, or get a sauté pan heating up.

Mix the salt and pepper into the flour.

Heat the oil in a sauce pan to 350°F.

Toss the shaved onions in the seasoned flour. Squeeze a little bit to coat well. Shake off excess flour with a sieve. Cook in small batches until golden brown. Reserve in a paper towel–lined bowl.

Heat a sauté pan to medium-high, and add oil before the pan gets hot.

Add the garlic, shallots, and green onions and sweat them. Add the vegetable medley (carrots, zucchini, peppers, fennel, mushrooms) before the garlic starts to brown.

Cook the vegetables until they come back up to a sizzle, and deglaze with some of the vegetable stock.

Cook the liquid down to almost dry. Keep hot while you finish the tuna.

Cooking the tuna: I often see instructions that tell you to cook tuna for said amount of time for said amount of weight. I don't like this because every fish is different—what might work for a 25-pound albacore might not work for a 10-pound albacore (because of different amounts of fat). Not every heat source is going to be the same, whether it is a charcoal fire, gas grill, or kitchen stove. I think you should watch, and touch it to get to know the tuna while cooking it. I think the best way to cook tuna is either on a flat, hot surface or a grated grill, like a backyard barbecue. When cooking the tuna you will see on the side of the fish that the meat will start to turn a white color. I like to watch it as the white color progresses up the side. If I have a piece of loin that is 3 inches in diameter, I like to let the white go up ¼ inch and turn it over toward me so I can watch the next side. With the last (third) side, you will be running blind but by the time you have cooked the first two sides you should have an idea of how long it should take. You can always cook it longer, but once it's overcooked, you can't cook the tuna less.

Putting it all together: If the vegetables look dry, add more of the vegetable stock. Divide the vegetables between four plates, top each plate with some of the "frizzled" onions, place your tuna squarely on top of the onions. Spoon some of the tomato saffron sauce on top of the tuna. Garnish with some fennel fronds. Enjoy.

Tomato Saffron Sauce

    1 (19-ounce) can whole tomatoes (the best you can buy)
    1 (19-ounce) can whole tomatillos
    1 pinch saffron
    1 tablespoon Hungarian sweet paprika
    1 tablespoon lemon herb seasoning

Open the cans of tomatoes and tomatillos and drain the liquid from the tomatillos into a saucepan.

Add the saffron to the tomatillo juice and bring to a boil. Remove from heat and let steep in the hot liquid for about 5 minutes.

Add all ingredients to a large enough container to be able to blend with a burr blender (or immersion blender). Chunky is okay, it doesn't need to be silky smooth.

Anthony's Barbecued Oysters with Citrus Garlic Chive Butter

Recipe Courtesy of Anthony's Homeport

(SERVES 2 TO 4 AS AN APPETIZER)

It's hard to beat the marvelous flavor of a plump Pacific oyster warm from the grill, its shell dripping butter, a gift ready to be tipped back and chased with your favorite adult beverage. Pick up a dozen the next time you're hosting a cookout. Or visit your local Anthony's and let them do the grilling.

    1 dozen Pacific oysters in the shell, preferably beach grown, rinsed in
       cold water, shell cleaned
    ¼ pound Citrus Garlic Chive Butter (see recipe)
    1 pound rock salt

Heat barbecue to 450°F–500°F, covered temperature (if using charcoal, have a 1- to 2-inch charcoal base).

Place clean oysters on barbecue grill (cover optional) and cook 3–5 minutes, until oysters spit, pop, or show signs of oyster liquor boiling inside—watch for it bubbling outside the edge of the shell.

Remove oyster from barbecue and let cool for a few seconds then pop open top shell.

Top oyster with 1 teaspoon seasoned butter and place oyster back on barbecue to melt butter or finish cooking if necessary.

Citrus Garlic Chive Butter
  ½ pound salted butter, softened to room temperature
  1 lemon, zested, then squeezed for juice
  ¼ cup chives, freshly chopped
  2 tablespoons minced garlic
  2–3 drops Tabasco
  1 sheet parchment paper

Whip butter until soft and add zest of one lemon. Stir in chives, garlic, lemon juice, and Tabasco, then spread butter on parchment paper. Roll into smooth log, removing all parchment creases.

Refrigerate (up to 3–4 days) or freeze (up to 30 days) until needed.

Arctic Char with Salsify, Crosnes & Rutabaga with Lemon Butter
Recipe Courtesy of Araxi Restaurant & Bar

(SERVES 4)

This dish is a perennial favorite at Araxi.

1 cup crosnes
1 tablespoon baking soda
4 cups duck fat
1 bay leaf
1 rutabaga, peeled and cut into ¼-inch slices
4 salsify roots

Bring a medium pot of water to a boil on high heat and add a generous pinch of salt. Add the crosnes, followed immediately by the baking soda (it will foam a bit then subside) and cook for 6 minutes. Drain in a colander, then place the colander under cold running water and rub the crosnes around the colander to loosen the skins. Peel off and discard the skins, then transfer the crosnes to a large bowl and refrigerate until chilled, about 30 minutes.

Melt the duck fat in a medium saucepan on low heat, then add the bay leaf and the rutabaga. Peel the salsify roots and add them to the pot. Increase the heat until small bubbles begin to form in the fat, then reduce the heat to low. Cover the vegetables with parchment paper and cook gently for 20 minutes. Using a slotted spoon, transfer the salsify to a small bowl and cook the rutabaga for a further 15 minutes. Transfer the rutabaga to the bowl of salsify. (The duck fat can be saved for 7 days in the fridge or frozen up to 1 month and used to confit other vegetables or duck.)

Arctic Char
4 (5-ounce) fillets Arctic char, skin on but bones removed
2 cloves garlic, thinly sliced
3 sprigs fresh thyme, leaves only
2 tablespoons grapeseed oil
1 tablespoon unsalted butter
⅛ cup lemon butter, melted (see recipe below)

Arrange the fillets, flesh side down, on a cutting board. Using a sharp knife, make five or six incisions, each 1-inch long, about a quarter of the way into the fish. Press a quarter of the garlic and a quarter of the thyme leaves into the incisions on each fillet.

Heat the grapeseed oil and the unsalted butter in a large saucepan on medium heat. Season the char with salt and pepper, then place the fish skin-side down in the pan and cook for 5–6 minutes, or until the skin is golden brown and crispy. Remove the pan from the heat, turn the fillets over, and allow the char to rest in the pan for 2–3 minutes. Transfer the fish to a plate and keep warm.

To serve: Place the rutabaga and salsify in a sauté pan on medium heat and allow them to caramelize in their own juices, about 5 minutes. Turn the vegetables over and add the crosnes. Heat for 3 minutes, or until the crosnes are warmed through. Divide the vegetables among four plates, top each serving with a fillet of Arctic char, then drizzle with the melted lemon butter. Serve immediately.

Lemon Butter

YIELDS 1 CUP
  1 cup unsalted butter at room temperature
  Juice of 2 lemons
  Zest of 1 lemon
  1 small hot red chili pepper, minced
  1 tablespoon chopped fresh parsley
  1 teaspoon chopped fresh cilantro
  Kosher salt

Cut an 11 x 18-inch sheet of parchment paper. Place all of the ingredients in a large bowl, add a pinch of kosher salt, and mix well to combine. Position the butter in the middle of the parchment paper and shape it into a log. Fold the bottom of the parchment paper over the butter, tuck in the sides of the paper like an envelope, then roll the paper away from you, encasing the butter in the parchment paper. Will keep refrigerated for up to 5 days or frozen for up to 2 weeks.

Basic Hawaiian Tuna Poke
Recipe Courtesy of Olympia Seafood Company

(SERVES 2 FOR DINNER, 6 FOR APPETIZERS OR AS A SIDE DISH)

Says Kira, "So yes, this traditional tuna dish is not cooked, but if you are a sushi fan or an adventurous eater, there is nothing better. The flavors and textures of basic poke [pronounced poe-kay] are simply superb and guaranteed to get you out of a winter funk faster than you can say 'macadamia.'"

⅓ cup soy sauce
1 tablespoon sesame oil
1 teaspoon honey
2 green onions, chopped
2 tablespoons wakame seaweed, chopped (optional, see Kitchen Note)
8 macadamia nuts, chopped
1 tablespoon toasted sesame seeds
½ teaspoon red pepper flakes (optional)
1 pound ahi (yellowfin tuna) or tombo (tropical albacore),
    cut into 1-inch cubes

In a large bowl, combine the soy sauce, sesame oil, honey, green onions, seaweed, nuts, sesame seeds, and red pepper flakes.

Stir to combine, then fold in the chopped tuna.

Let it sit in the refrigerator for about half an hour (if you can stand it) for the flavors to combine.

Serve with tortilla chips or wrap in nori (dried seaweed) for an appetizer, or sticky rice and avocado slices for a meal.

Kitchen Note: Wakame seaweed is full of vitamins and minerals. Find it at Asian markets, in the Asian section of larger grocers, at your local food cooperative in the bulk bins, or online. To prepare, Kira suggests you simply place the dried wakame in a dish of water. "In about 5 minutes, it rehydrates into a whole lot more seaweed than you thought you had! If you have kids in the vicinity, have them do this step—it's bordering on magical."

Black Cod or Salmon Kasuzuke
Recipe Courtesy of Uwajimaya

(SERVES 4)

It seems everyone in Seattle has their own version of this luscious dish, and for good reason: Its deep, nuanced flavor will convince anyone who tastes it that you're a seafood savant. If you lack the four days of marination this recipe calls for, or, have last-minute guests, pick up pre-marinated kasuzuke black cod in the Uwajimaya fish department to take and bake. Boom! Dinner, done.

4 (6-ounce) slices of fish fillet, black cod, salmon, snapper,
  or Chilean sea bass

For the marinade
½ cup kasuzuke (sake kasu, a by-product of the sake-making process,
  available in the seafood department of Uwajimaya)
2 tablespoons sake (rice wine)
3 tablespoons mirin
¼ cup water
3 tablespoons brown sugar (optional)
2 tablespoons miso (optional)

Generously salt fish, place in plastic container, and refrigerate overnight.

Mix kasuzuke, sake, and mirin, adding water as needed to make a paste.

Coat the fish with marinade mixture, cover and refrigerate for 3 additional days (or may be frozen at this point).

Scrape off marinade and broil both sides until nicely browned (approximately 4–5 minutes each side).

Chef Xinh's Clams in Hoisin Sauce
Recipe Courtesy of Chef Xinh Dwelley, Xinh's Clam and Oyster House

(SERVES 4)

This recipe from Taylor's Chef Xinh Dwelly uses fresh Manila clams to create a simple preparation that abounds in complex flavors. Serve as an entree or as an accompaniment to other dishes.

¼ cup butter
1 clove garlic, minced
1 medium onion, sliced
1 tablespoon lemongrass, chopped
3 tablespoons cooking sherry
1–2 stalks celery, chopped
3 tablespoons hoisin sauce
Juice of ½ lemon
2 tablespoons sesame seed oil
4–5 pounds Manila clams
1 green onion, chopped, for garnish

In a pan with a fitted lid (large enough to hold 5 pounds of clams) melt butter and brown the garlic. Add onion, lemongrass, sherry, celery, hoisin sauce, lemon juice, and sesame oil. Sauté lightly.

Add washed clams to mixture, mix well and cover. Bring to a boil and cook until clams are open. Sprinkle green onions on top, cover and cook for 3–5 minutes. Serve and enjoy!

Dungeness Crab–Crusted Halibut with Tomato Shallot Fondue

Recipe Courtesy of Ivar's Mukilteo Landing

(SERVES 4)

4 (5-ounce) halibut fillets
½ cup flour
Dungeness Crab Crust (see recipe)
½ cup panko bread crumbs
½ cup grated Parmesan cheese
1 tablespoon minced fresh parsley
1 cup Tomato Shallot Fondue (see recipe)
4 cups of your favorite garlic mashed potatoes
¼ cup olive oil
12 ounces fresh spinach
2 ounces butter
1 ounce shallots, minced
Salt and pepper, to taste
Herb Oil (optional, see recipe)

Lightly season halibut fillets, and then dredge the top surface of each fillet in flour (skin-side down).

Pat out about 2 ounces of crab crust onto the surface of the halibut fillets, making sure to spread evenly and cover entire surface.

Combine the panko bread crumbs, Parmesan cheese, and parsley in a small bowl, season to taste, then sprinkle this mixture over the top of the crab-crusted halibut fillets in an even layer. Pat down and set aside for 10 minutes to set up.

At this time make sure that everything else is prepared and ready to go: mashed potatoes hot, tomato fondue prepared and at room temperature, and herb oil at the ready (if using).

Preheat oven to 350°F. Heat a large ovenproof nonstick pan over medium heat and add olive oil to the pan.

When the oil just starts to smoke, carefully add the prepared halibut fillets with the crust side down. Cook for about 5 minutes or until a nice golden crust has formed.

Carefully turn fillets over and put pan in the oven for about 8 minutes or until halibut is just cooked through. While the halibut is in the oven, prepare the sautéed spinach in a nonstick pan: Melt the butter, then add the shallots, followed by the spinach. Season to taste and cook until spinach is wilted. Keep warm.

Remove halibut from pan and set on paper towels to drain.

For final plating, place about 6 ounces of mashed potatoes in a scoop shape in a large bowl or on a plate. Top carefully with 2 ounces of sautéed spinach, then top with a prepared halibut fillet. Push the halibut down a bit to secure it. Spoon the tomato shallot fondue around the plate and garnish with the herb oil. Serve immediately.

Dungeness Crab Crust
  1 tablespoon olive oil
  ¼ cup finely diced yellow onion
  ¼ cup finely diced red bell pepper
  ¼ cup finely chopped artichoke hearts
  ½ pound Dungeness crabmeat, drained well
  1 tablespoon minced fresh basil and parsley
  1 tablespoon lemon juice
  1 medium egg, whipped
  ¼ cup panko bread crumbs
  Salt and pepper, to taste

Note: This can be done the day before.

Lightly sauté the onion, peppers, and artichokes in the olive oil and cool.

Combine all ingredients in a mixing bowl, mix well, and cool for at least half an hour before using.

Tomato Shallot Fondue

Notes: This sauce can be made a day ahead; just make sure to serve at room temperature. The better the tomatoes, the better the sauce.

 1 cup finely sliced shallots
 ¼ cup extra-virgin olive oil
 1 cup seeded, julienned Roma tomatoes
 1 cup white wine
 1 teaspoon fresh minced thyme
 2 tablespoons unsalted butter
 Salt and pepper, to taste

Combine shallots and oil in a heavy-bottom pan, and simmer on low until shallots are caramelized. They should be a rich, light brown—don't burn them.

Add tomatoes and wine and simmer until wine is reduced and sauce has thickened.

Add thyme and butter, then season.

Stir slowly over low heat until butter has melted.

Herb Oil

 ½ cup chopped fresh basil, no stems
 ½ cup extra-virgin olive oil
 Salt and pepper, to taste

Combine ingredients in blender and puree. Serve immediately for best color.

Geoduck Crudo with Fennel & Radish
Recipes Courtesy of Anchovies & Olives

(SERVES 4)

This dish has become one of the restaurant's signatures. (Kitchen note: For those times you can't harvest your own, request geoduck from your local fishmonger. Or order online from Washington's Taylor Shellfish Farms or Marx Foods.) Unsure how to handle a clam that size? Seattle chef and *Good Fish* cookbook author Becky Selengut shows you how: search youtube.com for "how to clean a geoduck."

> 1 prepped geoduck siphon, halved lengthwise and sliced paper-thin
> Juice of 2 limes
> 4 Easter egg radishes, shaved with a mandoline
> 3 baby fennel, shaved with a mandoline
> 1 jalapeño chile, seeded and minced
> ¼ cup extra-virgin olive oil
> Kosher salt and freshly cracked black pepper

Combine the geoduck, lime juice, radishes, fennel, chile, and olive oil in a large bowl and toss gently.

Season to taste with salt and pepper.

Divide among four plates and drizzle the remaining juice over each portion.

Grilled Coho Salmon with Fennel Leek Jam, Candied Beets & Red Chard
Recipe Courtesy of Ivar's Mukilteo Landing

(SERVES 4)

Another best-seller from Ivar's Mukilteo Landing Executive Chef Steve Anderson.

> 2 pounds coho salmon, cut into four 7- to 8-ounce fillets
> Salt and pepper to taste
> 1½ pounds Roasted Fingerling Potatoes (see recipe)
> 8 ounces Red Swiss Chard Sauté (see recipe)
> ¾ cup Three Citrus Vinaigrette (see recipe)
> 1 cup Fennel Leek Jam (see recipe)
> 8 slices Candied Beets (see recipe)

Prepare all side dishes and sauce recipes ahead of time. Most can be done a day or two ahead.

Then get your barbecue grill hot. Ensure it's very clean or the salmon will stick. You may use either a gas, charcoal, or wood-fired grill, but wood will give the best flavor. Alternatively, fish may be cooked in a sauté pan with a little olive oil.

The salmon will cook quickly so preheat the fingerling potatoes in a 350°F oven and have the red chard ready to sauté.

Lightly season salmon fillets with salt and pepper and start grilling. As soon as you put the salmon on the grill, start sautéing the red chard. Fish should take no more than 4–5 minutes per side depending on thickness of the fish and temperature of your grill.

PHOTO COURTESY OF IVAR'S RESTAURANT

Once the salmon is done cooking, remove it from grill and begin plating.

The plate is set up with potatoes first and then sautéed red chard piled on the potatoes. Then spoon a little citrus vinaigrette on plate in front of the potatoes and top with the fish. Place a little dollop of the fennel leek jam on top of the fish. Garnish with a couple of slices of candied beets. Serve immediately.

Roasted Fingerling Potatoes
    1 pound fingerling potatoes, cut in half
    ¼ cup olive oil
    2 tablespoons shallots, minced
    1½ tablespoons garlic, minced
    1 tablespoon fresh thyme, chopped
    Salt and pepper to taste

Par cook potatoes in steamer and cool. Toss potatoes with remaining ingredients and roast in 350°F oven until golden brown. Serve immediately or hold in warm oven until needed.

Red Swiss Chard Sauté

2 teaspoons butter
1 teaspoon shallots, minced
2 ounces red swiss chard, cleaned and chopped
1 ounce white wine
Kosher salt and pepper to taste

Heat butter in pan and add minced shallots and sauté for 1 minute then add swiss chard. Add white wine and continue to sauté for 2 minutes then add salt and pepper to season upon completion. Entire process should take just under 5 minutes.

Three Citrus Vinaigrette

(MAKES ABOUT 1 PINT)
1 tablespoon lime juice
1 tablespoon lemon juice
2 tablespoons orange juice
2 tablespoons honey
2 tablespoons Dijon mustard
1 tablespoon shallots
1½ cups extra-virgin olive oil
Salt and pepper to taste

Combine all ingredients except the oil in a food processor or blender. With motor running, add oil slowly to emulsify. Taste and adjust seasoning if needed.

Fennel Leek Jam

(MAKES 2 CUPS)
The leftovers of the fennel leek jam can be used as an accompaniment to any fish or chicken dish. It can easily be frozen and used again as needed.

2 tablespoons olive oil blend
½ cup yellow onion, ¼-inch dice
¾ cup fennel bulb, ¼-inch dice
¾ cup leeks, tender part only, about 4 inches, chopped
1 tablespoon garlic, minced
¼ cup anise-flavored liqueur
1 tablespoon white wine vinegar

1 tablespoon brown sugar
2 tablespoons water
Kosher salt to taste
Black pepper to taste

Heat oil in heavy-bottom pot and add onion, fennel, and leeks. Saute until beginning to soften, don't brown. Add remaining ingredients and simmer on low for 45 minutes until vegetables are very soft. Puree mixture with a stick blender or in a food processor, then return to pan. Continue to cook until thickened like a jam, but don't over-reduce—it will thicken more as it cools. Adjust seasoning and cool before serving.

Candied Beets

2 quarts Candied Vegetable Syrup (see recipe)
2 each red beets
2 each yellow beets

Peel beets and cook them in a steamer until just cooked through. Let them cool completely. Slice the beets on a mandoline or cut into desired shapes, not too thick. Heat syrup in heavy bottom pot, add beets, and simmer on low for 1 hour until translucent. Strain off the syrup and reserve for later use. Lay beets out on a roasting rack with a sheet pan underneath. The beets must not be touching each other. Place rack into a preheated 180°F oven. Let beets dry 2 to 4 hours. (The time will vary depending on thickness of the beets.) When done the beets should be dry to the touch, not sticky but not brittle either.

Candied Vegetable Syrup

MAKES 1¼ GALLONS)

1 gallon water
8 cups sugar
3 each bay leafs
¼ ounce fresh thyme sprigs
¼ cup shallots, chopped
1 tablespoon black peppercorns
2 tablespoons lemon juice
2 tablespoons kosher salt

Combine all ingredients in heavy bottom pot and simmer for 30 minutes. Cool and reserve for later use.

Grilled Copper River King Salmon
Recipe Courtesy of Elliott's Oyster House

(SERVES 4)

 4 (6–8 ounce) fillets king salmon
 ¼ cup canola oil
 Kosher salt and pepper to taste
 2 ounces Pomegranate Butter (see recipe)
 1 bundle roasted Walla Walla asparagus
  (or your favorite local asparagus)
 1 cup Arugula Pesto (see recipe)
 12 ounces Roasted Potato and Sweet Onion (see recipe)
 1½ ounces pomegranate molasses
 ¼ cup pomegranate fruit arils (seeds)

Preheat grill and brush the grate, or set oven on low broil.

Brush salmon with a thin coat of canola oil and season with salt and pepper. For fish being grilled, place fish on the grill, skin side up; grill mark, turning fish 40 degrees after 2 minutes and then cook for another 2 minutes. Turn the fish over and repeat cooking an additional 4 minutes. For fish being broiled, cook to 120°F or until the flesh begins to turn opaque and starts to firm up. Total cooking time will be 7–10 minutes depending on the thickness of salmon used.

Remove; baste liberally with pomegranate butter and plate for service.

While the salmon is cooking, toss or rub the asparagus with a little of the oil and season liberally with salt and pepper. Then grill, turning frequently.

To plate, use a pastry or basting brush to spread pesto across the center of a plate from one end to the other. Place the asparagus diagonally across the pesto with the potatoes on top. Place the fish leaning over the potatoes, then drizzle some pomegranate molasses around the outside of the plate and sprinkle with pomegranate seeds.

Pomegranate Butter

(MAKES APPROXIMATELY ¼ POUND)

 ¼ pound butter
 3 tablespoons pomegranate molasses (available at many stores
  that supply Middle Eastern foods)
 1 tablespoon chives

¾ teaspoon kosher salt
⅛ teaspoon white pepper

Combine all ingredients and beat until well incorporated.

Arugula Pesto
(MAKES APPROXIMATELY 1¾ CUPS)
    4 cups baby arugula
    2 teaspoons peeled and chopped garlic
    3 tablespoons orange juice
    2 tablespoons lemon juice
    ¾ cup extra-virgin olive oil
    ½ cup toasted Oregon hazelnuts
    1 teaspoon kosher salt
    Ground white pepper to taste

Prepare an ice-water bath in a large bowl and bring a large pot of water
to a boil.

Put the arugula into a sieve, plunge into the boiling water, and stir for 15
seconds. Plunge sieve into the ice bath and stir until the arugula is cold.
Drain well and squeeze out excess water.

Chop the arugula well and place into a blender with the remaining
ingredients. Blend for at least 30 seconds but not until the pesto is warm, as
this will cause it to discolor.

Roasted Potato & Sweet Onion
(MAKES APPROXIMATELY 3 CUPS)
    3 tablespoons butter or oil, as you wish
    2 cups russet potato, diced small
    1 cup sweet or cipollini onion, diced small
    1 teaspoon kosher salt
    Ground white pepper to taste

Melt the butter in a pan and toss with remaining ingredients, then empty
pan onto baking sheet.

Cook in a 375°F oven. Turn the potatoes with a spatula after 6–7 minutes, and
continue cooking until the potatoes are tender and browned and onions are
caramelized.

Neah Bay Yelloweye Rockfish—Thai Style 5 Spice
Recipe Courtesy of RockCreek Seafood & Spirits

(SERVES 2)

    1 pound rockfish fillets, cleaned of sinew and sliced into
    ¾-inch paillards or rounds
    Kosher salt
    Ground black pepper
    Seasoned Wondra or Rice Flour (see recipe)
    3 tablespoons olive oil, divided
    2 tablespoons fresh ginger, peeled and diced
    1 cup oven-roasted cipollini onions
    1 cup shiitake mushrooms, halved and sautéed ahead of time
    2 cups Mushroom Stock (see recipe)
    2 tablespoons Thai 5-Spice Sauce (see recipe)
    1 tablespoon lemon juice
    Garnish of scallions thinly sliced lengthwise and cilantro sprigs

Season rockfish paillards or rounds with salt and pepper.

Dredge the fish in the seasoned flour.

In a stainless steel pan, on medium to high heat, add 2 tablespoons olive oil and bring to a smoke point.

Add rockfish to saute pan and roast on both sides until well caramelized.

Place the fish in a preheated oven set to 350°F to continue cooking while making the sauce.

Fish Braise

In a stainless steel pan, on medium to high heat, add 1 tablespoon olive oil.

Add ginger, cipollini onions, and shitake mushrooms. Saute the mixture for 30 seconds.

Add mushroom stock to the pan. Bring to a boil.

Add Thai 5-Spice Sauce, lemon juice. Season with salt and pepper.

Remove rockfish from oven and add to boiling stock. Cover and allow to slowly braise in stock for another 2–3 minutes on low heat.

Taste the stock to make sure there is enough Thai 5-Spice. Add more to your liking.

On a large platter, place the rockfish first and then follow with the remaining ingredients. Garnish with the long cut scallions and cilantro sprigs.

Mushroom Stock

   2 cups mushroom ends and pieces
   ½ cup fresh ginger
   1 quart light chicken stock

In a stainless steel pan, on medium to high heat, sauté mushroom ends. Add ginger and chicken stock to the mushrooms, bring to a slow simmer. Cover the pan and keep the stock at a slow simmer for 30 minutes.

5 Spice Sauce—Thai Style

   1 cup palm sugar or sugar in the raw
   2 tablespoons 5 spice powder
   ½ cup Madeira
   ½ cup white wine
   ½ cup Thai fish sauce
   ½ cup lime juice
   ½ cup water
   ¼ cup tamarind paste

In a stainless steel pot over medium heat, caramelize palm sugar, stirring frequently to prevent burning and keep it smooth.

As sugar starts to brown, add 5 spice powder, Madeira, white wine, fish sauce, lime juice, water, and tamarind paste.

Bring to a boil and stir until tamarind paste is dissolved.

Turn off the heat and let the mixture steep for 30 minutes.

Strain the mixture though a fine-mesh sieve or chinoise and put to the side.

Seasoned Wondra or Rice Flour

   1 cup Wondra or rice flour
   2 tablespoons kosher salt
   1 tablespoon ground white pepper
   1 teaspoon cayenne pepper

In a medium-size bowl, mix all of the ingredients together.

Pacific Fried Razor Clams
Recipe Courtesy of The Depot Restaurant
(SERVES 2)

Chef Lalewicz prefers his razor clams kept simple; the better to enjoy their sweet, meaty flavor, fresh from the beach, which is just a short walk from his restaurant. Locals like to coat their clams with finely crushed crackers. His favorite is Ritz, for a more buttery, salty finish.

    4 medium to large cleaned, fresh razor clams
    Seasoned Flour (see recipe)
    2 beaten eggs
    1 tablespoon water
    2 cups crushed panko bread crumbs
    4 tablespoons butter
    1 lemon, cut into wedges

Dredge razor clams in seasoned flour, then in egg wash, then in panko crumbs.

Add butter to a medium, heated frying pan. Add clams and fry for 2–3 minutes per side, or until golden brown.

Serve with fresh lemon wedges.

Seasoned Flour
    1 cup all-purpose flour
    1 teaspoon sea salt
    ¼ teaspoon cayenne pepper
    1 teaspoon sweet paprika

Combine all ingredients and mix until well incorporated.

Parmesan-Crusted Lingcod
Recipe Courtesy of Olympia Seafood Company

(SERVES 2)

Says Kira, "This quick and easy recipe translates to just about any white fish, but is especially nice with lingcod! Should you have any leftovers, they make excellent fish cakes. Flake up the cooked fish and combine with an equal amount of shredded cooked potato, some garlic and onion or herbs you like, and a bit of heavy cream. Roll the cakes in panko and fry quickly to brown and warm. Voilà!"

¼ cup crushed cornflakes
¼ cup shredded Parmesan
2 green onions, chopped
1 lemon (zest for the topping, then sliced for garnish)
Salt and black pepper
1 egg
1 pound lingcod, cut into 3–4 pieces

Mix the cornflakes, cheese, onion, lemon zest, salt and pepper and spread on a plate.

Beat the egg with a fork in a bowl. Dip cod pieces in the egg, then roll in the topping mixture, pressing firmly to get the fish coated.

Place on a baking sheet (we like to cover our sheet with foil and spray lightly with nonstick cooking spray for easy peasy cleanup). Bake at 400°F for about 12 minutes, or until fish flakes easily with a fork.

Serve with lemon wedges and tartar or remoulade sauce.

Petrale Sole Piccata with Tomato Concassé
Recipe Courtesy of The Depot Restaurant

(SERVES 2)

Delicate petrale sole is at its best with the briny, bright flavors of capers, lemon, and tomatoes. Chef Lalewicz recommends you enjoy your sole with rosemary mashed potatoes, pan-seared green beans, and a nice glass of Washington State Maryhill Pinot Gris.

2 tablespoons butter
1 tablespoon extra-virgin olive oil
2 large petrale sole fillets
1 cup all-purpose seasoned flour (see Pacific Fried Razor Clams for
   ingredients)
1 tablespoon chopped fresh garlic
Salt
Dash of black pepper
2 tablespoons crisp white wine (such as Pinot Gris)
1 tablespoon capers
1 tablespoon lemon juice
1 tablespoon Italian parsley
½ cup diced tomatoes
¼ cup fish stock

In a nonstick skillet, heat 1 tablespoon butter and extra-virgin olive oil on medium high heat.

Dredge sole fillets in flour on both sides and place in hot pan. Fry on one side for 1½ minutes, or until crust is formed. Turn over.

Add garlic, salt, pepper, wine, capers, lemon juice, and parsley. Cook until liquid is reduced and garlic is fully cooked.

Add tomatoes and fish stock, plus 1 tablespoon butter. Simmer until butter is melted.

Move fillets from pan to serving platter, and pour sauce over fish.

Ray's Boathouse Black Cod in Sake Kasu
Recipe Courtesy of Ray's Boathouse, Cafe & Catering

(SERVES 4)

This recipe is a classic at Ray's (and well worth the two days of marinating time!). Sake kasu is the lees, or residual yeast, from brewing sake, Japanese fermented grain alcohol. Used as a cooking paste, the kasu lends flavor to pickles, soups, and fish. You can usually find it near the okara (tofu lees) in a Japanese or Asian market.

2 (2½ pound) skin-on black cod fillets, cut into 4 serving pieces
⅓ cup kosher salt, more if needed
6 ounces (¾ cup) sake kasu paste
⅓ cup sugar
¾ cup water

Place black cod fillets skin-side down in a shallow glass baking dish. Sprinkle a generous layer of salt over the fish, cover, and refrigerate for 24 hours.

Rinse the salt from the fish and pat dry. Place fish skin-side down in a clean dish.

Using an electric mixer, beat the kasu paste and sugar until smooth. Slowly add water and mix until incorporated.

Pour the kasu mixture evenly over the fish, cover, and refrigerate for another 24 hours.

Prepare a charcoal or gas grill. When the grill is very hot, remove the black cod from the marinade, allowing the excess to drip off.

Grill fish until nicely browned and just cooked through, about 5 minutes per side.

Transfer to individual plates. Serve with steamed jasmine rice and grilled baby bok choy.

Sablefish Caramelized with Soy & Sake

Recipe Courtesy of Blue Water Cafe + Raw Bar (Yaletown)

(SERVES 4)

This recipe from Executive Chef Frank Pabst is among Blue Water Cafe's many treasures. Says Pabst: "Tamarind is a tart fruit that is used in chutneys and pickles, and is often ground to obtain a paste. It is available in many Asian food stores. This recipe also calls for mirin, a sweet cooking wine. Find it at an Asian supermarket."

Soy-Sake Marinade
½ cup sake
½ cup water
½ cup soy sauce
1 tablespoon brown sugar
1 tablespoon mirin

Orange-Tamarind Sauce
3 tablespoons olive oil
1 small carrot, sliced
1 rib celery, sliced (stock)
½ onion, sliced
3 garlic cloves, sliced
¼ jalapeño pepper, sliced
1-inch piece of ginger, sliced
1 teaspoon mustard seeds
1 teaspoon black peppercorns
1 sprig of thyme
1 bay leaf
¼ cup balsamic vinegar
¼ cup concentrated orange juice
2 tablespoons tamarind paste
4 cups chicken stock
8 kumquats, sliced and seeded
Zest of ¼ orange, julienned for
  garnish

Caramelized Sablefish
4 (6-ounce) sablefish fillets,
  skin on
1½ cups soy-sake marinade
10 ounces green beans
2 tablespoons unsalted butter
2 cups canola oil, for deep-frying
4 tablespoons flour
Pinch of cayenne pepper
4 shallots, thinly sliced on a
  mandoline

To make the Soy-Sake Marinade: In a small saucepan, bring all ingredients to a boil on high heat. Reduce the heat to medium-high and simmer until sugar is dissolved and alcohol has evaporated, about 2 minutes.

Remove from the heat, allow the mixture to cool, then refrigerate until well chilled.

To make the Orange-Tamarind Sauce: In a large saucepan, heat olive oil on medium heat. Add carrot, celery, onion, garlic, jalapeño, and ginger and sweat for 5–10 minutes until fragrant.

Add mustard seeds, peppercorns, thyme, bay leaf, vinegar, orange juice, tamarind paste, and chicken stock and cook until liquid has reduced by two-thirds, 20–30 minutes.

Strain the sauce through a fine-mesh sieve into a clean bowl, then season with salt and pepper. Add kumquats. Will keep refrigerated in an airtight container for up to 7 days.

To make the Caramelized Sablefish: Combine sablefish and soy-sake marinade in a resealable plastic zip-top bag and refrigerate overnight.

Heat a medium pot of salted water to a boil. Add beans and blanch for 2–3 minutes. Transfer the beans to a bowl and toss in butter. Season with salt and pepper.

Heat canola oil in a deep fryer or a deep pot to 300°F.

Mix flour and cayenne in a bowl. Toss shallot slices in this seasoned flour to dredge, then fry them in the oil until golden and crisp, about 30 seconds.

Remove the shallot slices from the oil and allow to drain on paper towels.

Remove the sablefish fillets from the refrigerator and allow them to warm to room temperature.

Turn the broiler on. Transfer the sablefish, skin-side down, to a cast iron pan and place it on the lowest rack under the broiler for 5–10 minutes until deeply caramelized. (The cooking time will depend upon the thickness of the fillets.)

To serve: Arrange a quarter of the green beans in the center of each of four plates. Using a metal spatula, lift each fillet from its skin and place the fish on the beans. Sprinkle each dish with a quarter of the fried shallots and finish with a quarter of the Orange Tamarind sauce and some orange zest.

Washington Chardonnay–Steamed Salmon

Recipe Courtesy of Seatown Seabar & Rotisserie

(SERVES 4)

Says Chef Tom Douglas: I love the way the aromatic steam created in this method of cooking subtly permeates the flesh of the fish. The rich flavor of a wild king or sockeye salmon makes it a perfect candidate for steaming, though you can steam any firm-fleshed fish.

PHOTO COURTESY OF TOM DOUGLAS RESTAURANTS;
PHOTO BY EVA MRAK-BLUMBERG

Steaming is a quick process, so be sure to keep an eye on your salmon, and don't let it overcook. If you're in the mood to pull one of your French cookbooks from the shelf, a classic beurre blanc, or butter sauce, made with the same Chardonnay you used for the steam, would be a good match. But a squeeze of lemon, a drizzle of good olive oil, and a sprinkle of sea salt may be the best to way to allow the flavor of the fish to shine through.

Chinese bamboo steamers work well and are not very expensive, but any steamer setup is fine here.

> 2 cups of your favorite Washington Chardonnay
> 2 cups water
> Zest of 1 lemon, removed in long strips with a vegetable peeler
> 8 sprigs fresh thyme
> 2 bay leaves
> 1½ pounds salmon fillet, preferably wild, cut into 4 portions

Place the Chardonnay, water, lemon peel, thyme, and bay leaves in the bottom of your steamer. Bring to a boil.

Lay the salmon fillets in the steamer basket and cover with the steamer lid. Steam until the salmon is just done, about 5–6 minutes.

Transfer the salmon portions to plates and serve.

Top Northwest Seafood Festivals

When you're surrounded by such abundance, there's always something delicious to celebrate or commemorate. Here are some regional gems.

Winter

The FisherPoets Gathering, Astoria, Oregon; coastradio.org; fisherpoets.org. There's no tale like a fish tale, especially from the lips of sea-weathered commercial fishermen and women who have seen it all. Each dark, wet February, old friends gather for a week to sing songs, tell stories, read poems, and play music.

Annual Blessing of the Fleet, Fishermen's Terminal, Seattle; ballardfirstlutheran.org. Every March at the start of halibut season, for generations, Ballard's First Lutheran Church holds its blessing of the fleet to pray for the safety of the hundreds of fishing crews who will make their way to Alaskan waters in search of halibut, crab, and many other denizens of the deep. Wish the fleet well and see Seattle's historic century-old halibut schooners, part of the nation's oldest continuously operating fishing fleet.

Newport Seafood & Wine Festival, Newport, Oregon; seafoodand wine.com. Since 1978, seafood fans, wine lovers, and chefs have gathered in this sparkling coastal city on Yaquina Bay to celebrate Oregon seafood, a wealth of divine regional wines, and the very best ways to enjoy them. Add art, crafts, photography, and pottery to the mix, and you've got yourself a party every February, with visitors from around the globe and often a waiting list for tickets.

Walrus & Carpenter Picnics, Shelton, Washington. What better way is there to spend a freezing winter evening than to wander tideflats beneath starry (or, more likely, drizzly) skies, shucking and slurping plump oysters plucked straight from their beds? The folks at Taylor Shellfish swear by it, and offer Champagne and seafood stew to thaw you out.

Spring

BC Spot Prawn Festival, Vancouver, British Columbia; chefstable society.com/spotprawnfestival. Kick off the start of spot prawn season in May with a spot prawn boil at the False Creek Fishermen's Wharf just west of Granville Island, hosted by the Chef's Table Society of British Columbia. Savor a plate of fresh-off-the-boat BC spot prawns while taking in cooking demos from Vancouver chefs. Then, put the recipes you learned to use; buy a bag of live, local, and sustainable spot prawns from the boat that pulls right up to the dock with the morning's catch. Doesn't get fresher than that!

Hood Canal ShrimpFest, Brinnon, Washington; facebook.com/ BrinnonShrimpfest. Since 1993, this north Hood Canal community has hosted the Hood Canal ShrimpFest each Memorial Day weekend, celebrating Hood Canal spot prawns and other local seafood with live music and family-friendly fun. Tides typically are low enough for easy harvest of clams and oysters on nearby public beaches at Dosewallips State Park.

Long Beach Razor Clam Festival, Long Beach, Washington; long beachrazorclamfestival.com. Here's your chance to wield a clam gun and take your limit: This pair of festivals celebrates the beloved bivalve with digging lessons, a big dig each evening as the tide goes out, a chowder taste-off, live entertainment, and a clam fritter cook-off by local

PHOTOS COURTESY OF LONG BEACH PENINSULA VISITORS BUREAU

culinary whizzes. There's even a contest for who digs the prettiest collection of clams. Truly something for everyone.

Penn Cove MusselFest, Coupeville, Whidbey Island, Washington; thepenncovemusselfest.com. The world-famous mussels are the star attraction at this longtime early-March event that features mussel-eating competitions, chowder tasting, tours of the Penn Cove Shellfish mussel farm by boat, beer and wine gardens, and activities for all ages along the historic Coupeville waterfront with a backdrop of chilly Puget Sound waters and the Cascade Mountains in the distance.

Summer

Allyn Days Salmon Bake & Geoduck Festival, Allyn, Washington; allynwa.com. This hometown hoedown organized by the Allyn Community Association takes place the third weekend of July at this Kitsap Peninsula town's waterfront park on Case Inlet. Enjoy baked salmon and try geoduck specialties prepared by area restaurants. Take in an oyster shucking contest and compete in the Geoduck Gallop mud run at low tide.

Ballard Seafood Fest, Seattle, Washington; seafoodfest.org. Since 1974 this Seattle neighborhood that's home to many a fishing family and the North Pacific Fishing Fleet has gathered in July to celebrate the return of salmon to the Ballard Locks, culminating in a mammoth salmon BBQ over an alder fire; in 2013, volunteers served more than 1 ton of grilled salmon. Yum!

Tillicum Village, Blake Island, Washington; argosycruises.com. Enchanting Northwest treasure or kitschy tourist trap? It depends whom you ask about this 4-hour cultural sightseeing cruise that whisks passengers from the Seattle waterfront to nearby Blake Island to partake in a traditional salmon bake over open fires in a giant cedar longhouse, then watch live dancing and hear local legends from storytellers. (Full disclosure: My fourth grade class and generations of other local kids absolutely loved it. So did my elderly aunts from Japan.) With James Beard Award winner and former Flying Fish chef-owner Christine Keff now leading the culinary program for Argosy Cruises, which operates the village, the daytrip could grow even more popular. This adventure is at its sparkling best in summer, when rain is less of a threat and daylight lingers well into the evening.

Fall

Clayoquot Oyster Festival, Tofino, British Columbia; oystergala .com. The third week of November, hundreds of oyster lovers make the trek to tiny Tofino on Vancouver Island's stormy west coast, where over 4 days they'll tip back some 8,000 bivalves to celebrate the start of the local harvest from the pristine waters of Clayoquot Sound, a UNESCO Biosphere Reserve. They'll don their best under-the-sea-themed costumes (think *Finding Nemo*, pirates, sea witches, and more) and party late into the night at the Mermaid's Masquerade held in the local community hall; explore local oyster farms tucked into serene inlets; and root for favorite local chefs at the Oyster Gala. It's all good fun in the name of "Keeping Tofino's population growing since 1997."

Feast Portland, Portland, Oregon: feastportland.com. This 4-day extravaganza of all things artisanal and Oregon showcases local culinary talent and ingredients alongside nationally recognized chefs and industry leaders. Past schedules have featured wine education, a speakers series on

topics from hunger to health care, a cookbook social, classes on how to roast your own coffee or fillet fish, and, of course, plenty of memorable bites.

Issaquah Salmon Days Festival, Issaquah, Washington; salmon days.org. Each fall, since 1970, this community in the Cascade foothills celebrates the return of spawning salmon up Issaquah Creek and the city's historic hatchery. In 2013, Salmon Days drew more than 185,000 festivalgoers, hosted a grand parade with 100-plus floats, and served almost 2 tons of salmon barbecued by the local Kiwanis Club. Yes, we love salmon.

OysterFest & West Coast Oyster Shucking Championship, Shelton, Washington; oysterfest.org. Washington State's official seafood festival draws thousands of hungry oyster fans to this historic logging and oystering community that's the westernmost city along Puget Sound, located on Oakland Bay. Hosted by the Shelton SKOOKUM Rotary Club Foundation, OysterFest features a seafood cookoff; nearly 100 food vendors, from barbecued oysters to seafood ceviche to corn on the cob; a Washington wine hall and microbrew tent; live music; and more than 500 dozen oysters to slurp during the shucking championship. (Champs typically can shuck two dozen in less than 2 minutes. Dang!)

Oyster New Year, Seattle, Washington; elliottsoysterhouse.com/ony. This perennially sold-out November bash at Elliott's Oyster House on the Seattle waterfront is widely considered one of the biggest fancy oyster parties on the West Coast and features more than 30 varieties of fresh local oysters, an expansive seafood buffet, live music, dozens of local wines and microbrews, even an oyster luge for the iciest of slurping. It's a chance to knock back oysters with the men and women who grow them and to celebrate oysters in all their briny goodness. Proceeds support the Puget Sound Restoration Fund, a nonprofit founded in 1997 dedicated to restoring marine habitat, water quality, and native species in Puget Sound.

Oyster Run, Anacortes, Washington; oysterrun.org. In 1981, Limp Lee and a few of his friends decided to go for a motorcycle ride at the end of summer and eat some oysters. The next year, more guys came along. Pretty soon, it was 200 guys. Three decades later, the event now billed as the "largest motorcycle run in the Pacific Northwest" starts in Anacortes and meanders through the Skagit Valley with stops all day at various biker-friendly joints, including oyster haunts Adrift in Anacortes, The Edison Inn in Bow, and Longhorn Saloon in Edison. Every fourth Sun in Sept.

Port Angeles Dungeness Crab & Seafood Festival, Port Angeles, Washington; crab festival.org. Each October this community along the Strait of Juan de Fuca celebrates the region's diverse bounty, its maritime traditions, and its favorite crustacean, named after the nearby village of Dungeness. Get cracking: Enjoy fresh Dungeness hot or cold with coleslaw and sweet corn, a clam chowder coo-koff, and a grab-a-crab tank derby.

Resources

Fishing & Shellfishing

Get supplies, gear, and licenses at most sporting goods, general, or hardware stores near the coast or major waterways. Then check each state or province's website for seasons, harvest limits, public beaches and waterways, species identification, how-to guides, cleaning instructions, recipes, and more.

Washington
Washington State Department of Fish and Wildlife
wdfw.wa.gov/fishing/shellfish/

Oregon
Oregon Department of Fish and Wildlife
dfw.state.or.us/resources/fishing/crabbing_clamming.asp

British Columbia
The BC Sport Fishing Guide
www.pac.dfo-mpo.gc.ca/index-eng.html

Classes & Workshops

Crabbing, Clamming & Oystering
Many coastal festivals, libraries, and parks departments offer how-to classes; inquire locally. Bainbridge Island's Parks Department (biparks.org) offers instructional outdoor adventures that have included shellfishing for geoducks and razor clams with foraging expert and author Langdon Cook.

Know Your Oysters
Rowan Jacobsen, longtime oyster aficionado and author of *A Geography of Oysters* shares his knowledge of regions with an interactive guide (oyster guide.com) to tasting notes, flavor, and place. This will help you know your Fanny Bay from Yaquina Bay, your Case Inlet from Dyes Inlet.

Seafood Canning
If you've got a big catch, check with your local cannery, smokehouse, or fish market for help with processing. Or, check with your local Slow Food group. Slow Food Seattle (slowfoodseattle.wordpress.com) holds a popular tuna canning workshop each year.

Index